AGRICULTURAL POLICY IN DISARRAY

VOLUME II

Edited by
**Vincent H. Smith, Joseph W. Glauber,
and Barry K. Goodwin**

AEI

AMERICAN ENTERPRISE INSTITUTE

ISBN: 978-0-8447-5019-4 (hardback)
ISBN: 978-0-8447-5020-0 (paperback)
ISBN: 978-0-8447-5021-7 (ebook)

American Enterprise Institute
1789 Massachusetts Avenue, NW
Washington, DC 20036
www.aei.org

*This volume is dedicated
to the memory of D. Gale Johnson,
whose seminal work on agricultural policy
has inspired the authors throughout their careers.*

Contents

Foreword

Americans admire our nation's farmers. Few industries require such discipline and hard work, and fewer still so clearly change millions of lives for the better each day. Unfortunately, our agricultural policies do not live up to such a high standard and poorly serve both farmers and the American public.

Agricultural Policy in Disarray is a collection of work that seeks to improve this. This two-volume compendium of 19 studies continues a storied AEI tradition: Dating back to the work of D. Gale Johnson and Hendrik Houthakker in the 1960s and 1970s, the Institute's scholars have examined the economic flaws and consequences of US agricultural policy for decades.

This work is a culmination of a three-year program of research, and it includes a wide range of studies, authored by prominent agricultural economists and written for a nontechnical audience. These evidence-based reports capture the complex, chaotic, and often internally inconsistent structure of US federal agricultural policy.

Today's policies have their roots in the 1930s New Deal legislation originally enacted to provide support for a struggling agricultural sector. But these policies have long outgrown their original purpose. By and large, US agricultural policies now merely transfer dollars from taxpayers to owners of financially sound farm businesses.

As the studies in this work document, agricultural interest groups have regularly found bipartisan support for their preferred policies in Congress, while other interested parties—such as agribusinesses and shipping companies—have used votes and campaign contributions to obtain favorable treatment. And although these policies serve desired ends for a select number of interests, they come at the expense of taxpayers, consumers, and especially families and children in poverty. Thus, the deepest flaw in agricultural policy today is not merely that it creates economic inefficiencies, whether involving the country's resource base, market mechanisms, long-run productivity growth, or US international trade relations; it is that the cronyism still present in our system reduces our ability to direct resources and opportunities to those who need them the most.

Agricultural Policy in Disarray is a self-recommending contribution to an underappreciated area of public policy. Without sacrificing substance, it breaks down the labyrinthine world of agricultural policy in accessible language, offering readers a clear understanding of both how and why scarce government resources are so frequently mismanaged. Anyone who gives this volume the attention it deserves will gain two valuable insights. The first is that most agricultural programs shrink the size of the economic pie while redistributing a larger share of that pie to special interests. The second is why these flaws in policy matter—because they ultimately limit opportunities for Americans who would benefit most from a smarter use of government resources.

If policymakers take the lessons of this volume seriously, they will find themselves equipped with actionable ideas for reforms that will reduce the damage being done by current policy. But more than that, these studies demonstrate how we can secure a dynamic and productive future for the agricultural sector, all while positioning our economy to lift up those on the margins. And it is ultimately this aspirational element that makes *Agricultural Policy in Disarray* so crucial to the policy conversation. Happy reading.

Arthur C. Brooks
President, American Enterprise Institute

Introduction

About 45 years ago, in 1973, D. Gale Johnson published a seminal study of agricultural policy. For his title, Johnson settled on *World Agriculture in Disarray* to reflect the chaotic incentives and economic inefficiencies created by the agricultural policies of many countries, including Australia, Canada, the European Union, Japan, New Zealand, and the United States.

Beginning in the mid-1980s with a set of radical reforms to New Zealand's and Australia's agricultural policies, many member countries of the Organisation for Economic Co-operation and Development initiated reforms to their agricultural policies. Those reforms involved reducing levels of support (measured percentages of the value of production) and changing how farm revenues are enhanced. The shift has been away from support tied to production and input use and toward either fixed payments or payments tied to the provision of environmental amenities. Not surprisingly, in those countries, farmers have generally become more entrepreneurial and efficient, and agricultural productivity has improved more quickly than in other countries whose programs have sustained inefficient farms and reduced incentives for innovation.

So what about the United States? While the United States appeared to be moving away from subsidies that distorted agricultural markets in the early and mid-1990s, since then the House and Senate Agriculture Committees that largely determine the structure of US farm programs have indulged in a 180-degree turn, boosting support to provide protection against falling market prices and revenues. In many ways, recent US policy initiatives, including several programs introduced in the 2014 Farm Bill, have only made matters worse. Most of those programs will likely remain unchanged, and possibly even be expanded, in any future US agricultural policy legislation.

These sacred cows include the two most expensive programs in terms of federal outlays on subsidy payments. One is a major new (in 2014) direct subsidy program that offers farm businesses a choice between two alternative methods by which they can obtain tax dollars. The other is the much older federal crop insurance program that benefits both farm businesses and, perhaps especially, crop insurance companies.

As a result, despite some major changes over the past four decades, in many respects US agricultural policy continues to vividly reflect the disarray about which Johnson wrote so elegantly almost half a century ago—hence the title of this two-volume examination of US agricultural policy, *Agricultural Policy in Disarray*, which includes 19 studies of a wide range of US agricultural policies authored by many of the world's leading agricultural economists.

The purpose of this work is to examine the complex and, in many ways, conflicted structure of contemporary US agricultural policy through a series of studies that are designed to be accessible to students, policymakers, and the general public. Each study examines a set of current programs that affect a particular subsector of the US agricultural economy (e.g., cotton, dairy, and sugar), a broader program area (e.g., conservation programs, the federal crop insurance program, and competition policy), or a major issue (e.g., domestic poverty alleviation) and evaluates the impacts of potential options for policy change.

Unfortunately, these studies are likely to be relevant for a long time, as the current chaotic amalgam of US agricultural programs appears unlikely to be altered in the near future. As this introduction is being written, the US House and Senate have passed separate versions of a new 2018 or 2019 Farm Bill. In the context of agricultural policy, the two draft bills are similar and essentially represent a "stay the course" approach. Both bills simply extend the current provisions of most agricultural subsidy programs while making some changes to, but maintaining overall funding for, conservation programs. Neither bill does anything substantive for public agricultural research funding. Therefore, in real terms, support is likely to continue to decline for one of the few initiatives that clearly generates widespread benefits for the economy as a whole.

Many of the studies reflect similar realities with respect to agricultural policy in the United States. First, policies are largely designed to benefit and are effectively determined by relatively small interest groups. Many of these organizations consist of farm businesses (e.g., the National Cotton Council and the American Soybean Association), producer organizations (e.g., the American Farm Bureau Federation and the National Farmers Union), and industries that service the agricultural sector, such as crop insurance companies and input supply organizations.

Second, other players in the agricultural policy process do include environmental and other more broadly focused interest groups (e.g., the World Wildlife Fund and the Sierra Club), but often the polices those groups seek involve payoffs to the agricultural sector (e.g., through paid land retirement programs and subsidies for changes to working-lands programs).

Third, little attention, if any, is paid to consumers or the poor in forming and implementing farm subsidy programs, despite assertions to the contrary from vested farm interest groups. Consumers, including the poor, are more likely to pay for farm programs either through higher taxes or higher prices for agricultural commodities because of tariffs and other forms of supply control. In fact, much of the recent debate on farm policy has focused on tightening work requirements for recipients of nutritional support and reductions in spending on such programs.

Fourth, US agricultural policies rarely take account of the international trade and trade relations implications associated with how they operate, notwithstanding that the US is a net exporter of agricultural commodities. Finally, in almost all cases, subsidy programs are intentionally structured to funnel federal funds to large farm businesses that in most cases would be financially successful without any help from the US taxpayer or consumer.

Volume I of this study focuses on policies and regulations intended to benefit farm businesses through direct subsidy payments (e.g., the federal crop insurance program), price controls (e.g., dairy marketing orders), and output restrictions through limits on domestic production or imports (e.g., the sugar program). It also examines the consequences of such policies on US trade relations. Volume II includes analyses of the effects of US domestic policies and international food aid programs on poverty and hunger (e.g., food stamp programs versus agricultural subsidies), the impacts of US conservation, environmental and renewable fuels programs and regulations, public agricultural research funding, the regulation of genetically modified (GM) technologies, and regulations affecting market operations, including agricultural commodity future markets and contracts.

As Vincent Smith et al. demonstrate in their detailed overview of contemporary US agricultural policy (Chapter 1, Volume I), in general, programs authorized by the 2014 Farm Bill channel substantial amounts of federal funds to households whose incomes and wealth are well above those of the average US household. Many of those programs also create incentives for farm businesses to operate in ways that waste economic resources, and the owners and managers of those businesses respond accordingly.

The issue of which farm businesses benefit from agricultural subsidy programs is considered in more detail by Anton Bekkerman, Eric Belasco, and Vincent Smith in Chapter 2 of Volume I. Using US Department of Agriculture (USDA) data, they examine the distribution of payments through the Agricultural Risk Coverage (ARC) and Price Loss Coverage (PLC) programs, which average over $6 billion a year, and crop insurance subsidy payments, which average just under $6 billion a year. Their analysis shows that farms in the top 10 percent of the crop sales distribution received approximately 68 percent of all crop insurance premium subsidies in 2014, and farms in the top 20 percent received more than 82 percent of ARC and PLC payments in 2015. Further, the astonishingly concentrated nature of those subsidy payments on the largest farm businesses was reflected by the fact that, in 2015, farms in the bottom 80 percent of crop sales received approximately the same total amount of ARC, PLC, and crop insurance subsidy payments as farms in the top 2 percent.

Vincent Smith, Joseph Glauber, and Barry Goodwin discuss the complex nature of the US federal crop insurance program in Chapter 3 of Volume I. They argue that, in effect, the US federal crop insurance program is a poster child for policies that waste economic resources, are poorly targeted, and involve substantial subsidies to an ancillary industry (the crop insurance industry) that, in response, becomes an effective and well-resourced lobby for the continuation and expansion of the program. From small beginnings, since 1981, the program has become a major source of subsidies for farmers, currently with more than 300 million acres and 130 crops enrolled in the program. In addition to being expensive—the program costs taxpayers over $8 billion a year, of which (one way or another) $2.5 billion is paid to crop insurance companies—as discussed by Bekkerman, Belasco, and Smith (Chapter 2, Volume I), federal crop insurance subsidies are targeted mainly to large farm businesses. Premium subsidies average about 60 percent, ensuring that a typical farm business receives more than $2 in indemnity payments for every $1 it pays in premiums. The program also encourages farmers to waste resources and has the potential to engage the US in World

Trade Organization (WTO) disputes with other countries over the trade impacts of US agricultural policy.

Two programs, ARC and PLC, were established by Congress in the 2014 Farm Bill. On a commodity-by-commodity basis, for a set of 17 "program commodities," many of which have received farm subsidies for seven or more decades, a farm business can select one of these two programs as a source of direct subsidy payments. In Chapter 4 of Volume I, Barry Goodwin explores the structure and economic implications of these PLC and ARC subsidy programs, which as discussed above involve income transfers averaging more than $6 billion annually. One important issue is whether subsidy payments made under these two programs are linked to current production decisions and therefore substantively affect resource-allocation decisions and distort markets. Payments under both programs are linked to historical production decisions within the period covered by the 2014 Farm Bill (2014–18) and therefore may appear to be decoupled from current production choices. However, as Goodwin notes, allowing farm businesses periodically to update their historical basis for payments, as in the 2008 and 2014 Farm Bills, reties such payments to current production choices. Such "recoupling" of support seems likely to occur in the future and raises substantial concerns regarding trade agreement obligations.

The US crop insurance and ARC and PLC programs are not the only elements of US agricultural policy that have spillover effects on global markets, with consequences for the country's international relations with other countries. Joseph Glauber and Daniel Sumner (Chapter 5, Volume I) examine the interactions between US agricultural programs and international trade in agricultural and food products, demonstrating that trade has always been important for US agriculture. However, over the past 50 years, US consumers and producers of agricultural commodities have become increasingly linked to global markets. Since the 1980s, several changes to US programs, many due to trade agreements and the WTO's influence, have lowered tariffs and increased trade, fostering income growth for farm businesses and lowering prices for consumers. Nevertheless, distortionary policies that are problematic for the US in its trade relations remain, and the impacts of some have expanded, which has adverse implications for global commodity prices and US trade relations. These include high tariffs for some commodities (e.g., sugar); substantial increases in price and income subsidies for other major commodities such as corn, soybeans, wheat, rice, peanuts, and milk; and the expansion of the federal crop insurance program.

Chapters 6–9 of Volume I focus on four sets of commodity-specific policies for sugar (Chapter 6), milk (Chapter 7), cotton (Chapter 8), and peanuts (Chapter 9). John Beghin and Amani Elobeid (Chapter 6) review the structure, welfare, trade, and world price implications of the US sugar program. The sugar program is a protectionist policy based on supply controls that increases the domestic price of sugar above the corresponding world price. It restricts imports of raw and refined sugar, depresses world sugar prices, and substantially changes the mix of sweeteners used in processed food. Domestic markets are distorted, sugar users are effectively taxed, and sugar producers are subsidized by the program. The welfare transfer to sugar growers and processors is quite large in the aggregate, hovering around $1.2 billion. Losses to households are diffused, about $11 per person per year, but are large for the population as a whole, in the range of $2.4–$4 billion. Gains to producers are concentrated in a few hands, especially in the cane sugar industry. Labor effects from lost activity in food processing are estimated to be between 17,000 and 20,000 jobs annually.

Daniel Sumner examines US dairy policy (Chapter 7, Volume I). Productivity gains in the US dairy industry, which now involves substantial exports of US dairy products, have shifted policies away from border protection, price supports, export subsidies, and government regulations. The 2014 Farm Bill terminated several outmoded programs but left some long-standing programs in place (e.g., marketing orders) and created new government programs. Those programs continue to be expensive for US consumers and taxpayers and create incentives for dairy farms to waste economic resources. They include dozens of high tariffs for specific dairy products and complex Federal Milk Marketing Orders that are costly to administer, and they generate resource misallocations within and beyond the dairy sector. A new income subsidy program was also introduced in 2014. The program is called the Margin Protection Program, which is notionally designed as a "risk-management insurance program."

Joseph Glauber examines cotton subsidies (Chapter 8, Volume I). They have been a major source of controversy in international trade relations and historically have been viewed as highly distortionary. However, as Glauber notes, among the reforms enacted in the 2014 Farm Bill, few were more significant than the changes made to the suite of federal subsidy programs for cotton. Direct and countercyclical payments were eliminated and replaced by a heavily subsidized supplemental insurance program, the Stacked Income Protection Plan (STAX), a program designed and promoted by the US cotton industry. The changes were made to resolve a long-standing trade dispute brought by Brazil to the WTO against US cotton price and income support programs. Subsequently, the US cotton industry became disenchanted with its own self-selected STAX program and pushed for access to the new ARC and PLC income and price support programs, which it eventually obtained for seed cotton. The seed cotton proposal was presented as a budget neutral initiative, but given the volatility of cotton prices, the potential for large subsidy payments exists. Moreover, the program clearly violates the US agreement with Brazil over cotton subsidies, will likely create market distortions, and could have detrimental effects on world prices. The new initiative is a classic example of a policy solely intended to benefit a relatively small but wealthy and politically influential interest group at a potentially substantial cost to US trade relations and other sectors of the economy.

Barry Goodwin and Vincent Smith examine the peanut program (Chapter 9, Volume I). They argue that the program is another compelling example of how relatively small, well-funded interest groups often successfully obtain funds from federal legislators. The peanut industry consists of about 6,000 generally affluent and financially secure farm businesses located in a small number of states. The peanut lobby's exceptional effectiveness in obtaining taxpayer funds is illustrated by the fact that between 2014 and 2016 peanut producers received, on average, over $340 an acre annually in taxpayer subsidies. Those payments amounted to almost half the total revenues farm businesses received from all sources of funds, almost matching their revenues from the sale of peanuts in the marketplace. Further, farm businesses raising peanuts enjoy exceptionally generous treatment in terms of limits on the subsidy payments they can receive. No other group of farm businesses, producing commodities such as rice, corn, and wheat, comes close to receiving such levels of government subsidies for a specific crop, and the program represents "an extreme among extremes" in the context of agricultural policy.

Farm interest groups have historically claimed that a major objective, if not the major purpose, of agricultural subsidy programs is to reduce rural poverty, especially poverty among farmers, and to mitigate urban poverty by lowering the prices paid by urban consumers for food. In the first study presented in Volume II (Chapter 1), Joseph Glauber, Daniel Sumner, and Parke Wilde review the current evidence about such impacts. They conclude that farm subsidy programs have little impact on food consumption, food security, or nutrition in the United States, despite any claims to the contrary. Further, as also discussed in Chapters 1 and 2 of Volume 1, the people whose household incomes are most improved by agricultural policies are the owners of large farm businesses, not struggling small-scale farmers or other rural families with low incomes who are at risk of poverty and hunger.

Farm bills include several nutrition assistance programs that do provide resources for low-income families. By a considerable margin, the Supplementary Nutrition Assistance Program (SNAP), examined by Diane Whitmore Schanzenbach (Chapter 2, Volume II), is the largest of these programs for both the number of people participating in the program and federal spending. Since 1960, SNAP has relied on the market system to increase access to nutrition by supplementing the resources that low-income families have to purchase food through regular channels of trade. The program is a cornerstone of the social safety net—estimated to have kept 8.4 million people, including 3.8 million children, out of poverty in 2014—and responds quickly to increased needs in times of economic downturns. Schanzenbach concludes that block granting the program would fundamentally undermine its ability to perform these benefits. However, access to SNAP is strictly time limited for able-bodied, unemployed adults without dependents during normal economic times and could be strengthened by doing more to assist participants with finding employment and rewarding work. Further, smart federal investments in monitoring could improve the program's integrity by reducing fraud and error. The SNAP program is frequently caught in the middle of debates between supporters and fiscal conservatives. The current debate over the 2018 Farm Bill is no different, with considerable rhetoric directed at restricting benefits through tighter work requirements, while many of the same legislators also argue that wealthy farmers in their constituencies need large subsidy payments.

Since 1954, the structure of US international food aid policy has largely been determined by farm bill legislation. Erin Lentz, Stephanie Mercier, and Christopher Barrett examine the current suite of food aid programs (Chapter 3, Volume II). They emphasize that US food aid programs have played a crucial role in saving and improving the lives of hundreds of millions of people around the world over the past 60 years. However, relative to other countries' food assistance programs, which have been extensively reformed over the past 30 years, the costs of US food aid are excessive, delivery of assistance is slow, and the programs have not kept pace with global emergency needs. They argue that three main opportunities exist to improve program efficiency and impact: (1) relaxing cargo preference requirements on shipments of US food aid, (2) expanding access to cash-based instruments rather than commodities, and (3) relaxing procurement requirements that compel food aid to be purchased in the US. Those changes are strongly opposed by the private companies that own US-flagged ships that benefit financially from cargo preference and the mandate to source food aid from the United States. Thus, even key elements of the current US international humanitarian food aid program represent a costly example of the role of rent-seeking by a small interest group at the expense of economic efficiency and, in this case, real lives.

Productivity growth is tied to, and in important ways driven by, public and private investments in research and development (R&D). Further, the productivity of private R&D investment is affected by public R&D investments, which continue to yield high rates of return for the economy as a whole. However, as Philip Pardey and Vincent Smith show (Chapter 4, Volume II), beginning in the 1980s the rate of growth in US public R&D investments slowed down in real terms, and since the mid-2000s public R&D spending has been shrinking. The United States now spends less on both public and private R&D than China does, and, significantly, as the rate of growth in US public R&D investments has declined, so too has the US agricultural sector's productive growth rate. Pardey and Smith suggest that one important reason for the slowdown in the growth and eventual decline of public R&D investments has been the willingness of agricultural interest groups to sacrifice spending on R&D to maintain or increase spending on direct subsidies to farmers.

Technology regulation can also substantially affect productivity growth by impeding or encouraging innovation. Gary Brester and Joseph Atwood (Chapter 5, Volume II) explore whether GM crops have been responsible for increased crop yields. Comparing US yields to EU yields (where GM crops are banned) provides evidence that GM technologies have increased crop yields in the United States. They conclude, however, that such yield and productivity increases are not a fait accompli. Rather, they result from the development of new technologies. Banning investments in and the use of yield-enhancing technologies has potentially serious consequences; food crop production will be lower than would otherwise be the case, and more water, land, and other inputs will be needed to increase global food production.

In the United States, some programs and regulations intended to sustain or reduce the degradation of natural resources are determined by the provisions of the conservation title in the farm bill and managed by the USDA. Other policies and regulations are established by non–farm bill legislation and fall under the purview of the US Environmental Protection Agency (EPA). These include the recent EPA Waters of the United States (WOTUS) rule and the Renewable Fuel Standard (RFS) that mandate the use of minimum annual levels of biofuels by the nation's transportation system.

Erik Lichtenberg (Chapter 6, Volume II) considers the conservation provisions of the farm bill. He points out that, from the beginning, conservation provisions in the farm bill have been linked with farm income support. Further, beginning in the mid-1980s, spending on conservation programs in the farm bill increased and has subsequently remained relatively stable, so conservation now accounts for about 30 percent of direct farm program payments. Farm bill conservation programs are justified as ways of preventing farmland degradation and mitigating environmental externalities, notably, damage to water quality, wildlife habitat, and air quality. Clear economic efficiency grounds exist for policies that address environmental externalities from agriculture, and the empirical evidence indicates that conservation programs have resulted in reductions in the environmental damage associated with farming and forestry. In addition, the USDA has made some progress in reorienting conservation programs toward environmental goals rather than mainly income enhancements for farm businesses. Thus, prioritizing conservation spending, as in the most recent farm bills, has had some positive outcomes. However, the conservation budget has not been allocated in ways that most efficiently improve environmental outcomes. Shifts in the allocation of federal funds among and within the different conservation programs could increase the efficiency of conservation spending in the sense of getting the most environmental-quality protection from the federal conservation budget.

In Chapter 7 of Volume II, Nathan Hendricks examines the issues associated with the WOTUS rule promulgated by the EPA under the provisions of the 2015 Clean Waters of the United States Act. The rule, which addresses water pollution, extends the jurisdiction of the 2015 act to all waters linked to navigable waters. He points out that many farm businesses do not know whether, as a result, they are subject to those provisions, and, if they are, then even simply obtaining permits for their operations is a costly endeavor. Further, nonpoint source pollution (emissions from sources that cannot readily be identified) is a major source of pollution in navigable waters, and the WOTUS rule does nothing to mitigate such emissions. Thus, Hendricks argues, a completely different market-based approach to reduce pollution and reach the optimal cost and benefit trade-off should be considered. As theorized by Ronald Coase in 1960, property rights should be assigned to either farm businesses (right to pollute) or environmentalists (right to clean water). They would then make contracts in which a party would accept not to exercise its rights fully in exchange for compensation. Hendricks argues that initial allocations of property rights could be established by state governments. Those governments would then be responsible for ensuring that parties comply with their contracts and use their resources to support the development of the organizations that would represent the interests of the different groups of individuals.

Aaron Smith (Chapter 8, Volume II) examines the viability and efficiency of the current RFS managed by the EPA. The RFS requires that biofuels such as ethanol and biodiesel be blended into the national transportation fuel supply. Nevertheless, the RFS is at a crossroads. Under the RFS, cellulosic biofuels would supposedly generate most greenhouse gas emissions reductions, and, as authorized by Congress, the RFS mandate requires immediate and substantial increases in their production. However, technologies have not been developed to make cellulosic biofuels cost-effective, and most biofuels continue to be produced from corn or soybeans. Moreover, the RFS now requires more biofuel than the fuel industry can easily absorb. Congress and the EPA, which administers the program, face important decisions about the future path of the RFS. Aaron Smith draws three lessons from the RFS that are relevant to government policymaking in this and other areas. First, in developing policies based on speculative assessments about future technologies, policymakers should account for uncertainty when making and implementing new programs. Second, they should not give regulators in government agencies too much discretion because it enables political forces and legal challenges to undermine policy. Third, policymakers should not mandate the use of things that do not exist.

Scott Irwin (Chapter 9, Volume II) examines regulatory and other issues associated with recent technological innovations and other changes that affect the way commodity futures markets function. A global uproar about speculation in commodity futures markets ensued after the spike in food commodity prices during 2007–08, which coincided with emerging large-scale participation by a new type of speculator in commodity futures markets: financial index investors. Some market participants, regulators, and civic organizations argued that the inflow into new commodity index investments was the principal driver of the spike in agricultural and energy prices. The subsequent policy debate focused on more restrictive speculation position limits in commodity futures markets. The issue was largely resolved when most of the evidence indicated that commodity index trading was at most a minor player in recent price spikes. As the commodity prices spiked, coincidentally a serious episode of convergence failures in grain futures and cash markets occurred. When contract rules were altered to raise artificially low storage rates, most problems disappeared, although more recent moderate non-convergence events suggest that the issue needs continued monitoring and that further increases in storage rates may be necessary. In addition, the transition from a telephone and open outcry trading platform to a computer and electronic order matching platform represents a major structural change in how futures markets operate. The issues associated with this shift are currently not well understood and are likely to be the subject of considerable research and regulatory attention in coming years.

Periodically, farm interest and other groups raise concerns about potential anticompetitive behaviors associated with contracting between farm businesses and downstream processors or upstream agribusiness input suppliers. Tomislav Vukina and Xiaoyong Zheng examine these issues in Chapter 10 of Volume II, focusing mainly on contracting in the livestock sector. They point out that two main types of contracts are widely used in the US agricultural sector: marketing contracts and production contracts, which are sometimes jointly described as alternative marketing arrangements (AMAs). They conclude that AMAs benefit not only farmers and packers by eliminating marketing timing and capacity underutilization risks but also consumers because such contracts provide consumers with better-quality products. The authors conclude that AMAs should not be banned by regulators but that regulators should protect spot markets, improve mandatory price reports, and leave tournament settlements of broiler contracts intact, all of which would enable markets to function more effectively. Policymakers should also support the 2012 Grain Inspection, Packers and Stockyards Administration rule regarding additional capital investment requirement and provisions regarding breaches of contract and suspension of delivery of animals, again to ensure the more efficient operation of markets.

In summary, the 19 studies included in this two-volume examination of US agricultural policy provide insights about a wide range of issues. Those issues range from the economic welfare effects and environmental consequences of direct and indirect agricultural subsidy programs such as crop insurance and the sugar program to the efficiency and effectiveness or ineffectiveness of environmental and conservation policies such as the Conservation Reserve Program and the RFS managed by the EPA. The relevance and consequences of international agricultural trade and trade policies are investigated, as are important issues about the impacts of agricultural subsidies on poverty and hunger in the United States (of which there are few, if any) and the efficiency of US international emergency food aid programs. The causes and consequences of the changing trajectory of public R&D funding are investigated, as are the potential impacts of different technology regulation regimes. And policy issues associated with the management of futures markets and the regulation of contracting are explored.

Finally, each of the studies, while using state-of-the-art knowledge, is designed to be accessible to the nonspecialist—students, policymakers, public interest groups, and the general public—and of interest to economists and graduate students seeking insights about contemporary US agricultural policies.

Section I

Poverty and US Agricultural Policy

1

Poverty, Hunger, and US Agricultural Policy: Do Farm Programs Affect the Nutrition of Poor Americans?

JOSEPH W. GLAUBER, DANIEL A. SUMNER, AND PARKE E. WILDE

Farm policy in what is now the United States began with trade barriers, taxes, and regulations in the earliest colonial times, when agriculture dominated the economy. The modern era of federal farm commodity subsidies began with the New Deal more than 80 years ago. Since then, subsidy programs, related international trade measures, and associated commodity regulations have been repeatedly modified. The current version of these programs operates under the provisions of the Agriculture Act of 2014 (the 2014 Farm Bill).

This chapter focuses on the economic consequences of current US farm subsidy policies for the food consumption and nutritional well-being of low-income Americans. We assess how the current policies affect prices paid by US food consumers and the incomes of poor households in the United States. The analysis involves two major steps. First, we outline the main farm commodity policies and programs in the United States and examine their impacts on commodity prices. Second, we consider the extent to which those farm policies affect incomes earned by poor households and the retail prices they pay for food.

We focus on the poor because they are potentially food insecure—vulnerable in that their incomes may be inadequate to cover food costs—making them especially vulnerable to high food prices. Shifts in food prices or marginal shifts in farm income subsidies are unlikely to affect food consumption patterns and the diets of middle-income and wealthy Americans. This is why we pay attention to defining which households are poor and how farm income and food price shifts may affect different urban and, especially, rural populations in poverty.

Scope and Focus

In this chapter, we examine the specific impacts of farm policies that address farm prices and incomes through commodity markets and related channels. We examine the claim that farm subsidy programs significantly affect food consumption and nutrition in the United States. For example, Robert Goodman claims that "government farm subsidies are necessary to protect the public from scarcity and high food prices."[1] Crop Insurance America argues, "It is in the public interest to have a financially stable agricultural sector that produces the nation's safe and affordable food and fiber supply and supports the rural economy. That necessitates the presence of a publicly supported safety net for farmers."[2] We explain in detail why such claims are unfounded.

In recent decades farm subsidies have taken various forms and are often considered farm "safety-net" programs. These policies include government payments to farmers, farm commodity price regulations and supports, and subsidized insurance or insurance-based programs, which are sometimes called risk-management programs. For a few commodities, such as sugar and orange juice, import barriers remain an important influence on commodity prices in the United States.

Many federal policies administered by the US Department of Agriculture (USDA) are beyond the scope of this study. Most importantly, we do not focus on the impacts of food and nutrition policy and programs, such as the Supplemental Nutrition Assistance Program (SNAP) and school lunch programs. These programs dominate the USDA budget and are important sources of income and food subsidies for the poor.

The USDA and the Food and Drug Administration have major roles in food inspection to assure safety and reduce the spread of plant and animal diseases. These agencies also regulate definitions of food ingredients and labeling. Their activities indirectly influence which foods are consumed, but those activities are outside our scope.

The USDA also engages in dozens of relatively small programs that have specific effects in selected markets and for particular groups of households and farmers. These range from support for farmers markets to grants to schools and community organizations for agricultural information. The USDA encourages people to "know your farmer" and supports "local" farm sales. At most, these sorts of activities likely have small, indirect effects on food consumption patterns and the nutrition status of the poor.

Farm commodity production in the United States has expanded rapidly even though input use in farm production has changed relatively little. Labor use on farms has declined, and purchased inputs and capital have risen only gradually. The rapid productivity improvements have been attributed to better human capital embedded in farm operators and research and development (R&D) funded by private firms and governments. Government-funded agricultural R&D has had a long history of improving farm productivity, expanding agricultural production, and reducing farm prices. We do not include impacts of government-supported (or government-performed) R&D among the farm policies considered here.

As for the study's scope, we focus on impacts on the poor in the United States. We do not consider the impacts of US farm policy on the poor in other countries. For example, we do not address the widely discussed issue of whether US subsidies lower global farm commodity prices, reducing the incomes of poor farmers in other countries who produce commodities that compete with US exports. That issue has been central to recent global controversies over US farm subsidies but is not examined here.

We should be clear at this stage about terminology for two key concepts and categories. First, we use the terms "farm commodity policy" and "farm policy" interchangeably to apply to a set of subsidy programs, trade barriers, commodity promotion programs, marketing regulations, land retirement, and related measures. As noted, this is not the full array of US agricultural policy, but rather an attempt to capture the important policy features that are generally referred to as farm programs. Second, we use the terms "low-income households," "household in poverty," and "the poor" interchangeably to refer to individuals, families, and similar food-consuming units in the United States who have relatively low access to resources with which to buy food. In most cases, we mean households with incomes below the official federal poverty guidelines, although we comment briefly on alternative poverty measures.

Our approach and findings are consistent with the sizable, broadly focused economics literature on obesity in the United States.[3] A smaller but still substantial literature has specifically examined the obesity impacts of US farm policy.[4] The literature has shown that farm subsidy, trade, and price support policies have had, and continue to have, small impacts on retail food prices. Some of these raise prices while others lower prices. The literature has also shown with several data approaches that US farm policy does not affect US obesity rates.

Linkages from Farm Policy to Food Consumption and Nutrition of the Poor

The farm policies we consider are directed to providing benefits for farm commodity industries and especially commodity producers. They deliver those benefits mainly through payments to farmers when prices, yields, or revenues are lower than those specified in the program rules. For over a dozen commodities (mostly grains and oilseeds), farmers now choose between commodity price–based payments or commodity revenue–based payments. Those producers, as well as producers of many other commodities—including fruits, nuts, and vegetables—are also eligible for highly subsidized crop insurance, often tied to farm revenue shortfalls rather than just crop yield shortfalls.

These programs are commodity based. As a result, they generate payments that are roughly proportional to a farm's expected revenue from the covered commodities. Small farms with small outputs therefore usually receive small payments. Many small farms report negative net farm incomes in most years, and their operators generally earn their livelihood from other sources. Indeed, operators of farms in all size categories tend to be relatively wealthy compared with most Americans. Very few who earn most of their income from farming are among the nation's low-income households. In the section that describes farm programs, we also examine the distribution of payments and related benefits in more detail.

The impacts of current farm policies on farm commodity prices are mostly indirect. Almost all government-set price floors that raise market prices have been eliminated in recent decades. Sugar price supports, implemented with the aid of trade barriers based on tariff-rate quotas, are the significant exception. For other commodities, farm programs add to expected revenue per unit and reduce the risk of income shortfalls associated with lower-than-expected yields and market prices, thereby increasing production incentives. At the same time, some of these enhanced incentives are not commodity specific, applying equally among many supported commodities. Those types of programs may therefore have only small overall impacts on the production of an individual commodity. The market price effects through supply response of all commodity policies depend on the array of commodity impacts and competition for land and other resources across crops. Effects on livestock commodity prices and retail prices are even more complex and indirect. We use prior research to assess the market price effects of commodity policies in the United States. We then examine the impacts on food prices paid by consumers.

Then we explore how the implied impacts on incomes and food prices affect the poor's food consumption patterns and nutrition. First, we consider the definition and extent of low-income households whose food consumption behaviors are the focus of this analysis. Measuring and identifying the extent of poverty is a complex topic that hinges especially on two concerns. First, what incomes should be considered, and in particular, how should we account for the value of noncash government benefits? Second, how should we account for geographic variations in the prices of goods and services? We briefly review alternative measurements of the poor in the United States, although for purposes of food and nutrition patterns, definitions do not matter much. Many households are poor enough that higher food prices and lower incomes will affect their diets.

We pay particular attention to two low-income groups that earn their livings from agriculture and therefore may be affected directly by farm subsidies. First, hired farmworkers may face reduced opportunities for employment and lower wages if farm subsidies are cut. Second, some farmers and farmland owners may themselves be poor. We also examine how changes in farm incomes may indirectly affect poor rural residents not working on farms in their communities. Despite their close linkage to agriculture, we find that farm policies are not structured or funded in ways that reduce poverty much even for these three groups. More generally, farm policy effects for these groups make only a minor contribution to broader efforts to reduce US poverty and consequent ill nourishment in the population at large.

Most hired farm employees in the United States work in fruits, vegetables, and other labor-intensive crops that receive a small share of the farm subsidy program budget and attention. As noted above, poor farm landowners and farm operators produce a small fraction of total farm output and receive little from farm subsidy policy. The effects on rural communities can be significant in some isolated cases, but farm income from subsidies is no longer a driver of rural incomes in the United States, if it ever was.[5]

For completeness, we note three additional broad or indirect effects of farm commodity subsidy policy on the incomes and welfare of low-income households and thereby on food consumption and nutrition patterns. First, since farm subsidies are mostly tax supported, they affect the tax bill of the poor. However, the share of the federal budget on farm programs is less than 1 percent, and many low-income households have low or negative income tax rates. Therefore, the effect of farm subsidies on the after-tax incomes of the poor is tiny.

Second, although the environment is not a focus of this study, we note that farm subsidy programs, such as crop insurance, affect the environment and the economy because farming has environmental consequences.[6] Hence, farm programs may affect the well-being of low-income households, especially in rural areas, because the poor generally live in less favorable areas that may be more vulnerable to negative environmental influences.

Third, and potentially most significantly, farm subsidy policies may affect federal tax-supported programs that directly benefit the poor, specifically those tied to food and nutrition and the USDA. Two offsetting forces are at play. To the extent that the federal government faces budget limits, different programs compete for spending. Thus, government expenditures on farm subsidies may reduce spending on general services that benefit the poor, especially SNAP subsidies, school lunch subsidies, and other food and nutrition programs in the USDA budget.

Offsetting the impacts of direct competition for the federal budget, political accommodation across subsidy programs may have positive effects on programs directly targeted to the poor. A long-held assumption is that food and nutrition programs and farm subsidies are part of an overall political bargain through which supporters of each type of subsidy agree tacitly to moderate their opposition to the others' programs in return for similar accommodation. This coalition may have been weakened during congressional debates over the 2014 Farm Bill. Still, in most years, farm subsidy spending and food and nutrition program spending are likely as much codependent as mutually competitive.

Overview and Road Map

Farm subsidy and other support programs were introduced in the 1930s as part of a massive federal effort to address the causes and consequences of the Great Depression. Farm price supports and supply controls were designed to increase farm incomes at a time when farmers were among the poor. These programs had significant short-run impacts on commodity prices and farm incomes in particular markets and locations. However, their success with respect to poverty relief in the 1930s is complex and controversial. These programs did raise prices temporarily and to that extent may have reduced nutritional well-being of the nonfarm poor.

Today, however, farm subsidy programs are clearly not poverty programs and cannot be usefully evaluated in that light. Farm commodity subsidies are also not food policy. We show that they have little influence on retail food prices in the United States. Farm subsidies may indirectly influence food consumption patterns of low-income households through impacts on household incomes. However, these are surely small relative to many other governmental and market economic factors.

In the first part of the chapter, we review the influence of farm commodity policies on farm prices and trace that effect to retail prices in the United States. We also consider their effects on net farm incomes and the distribution of net farm income by farm size. Then we examine the characteristics, food consumption, and nutrition status of US low-income households. We examine the rural poor and those with farm-related occupations in more detail. Finally, we link the previous two sections and draw the summary implications that have been highlighted above.

The Effects of US Agricultural Policies on Farm and Food Prices

The United States subsidizes farms and ranches and regulates farm commodity markets through a myriad of policies affecting prices, production, and farm incomes. While intervention in agricultural markets dates back to the early days of the republic (especially through trade policies), most farm policies have their roots in the New Deal legislation of the 1930s. Policies that often began as temporary "stabilization" measures to improve farm income in the 1930s have persisted to the present. The evolution of US policy can broadly be characterized as a move away from direct intervention in markets through purchases and supply controls toward support measures that more indirectly influence production. Recent policy shifts have emphasized risk-management programs through which, in some cases, producers contribute to funding through premium payments. That said, most of the measures originating in the 1930s continued in one form or another in 2016.

The federal government still uses tariffs and quotas to provide or augment protection for domestic prices (e.g., for sugar, orange juice, beef, and dairy products). We still have programs that boost domestic demand (the Special Supplemental Nutrition Program for Women, Infants, and Children (WIC) and SNAP) and export demand (export credit guarantees). We still restrict supplies or divert production to market segments (marketing orders and land retirement programs) and provide input subsidies (credit, conservation cost shares, and crop insurance). While many argue that the current policies distort markets less than did the old policies,[7] the amount of government outlays or price enhancement relative to open markets remains large for many commodities. The Congressional Budget Office projects that, if present policies continue, government spending for price and income support programs, conservation programs, and crop insurance will total $200 billion from fiscal year (FY) 2016 through FY2025.[8]

In this section we examine the range of federal programs that affect commodity and food prices. These include:

- Import restrictions, which protect domestic production from foreign competition;

- Supply management policies, which raise market prices by restricting supplies;

- Demand enhancement policies, which raise market prices by increasing demand;

- Export subsidy policies, which may raise domestic market prices by increasing exports;

Table 1. Average and Maximum US-Bound Tariff Levels for Selected Product Groups

Product Group	Average Tariff (Ad Valorem)	Maximum Tariff (Ad Valorem)
Animal Products	2.3	26
Dairy Products	16.6	188
Fruit, Vegetables, and Plants	4.9	132
Coffee and Tea	3.3	44
Cereals and Preparations	3.5	44
Oilseeds, Fats, and Oils	4.4	164
Sugars and Confectionery	12.3	55
Beverages and Tobacco	14.8	350
Other Agricultural Products	1.1	52
Fish and Fish Products	1.0	35

Source: World Trade Organization, *Trade Profiles 2015*, 2016, https://www.wto.org/english/res_e/publications_e/trade_profiles15_e.htm.

- Direct market price support, which typically raise market prices by taking production off the market;

- Direct payments to producers, sometimes tied to low market prices, which raise producer returns through income transfers;

- Input subsidies, which reduce input costs to producers; and

- Compensation programs such as crop insurance and disaster assistance, which assist producers during times of crop yield or revenue shortfalls.

This list of federal policies affecting agriculture examined is not comprehensive. Not covered here, but historically important, are:

- Federal land distribution policies, such as the Homestead Acts, which enabled access to virgin agricultural land;

- Water allocation rights, which tended to favor agriculture;

- Rural infrastructure development such as roads, canals, and railroads, which lowered costs of transporting agricultural commodities and inputs;

- Food safety laws, which protect consumers from foodborne illnesses; and

- Animal and plant health regulations, which help control plant and animal diseases.

Importantly, we do not examine the federal financing of agricultural R&D, which has led to large and sustained productivity gains.[9] Those gains have resulted in a significant decline in agricultural prices relative to prices of other goods in the economy over many decades.

Policies That Restrict Imports

Tariffs on agricultural imports date back to the early years of the United States. Originally, tariffs were primarily for revenue generation. By the latter half of the 19th century, tariffs were used to prevent agricultural imports (primarily from Canada) from weakening US prices.[10] By the late 19th century, the United States had become a major exporter of cotton, tobacco, and wheat.

Today, because of both unilateral and multilateral liberalization, US agricultural tariffs are among the lowest in the world (Table 1). The current trade-weighted average is 4.1 percent, and the simple (unweighted) average is 7.8 percent.[11] However, key exceptions include sugar, peanuts, orange juice, and dairy products.

The United States also uses domestic trade remedy laws, such as antidumping measures and countervailing duties, to protect selected products against imports from some countries. Currently, countervailing duties exist on a handful of products, including raw and roasted in-shell pistachios from Iran, fresh garlic from China, pasta from Italy and Turkey, honey from China, and numerous fresh fish and seafood products from China, Vietnam, India, Thailand, and Brazil.[12]

In addition, the United States has taken advantage of safeguard provisions under the World Trade Organization (WTO) Agreement on Agriculture that allow countries to impose temporary tariffs on certain imports in the event of price declines or import surges.[13] The United States has the right to impose safeguards on 189 products (mostly covering dairy and sugar tariff lines). While less frequently used in recent years, the US continues to apply safeguard provisions. In October 2015, for example, the United States imposed prohibitive tariffs on butter and sour cream imports for the rest of the 2015 calendar year.[14]

Nontariff barriers such as country-of-origin labeling requirements, quality standards, and sanitary and phytosanitary standards can also raise effective barriers to imports and raise prices. At the end of 2015, facing retaliation from Canada and Mexico, the United States ended its country-of-origin labeling regulations for certain muscle cuts of beef and pork after the WTO found these regulations violated agreements to avoid undue trade barriers.[15]

Acreage Controls

One traditional instrument used by the United States to raise farm prices, dating back to the 1930s New Deal legislation, has been mandatory and voluntary acreage supply control programs. Acreage control programs have generally been run in tandem with price and income support programs for grains, oilseeds, and cotton. The programs have been targeted to raise prices or control government outlays.[16] Annual acreage reduction programs were terminated by the 1996 Farm Bill.

Today, the principal land set-aside program is the Conservation Reserve Program (CRP). The CRP is a long-term land retirement program that pays annual rental payments in exchange for farmers removing environmentally sensitive land from agricultural production and improving the environmental quality of the land. CRP contracts are typically for 10–15 years. Since its first year of operation in 1986, the CRP has idled an average of 31 million acres annually. However, beginning in 2009, as their contracts matured, many farmers have opted to bring land out of retirement to take advantage of higher agricultural commodity prices. The 2014 Farm Bill restricted land enrollment in the CRP to 25 million acres. As of October 2015, 23.4 million acres were enrolled in the CRP.

Effectiveness of supply control efforts has been mitigated because producers generally retire less productive land. Thus, in percentage terms, production has fallen by less than the area idled. Much of the land currently enrolled in the CRP is in Great Plains states and is more suited for fallow cropping rotations and grazing. For example, between 2007 and 2015, the area enrolled in the CRP declined by 13.4 million acres, yet land planted to principal crops increased by only 5.3 million acres over the same period.

Marketing Quotas and Price Discrimination

Since the 1930s, the United States has implemented several programs that supported prices by limiting the amount of production that could be sold in the marketplace. The last of these programs, for peanuts, ended more than a decade ago. Marketing orders for several specialty crops remain, restricting the quantities that can be sold in higher-priced markets based on product characteristic or market (fresh vs. processed or domestic vs. export). Currently, the US operates marketing orders for 29 fruit, vegetable, and tree crops. Each order has quality restrictions, and 10 provide the authority for volume control.[17] Quality controls can raise the price of produce in domestic markets by diverting lower-quality produce to processed uses or destruction. Volume controls, however, have largely been suspended or are under review due to legal challenge (for example, raisins).

The Federal Milk Marketing Order (FMMO) system allows for explicit price discrimination between milk destined for fluid and soft products and more heavily processed products such as milk powders, butter, and cheese. The geographically based FMMOs (and the important California milk marketing order) set minimum prices to be paid by milk processors based on how the milk is used. These minimum farm milk prices change monthly with shifts in prices of major dairy commodities. Minimum milk prices for fluid beverage products differ geographically but tend to be about 10 percent to 40 percent above the minimum milk price for heavily processed products. Actual market prices paid to farmers tend to exceed the minimums, and not all regions are covered by marketing orders, so the impact of the marketing order system is muted. In 2014, milk marketed through federal orders accounted for 63 percent of all milk sold in the United States and 63 percent of fluid grade milk sold to US plants and milk dealers.[18] The California marketing order, which is similar to the federal orders, accounted for another 20 percent of US milk production.

Hayley Chouinard et al. conclude that eliminating the milk marketing orders would likely reduce fluid milk prices by 15.5 percent while increasing the price of cheese and other dairy products. They estimate that the FMMOs effectively cost the average US household $152.88 per year. The impacts on consumers vary by region, with the smallest effects in regions that have comparative advantages in milk production, such as the upper Midwest, Idaho, and California, because in these regions a low share of locally produced milk is used for beverages.[19]

Programs That Enhance Demand

The US agricultural policy portfolio contains several programs that boost demand for agricultural commodities, including commodity checkoff programs that promote products through generic advertising and commodity purchase programs such as those authorized under Section 32 of the Agricultural Adjustment Act Amendment of 1935. Costing more than $500 million per year and collected through the federal government's mandatory assessments on producers and importers in each industry, these checkoff programs are small in scale compared with private-sector advertising and marketing efforts but large compared with other government-supported communication efforts related to food and dietary guidance. The demand and price effects of these programs on food broadly are almost surely negligible.[20]

The United States spends over $100 billion annually on food-related programs to assist eligible low-income household families. These programs, including SNAP for low-income households, programs that target school children, and WIC, are described later.

Table 2. Total Purchases Under Section 32, FY2013

Commodity	Amount (Millions of $)
Turkey	$65.0
Chicken Products	$50.0
Potatoes	$25.0
Blueberries, Wild	$15.7
Blueberries, Cultivated	$15.0
Catfish Products	$ 9.9
Cranberries	$5.0
Lamb Products	$5.0
Grapefruit Juice	$3.8
Tomatoes	$3.6
Strawberries	$2.0
Total	$200.0

Source: US Department of Agriculture, Agricultural Marketing Service data, reproduced in Dennis A. Shields, "Farm and Food Support Under USDA's Section 32 Program," Congressional Research Service, November 18, 2014, https://www.fas.org/sgp/crs/misc/RL34081.pdf.

Section 32. Section 32 of the Agricultural Adjustment Act Amendment of 1935 is a permanent appropriation. Since 1935, it has set aside the equivalent of 30 percent of annual custom receipts to support the farm sector through purchasing surplus commodities and a variety of other activities.[21] In recent years, the annual appropriation has totaled about $9 billion. About $8 billion is transferred to the USDA's child nutrition account, with another $130 million transferred to the Department of Commerce for fishery activities. The remainder is used by the USDA to purchase agricultural commodities such as meats, poultry, fruits, vegetables, and fish—commodities that are not typically covered by price and income support programs. In FY2013, $718 million was spent on commodity purchases, including $518 million to supply USDA child nutrition programs and $200 million in "contingency" purchases of surplus commodities such as turkey, chicken products, and fruits and vegetables. These commodities were then distributed as "bonuses" to domestic food assistance programs such as soup kitchens, food banks, schools, and childcare centers (Table 2).

Checkoff Programs. Checkoff programs the USDA operates are mandated, grower-funded programs used for a variety of industry-enhancement programs including research, market development, and marketing strategies.[22] Currently, federal checkoff programs exist for a wide range of commodities including beef, lamb, pork, soybeans, sorghum, eggs, cotton, dairy, fluid milk, mushrooms, honey, peanuts, popcorn, potatoes, watermelon, cultivated blueberries, raspberries, Hass avocados, and mangos. In addition, federal marketing orders for a wide variety of primarily fruits, vegetables, and nuts are authorized to conduct promotion and research programs.

The impact of checkoff programs on commodity prices is likely small.[23] Commodity promotion expenditures generally amount to less than 1 percent of the total industry sales each year. Moreover, as Michael Wohlgenant points out, even if promotion efforts were effective in increasing demand and raising retail prices, producers may capture little of the benefits where the farm share of the retail price may be quite low.[24] As demand-enhancing policies, the impact of promotion programs is to shift food demand among products, not to increase food consumption overall.

Biofuel Policies. US biofuel policies have stimulated demand for biofuel feedstocks, mainly corn and soybeans. From 2005 to 2011, corn use for ethanol grew by about 3.4 billion bushels, accounting for over 40 percent of total corn use in 2011–12 (Figure 1). About 25 percent of soybean oil use goes to biodiesel production (Figure 2).

Bruce Babcock and Jacinto Fabiosa[25] emphasize that several other factors were crucial for ethanol's growth. First, the phaseout of methyl tertiary butyl ether as a gasoline additive in 2004 and 2005 boosted demand for ethanol as its replacement in oxygenated fuel markets. This growth in ethanol demand combined with existing demand subsidies and a limited supply of ethanol to increase ethanol prices, leading to wide processing margins in 2006 and 2007. Along with direct subsidies for the construction of ethanol-processing capacity, large margins spurred further investment in ethanol-production capacity. Second, the rapid rise in oil prices beginning in 2006 encouraged discretionary blending of ethanol as a substitute for gasoline.

The rapid rise in corn and other commodity prices in 2007–08 prompted concerns about the impact of ethanol on food prices both in the United

Figure 1. Corn Use for Ethanol

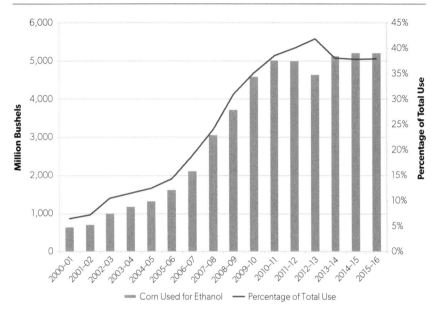

Source: US Department of Agriculture, Office of the Chief Economist, "World Agricultural Supply and Demand Estimates," various issues, http://www.usda.gov/oce/commodity/wasde/.

States and abroad. Many, like Brian Wright,[26] blame biofuel production for increased prices and volatility. Nicole Condon, Heather Klemick, and Ann Wolverton review a wide range of studies that considered the impact of ethanol production on corn prices during 2007–10.[27] Their meta-analysis concludes that about one-third of the price increase in corn prices over the period was likely due to increased ethanol production.

Since 2011, corn-ethanol production has remained relatively flat at about 13.5–14 billion gallons, reflecting automobile performance constraints, which limit ethanol penetration in motor fuel use at 10 percent (the so-called blend wall). As a result, corn use for ethanol remains at about 5.1 billion bushels per year and is not expected to grow much over the next 10 years (USDA baseline).

The current impact of the Renewable Fuel Standard (RFS) on corn prices is likely small. Ethanol remains price competitive as an octane enhancer in

Figure 2. Soybean Oil Use for Biodiesel

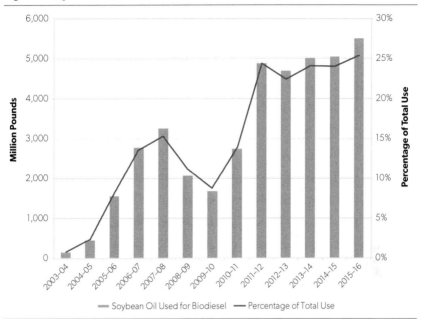

Source: US Department of Agriculture, Office of the Chief Economist, "World Agricultural Supply and Demand Estimates," various issues, http://www.usda.gov/oce/commodity/wasde/.

gasoline production.[28] Even with low oil prices, ethanol margins remain competitive, and ethanol production has remained above mandates under the RFS. Thus, eliminating the mandates would likely have little impact on ethanol production and hence corn use and prices, at least in the short run. (Wright has a somewhat different perspective.[29]) Competitiveness of ethanol without mandates and subsidies depends on the relative price relationship with alternative fuel sources.

Biodiesel production, however, is heavily influenced by the mandates and a biodiesel tax credit that provides a $1-per-gallon credit for blenders of biodiesel fuel. Under the 2016 RFS, mandates for biodiesel were set at 1.9 billion gallons. Without the mandates and tax credits, biodiesel production would unlikely be more than one-third of current levels. (A number of states and municipalities mandate biodiesel use.)

Export Policies

The United States has a long history of using subsidies to augment exports, including direct export subsidies, subsidized export credit, and food aid.[30] Under the Uruguay Round Agreement on Agriculture, the United States agreed to discipline its use of export subsidies. Since 1995, direct export subsidies have largely been limited to dairy. The 2008 Farm Bill eliminated the Export Enhancement Program, the primary export subsidy affecting commodities, and the 2014 Farm Bill eliminated direct export subsidies for dairy products. The United States agreed to reduce effective export credit subsidies as a part of the settlement with Brazil in the United States–Upland Cotton dispute.[31]

US foreign food aid has moved from primarily long-term commodity procurement (Title I) to primarily emergency and disaster food assistance and developmental programs to improve food security (Title II). Average spending on US international food aid programs during FY2006–13 was about $2.5 billion annually, with Title II activities averaging 76 percent of annual outlays.[32] The United States also provides about $200 million annually to promote US commodities overseas under the Market Access Program (MAP). As with the generic advertising programs, MAP's effectiveness in increasing demand for US products overseas is questionable.

Market Price Support

While price supports remain authorized for many commodities, they have been largely supplemented by income supports and safety-net policies such as crop insurance. To be effective, price supports require a policy mechanism to prevent the price paid to farmers from falling to a lower market equilibrium price. In the United States, price supports have been implemented using various combinations of direct government purchases, nonrecourse loans, and import barriers such as tariffs and quotas.

Historically, dairy prices were supported by direct purchases of dairy products such as cheese, butter, and nonfat dry milk. Purchased commodities were either delivered to low-income families under the USDA's nutrition programs or disposed of in foreign markets as food aid. Under the 2014 Farm Bill, dairy support prices were eliminated.

Nonrecourse loans have been available to grain, sugar, cotton, and oil-seed producers since the 1930s. With a nonrecourse loan, a producer has the opportunity to forfeit commodity pledged as loan collateral if market prices fall below the commodity's loan rate. Today, nonrecourse loans for most commodities are augmented by so-called marketing assistance loan provisions, which allow producers to repay nonrecourse loans at the lesser of the loan rate plus interest or the local market price. Thus, it is rare to see commodity forfeitures under the nonrecourse loan program.[33]

The exception is the sugar price support program, which continues to operate under a nonrecourse loan with no marketing assistance loan provisions. In some recent years, domestic sugar prices have been as much as twice the world price. Sugar imports increase the supply available in the US market and would tend to undermine support levels and lower domestic prices if unchecked by the US system of tariffs and import quotas. John Beghin and Amani Elobeid estimate that the removal of the sugar program would increase US consumers' welfare by $2.9 billion to $3.5 billion each year.[34] Since 2008, tariffs for sugar coming from Mexico have been zero under the North American Free Trade Agreement, which put pressure on US domestic sugar prices in late 2012 and 2013.[35] In response, the United States, with encouragement from the US sugar lobby, accused Mexico of subsidizing sugar exports to the United States. In December 2014, a suspension agreement with Mexico was announced in which Mexico agreed to limit exports to the United States in return for US agreement to suspend its countervailing duty and antidumping investigations.

Government Payments to Producers

Government payments supplement farm income through cash (or in-kind) transfers rather than through higher market prices.[36] After a long history with other variations of payment programs, the 2014 Farm Bill introduced price-based and revenue-based countercyclical payment programs that are based on historical rather than current plantings and provide income transfers whenever those prices or revenues fall below the administered price or revenue levels.

The impact of payments on production and prices largely depends on the degree to which the expected payments are linked to production and expected prices. Under current payment programs, payments are not tied directly to current production but determined by price or revenue outcomes and hence raise and smooth expected revenue from producing the covered crops. Researchers have pointed out that, by raising wealth and credit worthiness of eligible farms, such programs raise production.[37] Impacts of programs on production of any specific crop are further reduced to the extent that the main competitive crops are covered by similar subsidies.[38]

Input Subsidies

The US makes limited use of agriculture-specific production input subsidies (except to the extent that crop insurance is considered an input). The federal government assists farm borrowing at below-market interest on loans and offers some provisions specifically for beginning farmers, military veterans, and socially disadvantaged farm operators who might otherwise have limited access to credit. Demand for federal credit programs has declined significantly since the early 1980s when substantial underwriting changes were implemented to lower the probability of defaults.

Livestock producers who graze cattle, goats, and sheep on public lands benefit from implicit subsidies through grazing land improvement and irrigation infrastructure development, the full costs of which are not passed through to government-set grazing fees. Similarly, irrigation systems are priced to provide coverage of operating and maintenance costs (water delivery costs), but low-interest repayments and some loan forgiveness for physical infrastructure provide relief from full costs, so significant farm subsidies likely remain embedded in many water projects.

Cost-share programs for establishing conservation practices on agricultural land have supported implementation of farming practices and structures that reduce loss of fertility through soil erosion; facilitate improved drainage, water storage, and more efficient irrigation; and provide manure storage and assistance with meeting nutrient management regulations. Programs such as the Conservation Stewardship Program help cover input costs and income forgone for environmentally friendly practices that may reduce productivity or take years to achieve full production capacity.

The production effects of cost-share programs are difficult to calculate. First, some producers would have adopted such practices anyway. For example,

Roger Claasen et al. estimate that while additionality rates for practices such as nutrient management and buffer practices are above 80 percent, tillage practices are closer to 56 percent.[39] Second, while the impact of such subsidies for these practices on crop yields may be beneficial over the long run (thus potentially leading to lower prices), in the short run the impacts are likely minor.[40]

Disaster Assistance and Crop Insurance

Disaster assistance programs have provided compensation for production shortfalls from weather fluctuations and other natural events and from market revenue shortfalls due to combinations of yield and price declines. Losses from disease and disease management may also be compensated by the USDA.

In addition, the United States has offered crop insurance to producers since 1938. More recently, Congress has introduced an insurance-like program for dairy producers. These programs now constitute the largest budget outlay for farm subsidies in the United States.

The US crop insurance program has witnessed dramatic growth over the past 25 years. With an annual premium volume of over $9 billion, it is the largest agricultural insurance program in the world. For major row crops such as corn, wheat, soybeans, and cotton, participation is particularly high; producers typically insure over 85 percent of eligible acreage and generally at high coverage levels. The program has also encouraged the development of a myriad of products including revenue products, which insure against both price and yield declines; area-based products; and, more recently, margin products, which insure against declines in revenue or increases in input costs. Lastly, the 2014 Farm Bill has authorized supplemental coverage, which augments existing insurance coverage. With an annual estimated cost to the government of $8.5 billion, the US federal crop insurance program is the largest single farm subsidy program in the United States.[41]

When crop insurance is available and priced such that farms acquire coverage, risk-averse farms produce more. But the pure subsidy impact also matters. Recent papers by Bruce Babcock[42] and Xiadong Du, Hongli Feng, and David Hennessy[43] conclude that farmers do not pick coverage levels that maximize expected subsidy, nor do they demand full insurance coverage. However, over time, producers have tended to sign up for higher coverage levels for which the per-unit subsidies tend to be higher. Joseph Glauber[44] shows that average coverage levels for most row crops have grown significantly and continuously since the late 1990s, when subsidies were increased for higher coverage levels.

Measurement of impacts of the US crop insurance program has focused on planted area and the effects of insurance on input use. Barry Goodwin, Monte Vandeveer, and John Deal examined midwestern corn and soybean producers and wheat and barley producers in the Northern Plains and found that a 30 percent decrease in premium costs was likely to increase barley acreage by about 1.1 percent and corn acreage by less than 0.5 percent.[45] Soybean and wheat acreage showed no statistically significant impact. Ethan Ligon analyzed the impact of crop insurance on specialty crops and concluded that the introduction of crop insurance had a large and positive impact on tree crops but a negligible impact on non-tree crops.[46] Goodwin and Vincent Smith have questioned whether the results of earlier studies continue to be relevant given that subsidy levels are much higher now than when earlier research was conducted and that revenue policies have largely replaced yield coverages.[47] For example, the Goodwin, Vandeveer, and Deal study examined the effects of insurance subsidies over 1986–93, before enactment of major legislation in 1994 and 2000, which dramatically increased subsidy levels, and before the introduction of revenue insurance.[48] Jisang Yu, Aaron Smith, and Daniel Sumner find that crop insurance subsidies have had significantly positive impacts on acreages of major field crops. But the magnitudes of the implied acreage increases for these crops have been small (a few percent) as a share of acreage because crop insurance subsidies remain small relative to revenue per acre.[49]

Crop insurance likely has larger impacts on crop choice when insured crops compete against uninsured crops or when crops for which revenue insurance is available compete against crops with only yield insurance.

Overall Impacts Are Likely to Be Small

As discussed above, most price and income support policies in the United States provide little incentive to increase production of one crop relative to others. For example, insurance subsidies are generally available for most

Table 3. Farm Share of Retail Price, Selected Items

Item	Share (%)
Whole Milk	50
Cheddar Cheese	30
Ice Cream	15
Beef	52
Pork	30
Apples	32
Broccoli	24
Flour	26
Fresh Oranges	15
Orange Juice from Frozen Concentrate	24
Fresh Orange Juice	15
Bread	7
Grapefruit	12
Grapes	31
Iceberg Lettuce	21
Lemons	16
Peaches	26
Pears	22
Potatoes	15
Strawberries	44
Sugar	28
Tomatoes	27

Source: US Department of Agriculture, Economic Research Service, "Price Spreads from Farm to Consumer," October 20, 2016, http://www.ers.usda.gov/data-products/price-spreads-from-farm-to-consumer/.

competing crops, thus their elimination would not be expected to affect area or prices much.[50] The exceptions would be the dairy and sugar programs, for which elimination of the milk marketing order systems, elimination of sugar price support, and removal of protective tariffs would likely lower prices of fluid milk, sugar, and sugar-containing products.

If the Conservation Reserve Program were eliminated, 20–25 million acres of former cropland would be eligible to be planted. However, as we saw above, only a portion of this land would return to crops. Almost four million acres have been converted to trees, wetland restoration, or conservatory buffer practices. Moreover, a large portion of the CRP land is located in the northern and southern plains states where productivity is marginal. The overall effect would likely mean a small decrease in crop prices.

The impact of removing farm programs and subsidy policies on retail food would be smaller than the percentage impact on farm prices. The farm value of what a consumer purchases in a grocery store or restaurant is often quite small and depends on how much processing and marketing occur between the farm gate and the grocery shelf or food service table. For example, the farm value of whole milk was estimated at 50 percent in 2012, the farm value of cheddar cheese was 30 percent, and ice cream was 15 percent. Even for relatively unprocessed foods such as fresh oranges and pears, the farm value is small (Table 3) because marketing services for fresh items may be extensive.

The importance of the marketing margin is especially significant when considering the retail price impact of a change in the price of feedstuffs such as corn, soybeans, or other grains that are primarily fed to livestock or heavily processed before offered to consumers. Lower feed prices may cause producers to increase the size of their herds or flocks. But feed costs are only one component of livestock costs, and the farm share of beef and pork retail prices is itself 50 percent or less.

In considering the average basket of food purchased at home, the USDA Economic Research Service estimates that the farm share of the retail food dollar is about 17 percent.[51] Thus, even large changes in farm prices may have only modest impacts on food prices. Research by Leslie McGranahan[52] and James Mabli and Rosalie Malsberger[53] indicate that poorer households spend a larger share of their income on food and tend to spend more of their food dollars at home than away from home. Nonetheless, estimated impacts of eliminating farm subsidy programs would only minorly affect the prices of foods they purchase.

Linkages from Agriculture Commodity Policy to Poverty and Food Consumption of the Poor

Previously, we reviewed the impacts of farm policies on food prices. We now turn to the question of whether those policies affect either the extent of poverty or the food consumption and nutrition patterns of those who are poor. We begin by describing the extent of poverty and food consumption and nutrition patterns for low-income households. Then, we consider four hypothetical linkages between agriculture policy and poverty and food consumption in the United States affecting (1) food prices paid by poor households, (2) the poverty status of farm operators themselves, (3) the poverty status of farmworkers, and (4) poverty among other people in rural communities. Although these linkages are plausible hypotheses—and some are considered true by some policymakers or some of the public—we conclude that farm policy is at most a minor and indirect vehicle for addressing US poverty and nutrition of the poor. The previous section found that farm policy at most modestly affects farm commodity prices and that the overall impacts on food prices are tiny.

We explain at the end of this section that the impacts on food consumption are small for almost all foods. The populations whose incomes are most strongly affected by farm policy account for just a tiny fraction of US poverty. Poverty remains an important public policy issue in the United States, but farm programs are neither a significant cause of poverty nor the solution to poverty.

Poverty in the United States

Official estimates indicate that the share of the population in poverty in the United States fell rapidly from the 1950s to the early 1970s, but further improvements have been stubbornly elusive since that time. The federal government's official poverty measure counts household income from sources such as wages and salaries, investments, and government programs (excluding in-kind benefits such as housing subsidy, health insurance and services, and SNAP and other nutrition benefits). The measure compares household income to a poverty threshold, which varies by family composition. The threshold is updated each year for inflation. The average poverty threshold in 2014 for four-person households was $24,230.

In 2014, the official poverty rate—the percentage of people with household income below the threshold—was 14.8 percent (Table 4). However, some subpopulations are more commonly poor than others.

Table 4. Poverty Rates in the United States, 2014

	Persons (Thousands)	Poverty Rate (%)
Total	315,804	14.8
By Race		
White	244,253	12.7
Black	41,112	26.2
Asian	17,790	12.0
By Hispanic Ethnicity		
Hispanic	55,504	23.6
By Country of Origin		
US Born	273,628	14.2
Foreign-Born Citizen	19,731	11.9
Foreign-Born Noncitizen	22,444	24.2
By Age		
Under Age 18 (Thousands)	73,556	21.1
Ages 18 to 64 (Thousands)	196,254	13.5
Ages 65 and Older (Thousands)	45,994	10.0

Source: US Bureau of Labor Statistics, Current Population Survey, 2015.

By Age. Poverty is high for households with children. At one time, poverty was especially high among older Americans, but the United States has had much greater success over the decades in reducing poverty for older people than for children. One reason is that on average households headed by older Americans have more assets than households with children. In 2014, the poverty rate for people age 65 and over was 10.0 percent, while the poverty rate among people under age 18 was 21.1 percent (and exceptionally high compared with poverty rates in other advanced industrialized countries). Government benefits for the elderly are in the form of income that is measured in poverty criteria (Social Security benefits) and health care benefits that are not counted. Government benefits for households with children are mostly in the form of non-income benefits (housing, nutrition programs, and health care) that are not counted.

By Race and Ethnicity. Poverty is high for black and Hispanic Americans. In the United States, the poverty rate in 2014 was approximately twice as high for black people (26.2 percent) than for white people (12.7 percent). For Hispanic people, the poverty rate was 23.6 percent.

By Country of Origin. Poverty rates are high for noncitizens. For people born in the United States, the poverty rate in 2014 was 14.2 percent, and for naturalized citizens born elsewhere, the poverty rate was even lower (11.9 percent). The poverty rate was much higher for noncitizens, including those with and without legal documentation (24.2 percent).

Food Consumption and Nutrition for Low-Income Americans

Two leading nutrition concerns for low-income Americans are (1) food insecurity and hunger and (2) dietary quality. The federal government measures food insecurity using a nationally representative survey with 18 questions about symptoms of food-related hardship associated with not having enough resources to buy food. The USDA estimates that 14 percent of Americans lived in food-insecure households at some point during 2014.[54] In response to a direct question about going hungry, 4.6 percent of respondents reported going hungry during 2014 because of not having enough resources to buy food.[55] Evidence about actual food consumption behavior of these survey respondents is not available. Researchers therefore could not further investigate what precisely survey participants meant by these responses and whether differences in questionnaire responses correspond to food consumption differences.

Poor dietary quality and rising rates of overweight and obesity have been an important concern for Americans of all income levels for several decades. A large literature has compared dietary quality for low-income and higher-income Americans in particular.[56]

To address both food insecurity and dietary quality for low-income Americans, the United States has multiple major nutrition assistance programs. Some of these were discussed above in the context of programs that could raise market prices by raising food demand. The major nutrition programs include SNAP; child nutrition programs, such as the National

School Lunch Program (NSLP) and School Breakfast Program (SBP); and WIC.

The NSLP and SBP serve students attending 100,000 public and non-profit private schools and residential childcare institutions. In FY2014, the NSLP provided nutritionally balanced, low-cost or free lunches to more than 30 million children, while about 13.6 million children (many also enrolled in the lunch programs) participated in the SBP. Total spending on child nutrition programs was more than $19 billion in FY2014.[57]

Beginning in 2007, SNAP enrollment and spending soared due to the weak economy. In FY2014, more than 47.5 million people per month received SNAP benefits at an annual cost of $82 billion.[58] To receive benefits, households must qualify based on their income, expenses, and assets. SNAP benefits are targeted to those most in need. Households with lower income receive higher benefits up to a specified maximum. In 2013, SNAP participants represented 85 percent of eligible individuals.[59]

The WIC program provides food tied to nutritional services for low-income women, infants, and children younger than 5 who are at nutritional risk. WIC served an estimated 8.3 million people per month in FY2014 at an annual cost of $6.2 billion. WIC includes assistance to buy specific food items and required participation in nutrition-related information activities. After peaking in FY2010, the number of participants subsequently decreased by almost 10 percent due to declining numbers of US births.[60]

Nutrition assistance programs provide a partial buffer from the effects of food price variation and, especially, income shocks. Benefits under SNAP and child nutrition programs are indexed for inflation. The real value of in-kind WIC benefits also is held nearly constant. In addition to the food price inflation adjustment, SNAP benefits were increased on a one-time basis in 2009 to account for the poor economy, but this bump in benefits was subsequently whittled away and finally ended in 2014.

Some argue that the annual inflation adjustment for SNAP lags behind actual inflation by between 4 and 16 months because the adjustment is implemented each October based on food price data from several earlier months.[61] Offsetting this lag somewhat, the annual SNAP inflation adjustment has typically been slightly larger than the rate of food price inflation.[62] The cost-of-living adjustment for SNAP is pegged to the Thrifty Food Plan, which is more heavily weighted toward fruits and vegetables than the overall consumer price index (CPI) for food. Fruits and vegetables have experienced comparatively rapid price increases, so using the Thrifty Food Plan is slightly more favorable to SNAP participants than using the CPI. On balance, nutrition assistance programs offer low-income households more insulation from food price changes than they have from housing prices or most other prices that are important in their household budgets.

Extensive research has measured the association between participation in nutrition assistance programs and household food security and dietary quality, as well as other outcomes. The big challenge in such research is that eligible participants choose whether to participate in a program for many reasons, so simple participant/nonparticipant comparisons do not prove cause and effect.[63] Research that has sought to control for this self-selection challenge has provided clear evidence that SNAP improves household food security. As a recent example, in a longitudinal analysis James Mabli et al. investigated changes in the prevalence of food insecurity during the six months after low-income households began a spell of SNAP participation. They find a reduction in the rate of household food insecurity from 65.4 percent of new-entrant households to 60.8 percent of the six-month participants.[64]

For dietary quality, most research has not been able to address the self-selection challenge but instead more simply compares SNAP participants with low-income and higher-income nonparticipants.[65] In the large body of research making such comparisons, there is much evidence of poor dietary quality among all income groups and some evidence of lower dietary quality for SNAP participants than for nonparticipants. For example, among adults, the fraction with overweight and obesity is 72 percent for SNAP participants, 64 percent for low-income nonparticipants, and 64 percent for higher-income nonparticipants. The fraction of all calories classified as "empty calories" was 34 percent for SNAP participants, 32 percent for low-income nonparticipants, and 31 percent for higher-income nonparticipants.[66] A large systematic literature review found many studies showing no significant difference between SNAP participants and nonparticipants, some with lower dietary quality among the participants, and no conclusive demonstration of cause and effect.[67]

There is growing interest in research showing whether price incentives or food program changes can improve dietary quality for low-income program participants. Some of this research has used strong random-assignment research designs to address the self-selection challenge mentioned earlier. For example, the SNAP Healthy Incentives Pilot gave a 30 percent incentive for purchases of targeted fruits and vegetables, finding a moderate increase in daily targeted fruit and vegetable intake of 0.26 cup-equivalents per adult per day.[68]

Four Possible Linkages Between Farm Policy and Poverty

To understand the potential effects of farm policy on poverty and hunger, we first consider the effect on food prices for all poor households. Then, we consider specifically three subpopulations—farm operators, hired farmworkers, and rural residents—that farm policy is likely to more directly affect.

Linkage 1: Farm Policy and Food Prices for Households in Poverty

Hypothesis: Farm commodity policy may affect food prices, which in turn are important in the budgets of the poor. This is an important linkage to consider because the number of poor households is large—15.8 million households (14.8 percent of all households)—and of course all these households are food consumers.

In practice, this linkage is likely to be relatively small. First, we have seen that farm programs have only a small effect on farm prices. Second, the latest data show that farm prices represent an average of only approximately 10.5 cents out of a dollar of retail food spending.[69] Third, retail food expenditures are on average less than 10 percent of total per capita disposable income and about 17 percent for the poor. Fourth, as described above, nutrition assistance programs provide low-income households with a partial buffer from the effects of higher retail food prices.

At one time, poverty in the United States was conceptualized in terms of food needs. When the poverty rate was originally developed in the 1960s, researchers had access to good survey data on adequate food budgets but lacked information on other important spending categories, so the original poverty thresholds were determined by multiplying the cost of an adequate food budget by a factor of three. Based on similar reasoning, since 1977 the benefit formula for SNAP has assumed that participant households spend approximately 30 percent of their disposable income on food.

Today, a much smaller fraction of disposable income is spent on food.[70] This is still far below the 30 percent of spending assumed in the SNAP benefit formula and the one-third of spending assumed in the original construction of the poverty rate.

Variations in the price of housing may have larger consequences for the household budgets of low-income Americans. Based on a commonly used standard for housing affordability, SNAP households whose shelter costs exceed 50 percent of their net income are permitted a deduction that has the effect of increasing their benefits. More than 70 percent of SNAP households can claim this deduction.[71]

In federal government statistics, food-related hardship is measured using the prevalence of "household food insecurity," based on an 18-item survey about experiences of not having enough food.[72] The most powerful predictor of food insecurity, as measured by the survey, is household income. Consistent with actual consumption observations, the rate of food insecurity was high for poor households (39.5 percent) and much lower for middle-income and high-income households (6.3 percent). Low income in general, rather than something about food in particular, may be considered the fundamental source of food insecurity and hunger.[73]

Linkage 2: Farm Policy and Poverty for Farm Operators

Hypothesis: Farm policy could affect US poverty and nutrition of the poor by lifting farm operators out of poverty. At earlier stages of US history and in many low-income countries today, farm operators' households have been a large population at high risk of poverty.[74] An explicit goal of US farm policy is to raise farm incomes, so perhaps it also could reduce poverty.

As with Linkage 1, this linkage is not strong in practice. First, the commercial family farms that produce most of the food in the United States and receive most of the benefits from farm programs are owned and operated by households with high farm incomes and wealth. Second, farm incomes are only part of total household incomes. Farm operators, including those operating small part-time farms, have comparatively high total household incomes on average. Third, farm households are a small fraction of all US households, less than 2 percent. Given that relatively few farm households are poor, farm households represent an especially small fraction of US households in poverty. The effect of farm policy on farm operators' incomes is of little consequence for US poverty more broadly, and, as a result, farm policy has little impact on the nutrition of the poor.

To illuminate the issues, we examine the evidence on farm incomes and household incomes for farm operators overall and in particular categories, and we contrast the characteristics of US farm operator households and the characteristics of US households in poverty.

Income for Farm Operator Households, Overall and by Farm Type. In most years, the USDA estimates report that farm operator households have median incomes that are about as high as those of nonfarm households. To interpret these data, we note first that a farm is defined to include operations that grew or could have grown agricultural output worth $1,000. This definition is based on gross revenue (or normal-year revenue in case of low yields or other shortfall). USDA data show that most low-gross-revenue farms generate negative net cash revenues (incomes from sales are lower than reported costs) and contribute negatively to household income (but also reduce the household's tax liabilities). For two decades, median incomes of farm households have been above those of nonfarm households, and the gap has widened in the past decade (Figure 3).

It is useful to distinguish among farm types, to make sure that these average statistics do not disguise hardship among a particular subpopulation such as small farmers. Likewise, it is useful to separate farm and nonfarm sources of income, to make sure that one does not give an overoptimistic interpretation if struggling farmers must take second jobs or if those with mainly low-wage nonfarm employment operate farms as a second source of income. The USDA distinguishes three broad[75] categories:

- **Large-scale family farms (annual gross cash farm income of $1 million or more).** The 6,853 "very large" family farms and 62,706 "large" family farms represent just 3.3 percent of all farms by number, but they produce most of the food grown in the United States and receive

Figure 3. Household Income: Median Farm Operator vs. Median US, 1991–2014

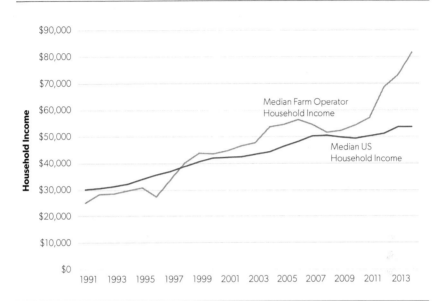

Note: Differences between farm operator income estimates from 2012 to 2014 and estimates from prior years reflect changes in survey methodology and implementation associated with the 2012 Agricultural Resource Management Survey, in addition to changes in the economic situation of farm households.
Source: US Department of Agriculture, Economic Research Service and National Agricultural Statistics Service, Agricultural Resource Management Survey; and US Census Bureau, Current Population Survey. Data were revised May 2, 2016.

most of the agricultural subsidies. In 2014, the median annual household income (including farm and nonfarm sources) was $1,183,000 for the "very large" family farms and $368,000 for the "large" family farms, far above the average income for nonfarm households. More than one household often owns and operates farms in this category.

- **Midsize family farms (annual gross cash farm income from $350,000 to $999,999).** Annual household income (including farm and nonfarm sources) was $185,000.

- **Small family farms (annual gross cash farm income less than $350,000).** Some 281,000 of these farms (13.5 percent of all farms) are "retirement farms," in which net farm income is low or negative, but average household income from other sources is above the national average for nonfarm households. Another 943,137 (45.4 percent of all farms) are "off-farm occupation farms," whose operators report a major occupation other than farming. The remaining 635,000 small family farms (30.6 percent of all farms) are "farming-occupation farms." This last group is the one whose risk of poverty is sometimes mentioned as part of the motivation for farm programs. Most of these farms generate very low farm revenue; in 2012 about half of all farms had gross farm revenue of less than $10,000.[76]

Characteristics of Farm Operator Households. In general, owning or operating a farm in the United States requires considerable experience and assets. US family farms have consolidated over the years into fewer and larger farms.

The USDA Economic Research Service reports that 95.4 percent of farm operators were white and only 1.6 percent were black or African American. Hispanic Americans (of any race) represented only 3.2 percent of farm operators. Robert Hoppe and James MacDonald[77] estimate that 33 percent of farm operators in 2014 were at least 65 years old. By comparison, only 12 percent of self-employed workers in nonagricultural businesses were at least 65 years old.

Poverty Among Farm Operators. Neither the USDA nor any other government agency publishes an official poverty rate for farm operators using the same methodology that is used for the general population. Because the number of farmers in the sample is too small, the Current Population Survey used in official poverty statistics does not provide estimates for farm operator households. However, the USDA does estimate the number of what they call "limited-resource farms" based on low farm income combined with "insufficient" off-farm income for the operator's household. The USDA classifies approximately 153,000 farms (7.4 percent of all farms) as limited-resource farms.[78] These limited-resource farm households represent a tiny fraction (less than 1 percent) of all US households in poverty.

Hisham El-Osta and Mitchell Morehart[79] used data from the Agriculture Resource Management Survey to study the determinants of poverty among farm operators. They found that poverty was lower for farm households with a household head who was older or white and that poverty was lower for farm households in metropolitan counties, which often include some rural areas. Poverty was lower for households that participated in government programs or had off-farm income.

While larger farms receive most agriculture program benefits, the USDA has a small program targeted more directly at "socially disadvantaged limited-resource farmers," providing outreach and support in applying for farm program benefits. This program, known as Section 2501, is administered by the USDA's Office of Advocacy and Outreach (OAO). It provides about $20 million per year to organizations that conduct outreach with the target population of farms.[80] A blistering report in 2015 from the USDA's Office of Inspector General (OIG) found "a pattern of broad and pervasive mismanagement of OAO grant funds." The report said that grant approval processes were "informal and undocumented" and "regulatory processes were disregarded."[81] The OIG recommended that USDA administrators "more closely monitor OAO's administration of this program" and reported that the department "has been developing and implementing internal controls as a result of our prior audit work."

In summary, even after distinguishing by farm type, most farm operator households are not at risk of poverty. Agricultural program benefits are related to current or historical production levels, which means that larger farms receive most program benefits. It is not politically feasible or economically practical to retarget the major farm programs toward the relatively few small full-time farms whose operators are at greater risk of poverty. Overall, if the goal is to reduce poverty in the United States, focusing on farm operator households is unlikely to have much impact.

Linkage 3: Farm Policy and Poverty for Farmworkers

Hypothesis: Farm policy could affect poverty for farmworkers, either by directly affecting wages and working conditions or by affecting the demand for farm labor.

People who work as hired laborers on US farms are at greater risk of poverty than farm operators. Compensation and working conditions for farmworkers are determined by supply and demand in labor markets. Farm policy could have some influence on labor demand, but it remains just one small factor among many that influence poverty for farmworkers. The evidence about the poverty status of farmworkers is as follows.

Farmworkers in the United States. Of the 676,000 farm laborers and supervisors, the USDA estimates that 50 percent are Hispanic, 47 percent are foreign born, and 41 percent are noncitizens. All these characteristics are associated with higher risk of poverty. These patterns vary by agricultural industry. For hired crop farmworkers in particular, only 29 percent are from the United States (including Puerto Rico), while 68 percent are from Mexico. The USDA estimates that almost half of hired crop farmworkers lack legal authorization, another 19 percent hold green cards or other forms of work authorization, and approximately 33 percent are US citizens (Table 5).[82] Farm work often involves physical labor that many workers cannot sustain as they age. In contrast with the large number of older farm operators, only 30 percent of farmworkers are over 44 years of age.

Estimated median wages are low for some of the highest-employment categories of farm work. The estimated median hourly wage in 2011 was $8.99 for crop farmworkers and $9.17 for agricultural graders and sorters. By comparison, in nonfarm sectors, the median hourly wage was higher than for farmworkers, even for low-wage occupations: $9.32 for maids and housekeepers and $14.30 for construction laborers.

Effects of Farm Policy on Farm Labor Markets. Wages and working conditions are determined by the supply of and demand for farm labor. All else equal, wages are expected to rise when the labor supply is constrained or when labor demand is high. Each agriculture sector's demand for labor depends in part on the economic market for that sector's products. For example, if consumer demand for tomatoes rises, we can expect an increase in the labor demand for workers to harvest tomatoes.

As noted previously, farm policy can affect markets for agricultural products in several directions. Farm payments tied to output increase incentives for increased production, leading to higher demand for labor. Likewise, commodity promotion or generic advertising programs could enhance the demand for farm products, and hence demand for farm labor. On the other hand, supply controls, or the supply limitations in land retirement programs such as the CRP, reduce the demand for labor.

Table 5. Demographic Characteristics of Hired Farmworkers and All Wage and Salary Workers, 2012

Item	Farm Laborers and Supervisors	Farm Managers	All Hired Farmworkers	All US Wage and Salary Workers
Number	676,000	111,000	787,000	142,653,000
Percentage Male	82	81	82	53
Median Age in Years	34	38	35	42
Percentage Under Age 25	27	15	25	13
Percentage Over Age 44	30	41	31	44
Percentage Married	51	61	53	56
Percentage White (Race)	91	96	92	81
Percentage Hispanic (Ethnicity)	50	16	45	15
Percentage Foreign Born	47	11	42	16
Percentage with US Citizenship	59	91	64	91
Percentage with Less Than Ninth Grade Education	31	6	27	3
Percentage with Some College	20	51	25	64

Source: US Department of Agriculture, Economic Research Service, "Farm Labor: Background," September 27, 2016, http://www.ers.usda.gov/topics/farm-economy/farm-labor/background.aspx.

However, in the United States, the major farm commodity and land retirement programs are focused on field crops, which have a comparatively high level of mechanization and low labor demand per acre, output unit, or dollar of output value. By contrast, specialty crops, including major fruit and vegetable crops, which have much less connection with farm programs, have comparatively less mechanization and higher labor demand per acre, output unit, or dollar of output value. Overall, farm programs are not focused on the farm commodities that matter the most for farm labor. Farm policy is therefore unlikely to majorly affect wages and working conditions for farmworkers.

Immigration Policy and the Supply of Farm Labor. US immigration policy is central to the supply of farm labor. Policies that reduce immigration place constraints on farm labor supply, leading to higher wages for workers who do make it to the United States (while leaving other would-be workers to find employment as best they can in their home countries). Conversely, policies that permit immigration allow more people to find employment in the United States, but the increased labor supply puts downward pressure on wages. As a result, US farm interest groups closely monitor immigration policy and actively participate in policy discussions.

Legal immigration is possible through several visa designations. Major nonagricultural visa designations include H-1a (skilled technical workers sponsored by a particular employer) and H-2b (seasonal or temporary nonagricultural workers). An important agricultural visa designation is H-2a (seasonal or temporary farmworkers).[83] Farm employers have shown increasing interest in hiring H-2a workers, but the program has a reputation for being cumbersome, requiring several years of dedicated effort to master the paperwork requirements and learn to use the program efficiently.[84]

The role of undocumented immigrants remains important as a part of the farm labor force. When authorities more vigorously enforce immigration rules, employers report disruptions in farm labor supply and farm production. For example, local governments may develop agreements with the US Department of Homeland Security under Section 287(g) of the Immigration and Nationality Act, allowing local authorities to perform immigration law functions. When these Section 287(g) agreements are adopted, farmworkers' wages rise, farm output decisions change, and farm profitability falls "in a manner consistent with farm labor shortages."[85]

In recent years, because of market conditions in Mexico and immigration policies in the United States, agricultural labor supply has been constrained, and wages have been rising.[86] Farms have responded by adopting technologies and practices that allow more output per worker (through mechanical and biological technology) and shifting to crops that use less labor per unit of value.

Strategies for Increasing Farmworker Wages and Improving Working Conditions. Increased farmworker incomes have been a goal for farm labor organizations for many years. Some labor organizations have expanded beyond traditional advocacy focused on farm operators because the farm operators face highly competitive output markets and may be unable to raise wages on their own. Instead, these organizations have developed campaigns focused on branded food companies downstream, which may be simultaneously more vulnerable to bad publicity and more able to encourage higher wages by offering higher prices for output.

In addition to labor advocacy, new reports suggest that farm wages have increased somewhat in recent years due to tightening labor markets in Mexico, combined with stronger enforcement of immigration rules in the United States.[87] One consequence of the inability to pass immigration reform legislation through Congress may be tighter farm labor markets in the United States, causing concern for farm employers but some wage improvements and perhaps eventual poverty reductions and consequence improvements in diets for farmworkers.

Linkage 4: Farm Policy and Poverty in Rural Communities

Hypothesis: Farm policy could affect poverty in rural communities by supporting farms and enhancing local economic activity. This economic activity could increase demand for local goods and services, raising wages and reducing poverty.

Farm policy is an indirect way of addressing poverty in rural communities. Farm programs are not strongly focused on generating employment, and most employment in rural communities is not related to agriculture.

The evidence from national statistics on poverty in rural communities, presented below, indicates that some measures show higher poverty rates in rural communities, while other measures show higher poverty rates in urban communities. The following review of initiatives for enhancing economic activity and wealth creation in rural communities demonstrates that most are focused on nonfarm sectors of the economy.

Poverty in Nonmetropolitan Communities. Poverty rates in the United States are higher in the principal cities than in other areas. Among the approximately 316 million residents of the United States in 2014, 84 percent lived in metropolitan statistical areas, while 16 percent lived in nonmetro areas. (Note that "metropolitan" is related to "urban," and "nonmetro" is related to "rural," but the terms are not identical. Some metropolitan counties have rural hinterlands, and, conversely, some towns in nonmetro areas have an urban character.)

The poverty rate is much higher in the principal cities (19.0 percent) than in other metro areas (11.9 percent), including suburbs or rural areas

Table 6. Median Income and Poverty Rates in Metropolitan and Nonmetropolitan Areas of the United States, 2014

| Item | Total | Metropolitan | | | Nonmetro |
		Total Metro	Principal City	Other	
People (Thousands)	316,168	266,071	99,298	166,733	50,097
Households (Thousands)	124,587	104,009	40,578	63,431	20,578
Median Household Income ($)	53,657	55,855	47,850	61,600	45,482
Poverty, Official (%)	14.9	14.5	19.0	11.9	16.6
Poverty, Supplemental (%)	15.3	15.8	20.2	13.1	12.8

Note: The official poverty rate takes account of wages and nonwage income but does not include in-kind benefits such as SNAP benefits as income. The supplemental poverty measure counts some in-kind benefits as income and includes a geographic adjustment for housing costs, among other changes.
Source: Carmen DeNavas-Walt and Bernadette D. Proctor, "Income and Poverty in the United States: 2014," US Census Bureau, September 2015, http://www.census.gov/library/publications/2015/demo/p60-252.html; Kathleen Short, "The Supplemental Poverty Measure: 2014," US Census Bureau, September 2015, https://www.census.gov/content/dam/Census/library/publications/2015/demo/p60-254.pdf; and US Census Bureau, Current Population Survey, Annual Social and Economic Supplement.

in metropolitan counties (Table 6).[88] The official poverty rate in nonmetro areas fell in the middle (16.6 percent) but is higher than the average for the United States as a whole (14.9 percent).

Many proposals have been put forward to improve the measurement of poverty.[89] Building on these suggestions, in recent years the federal government has published a supplemental poverty measure. Among other changes, the supplemental poverty measure uses different approaches for taxes, which are significant for low-income households that receive the earned income tax credit; in-kind government program benefits, which are significant for low-income households that receive SNAP and other nutrition benefits; and housing costs, which may be lower on average in nonmetro areas. In contrast to the official poverty measure, poverty rates using the supplemental measure are substantially lower in nonmetro areas. In 2014, the supplemental poverty rate was 15.8 percent in metro areas and 12.8 percent in nonmetro areas (Table 6).[90]

In nonmetro areas, as in metro areas, poverty rates are higher for non-Hispanic, African American, and Hispanic residents than for white residents and higher for female-headed households with children and no spouse present than for other family types.[91] While there are some differences in the trajectory and timing of the ongoing economic recovery, the basic patterns of poverty appear similar in metro and nonmetro areas.

Employment Generation and Wealth Creation in Rural America. In the first few years following the Great Recession of 2008–09, employment was slow to grow in both metro and nonmetro areas. By 2012–13, employment conditions had begun to improve in metro areas but remained stagnant in nonmetro areas. By 2014 and the first half of 2015, there were employment gains in both metro and nonmetro areas, but rural areas continue to experience population out-migration.[92]

Farming is responsible for only 6 percent of all employment in nonmetro areas and 1 percent of employment in metro areas. Several other sectors employ more people, even in nonmetro areas. In nonmetro areas, services are responsible for 41 percent of all employment; trade, transportation, and utilities for 17 percent; government for 16 percent; and manufacturing for 11 percent (Figure 4).[93]

In a recent multiauthor volume on rural wealth creation, Steven Deller observes that rural development policy focused in the past on agriculture because agriculture "was considered the economic base of rural areas. While this was perhaps true before World War II, most rural areas outside the Central Plains have now diversified into manufacturing, tourism and recreation, and service-based industries."[94] It makes sense that local communities and USDA programs alike have shifted toward many other sectors for both employment and wealth creation.

In summary, most poor Americans do not live in rural areas, and for reducing poverty in rural areas, the primary focus is on employment sectors other than agriculture. Of the approximately 47.1 million Americans in poverty in 2014, according to the official measure, just 8.3 million (18 percent) lived in nonmetro areas. Using the supplemental poverty measure, which takes account of lower housing costs in some areas, the fraction of poor people found in nonmetro areas is even smaller. Farming is responsible for about 6 percent of employment in nonmetro areas, while other industries such as manufacturing are more important in those areas. The USDA does many things to promote rural development, but the agriculture

Figure 4. Distribution of Nonmetro and Metro Employment by Industry Group, 2014

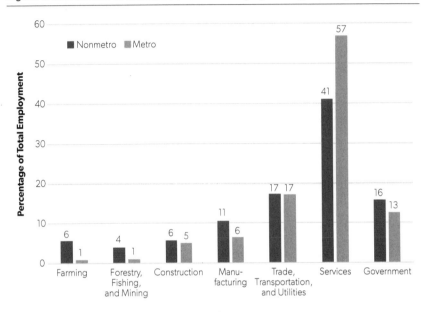

Note: Employment is full-time and part-time jobs, by place of work.
Source: US Department of Agriculture, Economic Research Service, 2016.

subsidy programs are not central to that effort. And despite the many programs, the USDA devotes relatively little of its budget to this effort.[95]

Overview of the Implications of Farm Subsidies on Poverty and Consequent Food Consumption of the Poor

The previous sections have documented the limited role of farm policy in US poverty even for the subpopulations of those in poverty that are most linked to farming. By definition, the overall effects of farm subsidies on incomes of those in poverty in the United States are much smaller than these impacts on the most affected subgroups.

Given that incomes of these groups of poor households are unlikely to be much influenced by farm policy, the consequences for food consumption and nutrition are smaller and more indirect. The response of food consumption to changes in income is less than one-to-one in percentage terms. In economic terms, the income elasticity for food products are below 1.0, and that is especially true for staple foods.[96] For many food groups, the income elasticity is close to zero, suggesting no more is purchased as income rises.[97] Low-income households have higher income elasticities for food, but they are still low for basic food products and higher for high-priced items.

Thus, while farm subsidies transfer income from taxpayers to farm resource owners, most of the direct beneficiaries are relatively wealthy. The impacts on indirect beneficiaries, farmworkers, rural residents, and those in other farm-related occupations receive little additional income from farm programs, and their food consumption and nutrition are almost unaffected by income effects of farm subsidies.

Summary and Conclusions

The introduction outlined two channels of influence from farm subsidy programs to food and nutrition of the poor. Farm commodity subsidy programs in the United States have limited potential to affect retail food prices. Most farm subsidy programs have at most small impacts on overall US production of farm commodities, even though they may increase acreage and production of some crops relative to others. For example, farm programs, including risk-management programs, may encourage acreage of feed grains, oilseeds, and cotton relative to other crops. But even for these, land retirement under the CRP offsets these acreage impacts.

Moreover, these crops are far removed from the food items in which they are an input. For example, soybeans are mostly either exported or used as livestock feed. Therefore, any impact on meat prices, for example, is indirect and small. Even for livestock feed, much of the impact of subsidies would be to expand grain acres at the expense of hay or other forage acreage, so the net impact on the cost of production of beef or milk, for example, is mixed. On net, the impact of these programs on US consumer prices is surely tiny.

Some policies clearly raise consumer prices. For example, trade barriers raise the price of sugar and sugar-containing foods above what they would be if imports of raw or refined sugar entered the United States more freely. But sugar is a small share of the total food budget, and some nutritionists would argue that raising the cost of sugar-containing processed food products may improve the nutrition of the poor. After several rounds of tariff reductions and free trade agreements, most tariffs on food items are relatively low. But trade barriers also raise prices of orange juice and fresh market tomatoes.

The impact of the complex array of dairy policy on milk product prices deserves special notice. After decades of propping up US milk prices, trade barriers and export port subsidies now have no significant impact on prices of retail prices. Farm price supports that raised dairy prices have also been eliminated. The new risk-management program has the potential to raise milk production overall and lower US prices for dairy products slightly. At the same time, the elaborate array of marketing regulations raises the prices of milk used for beverage products and slightly depresses the price of more heavily processed dairy products and ingredients, such as cheese, milk powders, and butter, which are sold domestically or exported. Despite the complicated array of policies, the new result is no significant effect on prices and consumption of dairy products by the poor in the United States.

The bottom line is clear. Farm subsidies and related land retirements, market regulations, and trade policies have an array of small and offsetting impacts on farm commodity prices. When these impacts are filtered through the supply chain, the impacts on retail prices and food consumption are surely tiny.

The second way farm subsidies could, in theory, affect food consumption and nutrition of the poor is through incomes and therefore the budgets that poor households have available for food expenditures. Large and important USDA programs provide income assistance and food-specific aid to low-income households that reduce poverty and lower the relative cost of food. These programs—SNAP, school meals, WIC, and related programs—make additional resources available to enhance food consumption of the poor. Although operated by the USDA with authorization and oversight from the same committees in Congress, these programs are distinct from the farm programs.

The farm programs themselves have almost no impact on incomes of the poor in the United States. That lack of impact is by design. The bulk of farm subsidy benefits are roughly proportional to output of bulk commodities, so these benefits go to large commercial-sized farms. That means that farmland owners and operators of large farms tend to receive these benefits, and few of these owners or operators are poor or food vulnerable. We find that farm subsidies have slight impacts on incomes of the relatively few farm operators living in poverty because they produce little farm output.

Farm employees also gain little. Impacts on wages through increased demand for labor may be slightly positive in the short run. But the most labor-intensive crops receive the smallest subsidy. Even where trade barriers raise acreage, such as in sugar or fresh market tomatoes, elastic labor supplies and farmworker immigration programs minimize any positive wage impacts. Finally, farm income and employment are small shares of the rural economy almost everywhere in the United States. Even with multiplier impacts that affect nonfarm employment and income opportunities, farm subsidies do little for rural poverty in the long run and thus have tiny impacts on food consumption and nutrition of vulnerable households. Food and income assistance are far more important than farm subsidies for poor rural households.

Our bottom line is that, despite occasional claims to the contrary, farm subsidy programs have little impact on food consumption, food security, or nutrition in the United States.

Notes

1. Robert W. Goodman, "Should Washington End Agriculture Subsidies? No," *Wall Street Journal*, July 12, 2015, http://www.wsj.com/articles/should-washington-end-agriculture-subsidies-1436757020.

2. Crop Insurance America, "Just the Facts: How Does Crop Insurance Benefit the Public?," 2016, http://www.cropinsurancein-america.org/about-crop-insurance/just-the-facts/.

3. Eric A. Finkelstein and Laurie Zuckerman, *The Fattening of America: How the Economy Makes Us Fat, If It Matters, and What to Do About It* (Hoboken, NJ: John Wiley & Sons, 2008).

4. Julian M. Alston, Daniel A. Sumner, and Stephen A. Vosti, "Farm Subsidies and Obesity in the United States: National Evidence and International Comparisons," *Food Policy* 33, no. 6 (December 2008): 470–79; Abigail M. Okrent and Julian M. Alston, "The Effects of Farm Commodity and Retail Food Policies on Obesity and Economic Welfare in the United States," *American Journal of Agricultural Economics* 94, no. 3 (April 2012): 611–46; and Julian M. Alston, Joanna P. MacEwan, and Abigail M. Okrent, "The Economics of Obesity (Policy)," *Annual Review of Resource Economics* (2016).

5. Mary Ahern, "Rural Development Policy in the Farm Bill," in *The Economic Welfare*

and Trade Implications of the 2014 Farm Bill, ed. Vincent H. Smith (Bingley, UK: Emerald Group Publishing, 2015).

6. See, for example, Daniel A. Sumner and Carl Zulauf, "Economic and Environmental Effects of Agricultural Insurance Programs," Council on Food, Agricultural and Resource Economics, July 2012, http://www.cfare.org/publications/the-conservation-crossroads-inagriculture.

7. Carl Zulauf and David Orden, "The US Agricultural Act of 2014: Overview and Analysis," International Food Policy Research Institute, December 10, 2014, https://www.ifpri.org/publication/us-agricultural-act-2014-overview-and-analysis; and Bruce A. Babcock and Jacinto F. Fabiosa, "The Impact of Ethanol and Ethanol Subsidies on Corn Prices: Revisiting History," Iowa State University, Center for Agricultural and Rural Development, April 2011, http://www.card.iastate.edu/products/publications/synopsis/?p=1155.

8. Congressional Budget Office, "CBO's January 2016 Baseline for Farm Programs," January 25, 2016, https://www.cbo.gov/sites/default/files/51317-2016-01-USDA.pdf.

9. Julian M. Alston et al., *Persistence Pays: US Agricultural Productivity Growth and the Benefits from Public R&D Spending* (New York: Springer, 2010); and Julian M. Alston and Philip G. Pardey, "Agriculture in the Global Economy," *Journal of Economic Perspectives* 28, no. 1 (Winter 2014): 121–46.

10. F. W. Taussig, *The Tariff History of the United States* (New York: J. P. Putnam's Sons, 1910).

11. World Trade Organization, *Trade Profiles 2015*, 2016, https://www.wto.org/english/res_e/publications_e/trade_profiles15_e.htm.

12. US International Trade Commission, "Antidumping and Countervailing Duty Orders in Place as of September 16, 2016," 2016, http://usitc.gov/sites/default/files/trade_remedy/documents/orders.xls.

13. Qualifying products are restricted to those products that were tariffed during the Uruguay Round.

14. World Trade Organization, "The Agriculture Committee and Implementation of Commitments: Documents and Data," s.v. "Notifications on Special Safeguards Under Articles 5.7 and 18.2," 2016, https://www.wto.org/english/tratop_e/agric_e/ag_work_e.htm.

15. US Department of Agriculture, Agricultural Marketing Service, "Removal of Mandatory Country of Origin Labeling Requirements for Beef and Pork Muscle Cuts, Ground Beef, and Ground Pork," *Federal Register* 81, no. 41 (March 2, 2016): 10755–61.

16. Bruce L. Gardner, *American Agriculture in the Twentieth Century* (Cambridge, MA: Harvard University Press, 2002).

17. Volume control remains authorized for almonds, dates, hazelnuts, prunes, raisins, walnuts, tart cherries, Florida citrus, cranberries, and spearmint oil.

18. US Department of Agriculture, Agricultural Marketing Service, "Measures of Growth in Federal Milk Orders," September 30, 2016, 3, https://www.ams.usda.gov/sites/default/files/media/FMMO%20Measures%20of%20Growth%201950%20-%202014.pdf.

19. Hayley H. Chouinard et al., "Milk Marketing Order Winners and Losers," *Applied Economic Perspectives and Policy* 32, no. 1 (Spring 2010): 59–76, http://aepp.oxfordjournals.org/content/32/1/59.full.

20. Julian M. Alston, James A. Chalfant, and Nicholas E. Piggott, "The Incidence of the

Costs and Benefits of Generic Advertising," *American Journal of Agricultural Economics* 82, no. 3 (August 2002): 665–71; and Gary W Williams and Oral Capps Jr., "Measuring the Effectiveness of Checkoff Programs," *Choices* 21, no. 2 (2006): 73–78.

21. Dennis A. Shields, "Farm and Food Support Under USDA's Section 32 Program," Congressional Research Service, November 18, 2014, https://www.fas.org/sgp/crs/misc/RL34081.pdf.

22. The Agricultural Marketing Agreement Act of 1937 and several "stand-alone" acts, such as the Beef Promotion and Research Act of 1985, establish the federal statutes for checkoff programs. Williams and Capps, "Measuring the Effectiveness of Checkoff Programs."

23. Williams and Capps, "Measuring the Effectiveness of Checkoff Programs."

24. Michael K. Wohlgenant, "Retail-to-Farm Transmission of Generic Advertising Effects," *Choices* 21, no. 2 (2006): 67–72.

25. Babcock and Fabiosa, "The Impact of Ethanol and Ethanol Subsidies on Corn Prices."

26. Brian Wright, "Global Biofuels: Key to the Puzzle of Grain Market Behavior," *Journal of Economic Perspectives* 28, no. 1 (Winter 2014): 73–98.

27. Nicole Condon, Heather Klemick, and Ann Wolverton, "Impacts of Ethanol Policy on Corn Prices: A Review and Meta-Analysis of Recent Evidence," *Food Policy* 51 (February 2015): 63–73.

28. Scott Irwin and Darrel Good, "Further Evidence on the Competitiveness of Ethanol in Gasoline Blends," *farmdoc daily*, January 30, 2015, http://farmdocdaily.illinois.edu/2015/01/further-evidence-on-competitiveness-of-ethanol.html.

29. Wright, "Global Biofuels."

30. Christopher B. Barrett and Erin C. Lentz, "Highway Robbery on the High Seas," *Hill*, May 29, 2014, http://thehill.com/blogs/pundits-blog/transportation/207565-highway-robbery-on-the-high-seas.

31. Randy Schnepf, "Status of the WTO Brazil-U.S. Cotton Case," Congressional Research Service, October 1, 2014, http://nationalaglawcenter.org/wp-content/uploads/assets/crs/R43336.pdf.

32. Randy Schnepf, "US International Food Aid Programs: Background and Issues," Congressional Research Service, April 1, 2015, https://www.fas.org/sgp/crs/misc/R41072.pdf.

33. Forfeitures may occur due to payment limitations (nonrecourse loans are not subject to payment limits unlike marketing loan gains) or when repayment prices do not reflect local market conditions (e.g., peanuts).

34. John C. Beghin and Amani E. Elobeid, "The Impact of the US Sugar Program Redux" (working paper, Iowa State University Center for Agricultural and Rural Development, 2013), http://lib.dr.iastate.edu/card_workingpapers/574.

35. Gary W. Brester, "20 Years in, NAFTA Finally Sours the US Sugar Program," American Enterprise Institute, September 4, 2014, http://www.americanboondoggle.com/20-years-in-nafta-finally-sours-the-us-sugar-program/.

36. In-kind payments are payments made in the form of commodities rather than cash.

37. Erik J. O'Donoghue and James B. Whitaker, "Do Direct Payments Distort Producers' Decisions? An Examination of the Farm Security and Rural Investment Act of 2002," *Applied Economic Perspectives and Policy* 32, no. 1 (Spring 2010): 170–93.

38. Daniel Sumner questioned whether provisions that allow producers to update acreage bases and yields effectively link even "decoupled" payments to planting decisions. Daniel A. Sumner, "Implications of the USA Farm Bill of 2002 for Agricultural Trade and Trade Negotiations," *Australian Journal of Agricultural and Resource Economics* 47, no. 1 (March 2003): 117–40. Nathan Hendricks and Daniel Sumner showed that updating made little difference when all relevant commodities had similar subsidies available. Nathan P. Hendrick and Daniel A. Sumner, "The Effects of Policy Expectations on Crop Supply, with an Application to Base Updating," *American Journal of Agricultural Economics* 96, no. 3 (April 2014): 903–23.

39. Roger Claasen et al., "Additionality in US Agricultural Conservation and Regulatory Offset Programs," US Department of Agriculture, Economic Research Service, July 2014, http://www.ers.usda.gov/publications/err-economic-research-report/err170.aspx.

40. Erik Lichtenberg, "Conservation, the Farm Bill and US Agri-Environmental Policy," in *The Economic Welfare and Trade Relations Implications of the 2014 Farm Bill*, ed. Vincent H. Smith (Bingley, UK: Emerald Publishing Group, 2016): 31–42.

41. Congressional Budget Office, "CBO's January 2016 Baseline for Farm Programs."

42. Bruce A. Babcock, "Using Cumulative Prospect Theory to Explain Anomalous Crop Insurance Coverage Choice," *American Journal of Agricultural Economics* 97, no. 5 (October 2015): 1317–84.

43. Xiaodong Du, Hongli Feng, and David A. Hennessy, "Rationality of Choices in Subsidized Crop Insurance Markets," Iowa State University, Center for Agricultural and Rural Development, February 2014, http://www.card.iastate.edu/products/publications/synopsis/?p=1219.

44. Joseph W. Glauber, "The Growth of the Federal Crop Insurance Program, 1990–2011," *American Journal of Agricultural Economics* 95, no. 2 (January 2013): 482–88.

45. Barry K. Goodwin, Monte L. Vandeveer, and John L. Deal, "An Empirical Analysis of Acreage Effects of Participation in the Federal Crop Insurance Program," *American Journal of Agricultural Economics* 86, no. 4 (November 2004): 1058–77.

46. Ethan Ligon, "Supply and Effects of Specialty Crop Insurance," in *The Intended and Unintended Effects of U.S. Agricultural and Biotechnology Policies*, eds. Joshua S. Graff Zivin and Jeffrey M. Perloff (Chicago: University of Chicago Press, 2012), 113–42.

47. Barry K. Goodwin and Vincent H. Smith, "The Effects of Crop Insurance and Disaster Relief Programs on Soil Erosion: The Case of Soybeans and Corn," in *Risk Management and the Environment: Agriculture in Perspective*, eds. Bruce A. Babcock, Robert W. Fraser, and Joseph N. Leakakis (Dordrecht, Netherlands: Kluwer Academic Publishers, 2003), 181–95.

48. Joseph W. Glauber, "Crop Insurance Reconsidered," *American Journal of Agricultural Economics* 86, no. 5 (December 2004): 1179–95.

49. Jisang Yu, Aaron Smith, and Daniel A. Sumner, "The Acreage Effects of the Premium Subsidy in the U.S. Federal Crop Insurance Program" (working paper, University of California Agricultural Issues Center, 2016), http://aic.ucdavis.edu/research1/policy.html.

50. Goodwin and Smith, "The Effects of Crop Insurance."

51. Jessica Kelly, Patrick Canning, and Alfons Weersink, "Decomposing the Farmer's Share of the Food Dollar," *Applied Economic Perspectives and Policy* 37, no. 2 (June 2015): 311–31.

52. Leslie McGranahan, *Food Inflation and the Consumption Patterns of US Households*, Federal Reserve Bank of Chicago, October 2008, https://www.chicagofed.org/publications/chicago-fed-letter/2008/october-255.

53. James Mabli and Rosalie Malsberger, "Recent Trends in Spending Patterns of Supplemental Nutrition Assistance Program Participants and Other Low-Income Americans," *Monthly Labor Review*, September 2013, http://www.bls.gov/opub/mlr/2013/article/mabli-malsberger.htm#.

54. Alisha Coleman-Jensen et al., "Household Food Security in the United States in 2014," US Department of Agriculture, Economic Research Service, September 2015, https://www.ers.usda.gov/publications/pub-details/?pubid=45428.

55. Alisha Coleman-Jensen et al., "Statistical Supplement to Household Food Security in the United States in 2014," US Department of Agriculture, Economic Research Service, September 2015.

56. Elizabeth Condon et al., *Diet Quality of Americans by SNAP Participation Status: Data from the National Health and Nutrition Examination Survey, 2007–2010*, US Department of Agriculture, Food and Nutrition Service, May 2015, http://www.fns.usda.gov/sites/default/files/ops/NHANES-SNAP07-10.pdf.

57. US Department of Agriculture, Food and Nutrition Service, "Child Nutrition Tables," 2015, http://www.fns.usda.gov/pd/child-nutrition-tables.

58. US Department of Agriculture, Food and Nutrition Service, "Supplemental Nutrition Assistance Program (SNAP)," 2015, http://www.fns.usda.gov/pd/supplemental-nutrition-assistance-program-snap.

59. Esa Eslami, *Trends in Supplemental Nutrition Assistance Program Participation Rates: Fiscal Year 2010 to Fiscal Year 2013*, US Department of Agriculture, Food and Nutrition Service, August 2015, http://www.fns.usda.gov/snap/trends-supplemental-nutritionassistance-program-participation-rates-fiscal-year-2010-fiscal-1.

60. Victor Oliveira, "The Food Assistance Landscape: FY 2014 Annual Report," US Department of Education, Economic Research Service, March 2015, http://www.ers.usda.gov/publications/eib-economic-information-bulletin/eib137.aspx.

61. Julie A. Caswell and Ann L. Yaktine, eds., *Supplemental Nutrition Assistance Program: Examining the Evidence to Define Benefit Adequacy* (Washington, DC: National Academies Press).

62. Parke E. Wilde, "The New Normal: The Supplemental Nutrition Assistance Program (SNAP)," *American Journal of Agricultural Economics* 95, no. 2 (January 2013): 325–31.

63. Parke E. Wilde, "Measuring the Effect of Food Stamps on Food Insecurity and Hunger: Research and Policy Considerations," *Journal of Nutrition* 137, no. 2 (February 2007): 307–10.

64. James Mabli et al., *Measuring the Effect of Supplemental Nutrition Assistance Program (SNAP) Participation on Food Security*, US Department of Agriculture, August 2013, http://www.fns.usda.gov/measuring-effect-snap-participation-food-security-0.

65. Tatiana Andreyeva, Amanda S. Tripp, and Marlene B. Schwartz, "Dietary Quality of Americans by Supplemental Nutrition Assistance Program Participation Status: A Systematic Review," *American Journal of Preventive Medicine* 49, no. 4 (October 2015): 594–604; and Condon et al., *Diet Quality of Americans by SNAP Participation Status*.

66. Andreyeva, Tripp, and Schwartz, "Dietary Quality of Americans by Supplemental Nutrition Assistance Program Participation Status"; and Condon et al., *Diet Quality of Americans by SNAP Participation Status.*

67. Andreyeva, Tripp, and Schwartz, "Dietary Quality of Americans by Supplemental Nutrition Assistance Program Participation Status."

68. Susan Bartlett et al., *Evaluation of the Healthy Incentives Pilot (HIP): Final Report,* US Department of Agriculture, Food and Nutrition Service, September 2014, http://www.fns.usda.gov/snap/healthy-incentives-pilot-final-evaluation-report.

69. US Department of Agriculture, Economic Research Service, "Food Prices and Spending," https://www.ers.usda.gov/dataproducts/ag-and-food-statistics-charting-the-essentials/food-prices-and-spending.aspx.

70. Caswell and Yaktine, *Supplemental Nutrition Assistance Program.*

71. Caswell and Yaktine, *Supplemental Nutrition Assistance Program.*

72. Coleman-Jensen et al., "Household Food Security in the United States in 2014."

73. Parke E. Wilde, "America's Hunger Problem: What's Really Going On," *Politico,* September 9, 2015, http://www.politico.com/agenda/story/2015/09/americas-hunger-problem-whats-really-going-on-000222.

74. Carolyn Dimitri, Anne Effland, and Neilson Conklin, "The 20th Century Transformation of US Agriculture and Farm Policy," US Department of Agriculture, Economic Research Service, June 2005, http://www.ers.usda.gov/publications/eib-economic-informationbulletin/eib3.aspx.

75. Robert Hoppe and James M. MacDonald, "America's Diverse Family Farms: 2015 Edition," US Department of Agriculture, Economic Research Service, December 2015, http://www.ers.usda.gov/publications/eib-economic-information-bulletin/eib-146.aspx.

76. US Department of Agriculture, *2012 Census of Agriculture,* May 2014, https://www.agcensus.usda.gov/Publications/2012/.

77. Hoppe and MacDonald, "America's Diverse Family Farms."

78. Hoppe and MacDonald, "America's Diverse Family Farms"; US Department of Agriculture, Economic Research Service, "Beginning & Disadvantaged Farmers," October 8, 2014, http://www.ers.usda.gov/topics/farm-economy/beginning-disadvantaged-farmers.aspx.

79. Hisham S. El-Osta and Mitchell J. Morehart, "Determinants of Poverty Among US Farm Households," *Journal of Agricultural and Applied Economics* 40, no. 1 (April 2008): 1–20.

80. National Sustainable Agriculture Coalition, "Outreach and Assistance for Socially Disadvantaged and Veteran Farmers and Ranchers (Section 2501)," October 2014, http://sustainableagriculture.net/publications/grassrootsguide/farming-opportunities/sociallydisadvantaged-farmers-program/.

81. US Department of Agriculture, Office of Inspector General, "Section 2501 Grants Awarded FYs 2010–2011," March 2015, https://www.usda.gov/oig/webdocs/91099-0003-21.pdf.

82. US Department of Agriculture, Economic Research Service, "Farm Economy," October 30, 2014, http://www.ers.usda.gov/topics/farm-economy/.

83. Stephanie Mercier, "Employing Agriculture: How the Midwest Farm and Food Sector Relies on Immigrant Labor," Chicago Council on Global Affairs, December 2014,

http://www.agri-pulse.com/uploaded/Midwest-Agriculture-Immigration.pdf.

84. Zhengfei Guan et al., "Agricultural Labor and Immigration Reform," *Choices* 30, no. 4 (2015), http://www.choicesmagazine.org/UserFiles/file/cmsarticle_476.pdf.

85. Genti Kostandini, Elton Mykerezi, and Cesar Escalante, "The Impact of Immigration Enforcement on the U.S. Farming Sector," *American Journal of Agricultural Economics* 96, no. 1 (January 2014): 172–92.

86. Philip Martin, "Immigration and Farm Labor: Policy Options and Consequences," *American Journal of Agricultural Economics* 95, no. 2 (January 2013): 470–75; and Maoyong Fan et al., "Why Do Fewer Agricultural Workers Migrate Now?," *American Journal of Agricultural Economics* 97, no. 3 (April 2015): 665–79.

87. Guan et al., "Agricultural Labor and Immigration Reform."

88. Carmen DeNavas-Walt and Bernadette D. Proctor, "Income and Poverty in the United States: 2014," US Census Bureau, September 2015, http://www.census.gov/library/publications/2015/demo/p60-252.html; and Kathleen Short, "The Supplemental Poverty Measure: 2014," US Census Bureau, September 2015, https://www.census.gov/content/dam/Census/library/publications/2015/demo/p60-254.pdf.

89. Short, "The Supplemental Poverty Measure."

90. Short, "The Supplemental Poverty Measure."

91. Lorin D. Kusmin, "Rural America at a Glance: 2015 Edition," US Department of Agriculture, Economic Research Service, January 2016, http://www.ers.usda.gov/publications/eib-economic-information-bulletin/eib-145.aspx.

92. Kusmin, "Rural America at a Glance: 2015 Edition."

93. US Department of Agriculture, Economic Research Service, "Rural Employment & Population," http://www.ers.usda.gov/topics/rural-economy-population/.

94. Steven C. Deller, "Strategies for Rural Wealth Creation: A Progression of Thinking Through Ideas and Concepts," in *Rural Wealth Creation*, eds. John L. Pender et al. (New York: Routledge, 2014).

95. Ahern, "Rural Development Policy in the Farm Bill."

96. Abigail M. Okrent and Julian M. Alston, "Demand for Food in the United States: A Review of the Literature, Evaluation of Previous Estimates, and Presentation of New Estimates of Demand" (working paper, Giannini Foundation of Agricultural Economics, Berkeley, CA, April 2011), http://giannini.ucop.edu/Monographs/48-FoodDemand.pdf.

97. Okrent and Alston, "Demand for Food in the United States."

2

The Future of SNAP: Continuing to Balance Protection and Incentives

DIANE WHITMORE SCHANZENBACH

The Supplemental Nutrition Assistance Program (SNAP), formerly known as the Food Stamp Program, makes up the lion's share of the farm bill, totaling approximately 80 percent of its spending.[1] In 2017, 12.9 percent of the population participated in the program, with $63.6 billion spent on benefits.

SNAP is an efficient and effective program. It is designed to work in conjunction with the free market through the normal channels of trade by supplementing the cash resources that a family has to purchase food, so that between SNAP and their other income, a family can purchase an adequate diet. Average monthly benefits in 2017 amounted to $255 per household, or $126 per person—about $4.20 per person per day. Benefits can be used to purchase most foods at grocery stores and farmers markets that are intended to be taken home and prepared, excluding goods such as hot foods intended for immediate consumption, vitamins, paper products, pet foods, alcohol, and tobacco. Benefits typically are paid once per month on an electronic benefits transfer card that can be used in a checkout line like a debit card.

An important goal of SNAP is to address food insecurity—that is, having inadequate or uncertain access to enough food for an active, healthy lifestyle. In 2016, 12.3 percent of households overall were food insecure at some point over the year, and 16.5 percent of households with children experienced food insecurity. As shown in Figure 1, food insecurity rates increased approximately 30 percent during the Great Recession, rising by more than would have been expected from families' declines in income alone.[2] Food insecurity has declined markedly over the past few years but nonetheless remains elevated over prerecession levels. SNAP has been shown to reduce food insecurity.[3]

Figure 1. Food Insecurity Rates, by Group

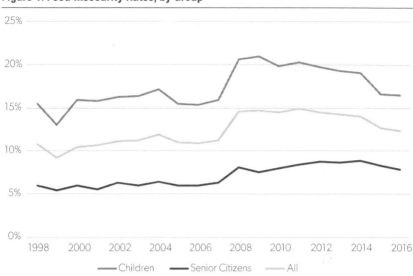

Source: US Department of Agriculture, Economic Research Service, "Food Security in the US," https://www.ers.usda.gov/topics/ food-nutrition-assistance/food-security-in-the-us/key-statistics-graphics.aspx#trends.

Figure 2. SNAP Participation and Expenditures

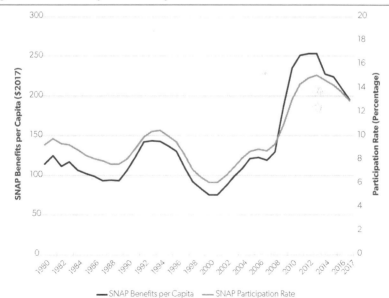

Source: Author's calculations using data from the US Department of Agriculture, Food and Nutrition Service and the Bureau of Labor Statistics.

Figure 3. Relationship Among Income, SNAP, and Food Spending

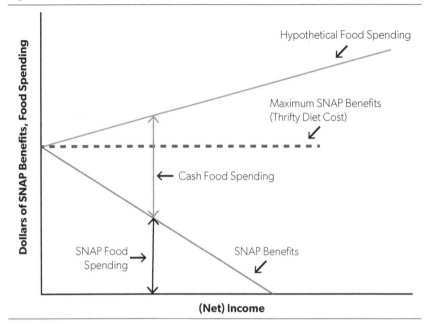

Source: Hilary W. Hoynes, Leslie McGranahan, and Diane Whitmore Schanzenbach, "SNAP and Food Consumption," in *SNAP Matters: How Food Stamps Affect Health and Well-Being*, eds. Judith Bartfeld et al. (Palo Alto, CA: Stanford University Press, 2015).

The earned income tax credit (EITC) and SNAP are the cornerstones of the social safety net. In 2015, SNAP kept 8.4 million people, including 3.8 million children, out of poverty, after correcting for undercounted benefits in the Current Population Survey.[4] Because the EITC is designed to provide benefits only when a household has an employed worker, its effectiveness is limited in times of high unemployment.[5] On the other hand, SNAP can both support work when it is available and serve as insurance, propping up food consumption levels during periods of unemployment. While SNAP payments and caseloads increased in the wake of the Great Recession, the caseload has begun to fall slowly since its peak in 2013, and the Congressional Budget Office (CBO) predicts that it will fall further in the coming years in response to a strengthening economy.[6] This chapter will lay out facts and recent research findings on SNAP and propose potential policy reforms.

Background on SNAP

Figure 2 presents SNAP participation and expenditures over time. Total expenditures (in inflation-adjusted 2016 dollars) increased from $25.9 billion in 1990 to $78.4 billion in 2013, falling to $63.6 billion in 2017. Over the same period, average monthly participation grew from 20 million persons in 1990 to a peak of 47.6 million in 2013, declining to 42.1 million in fiscal year (FY) 2017. As a share of the total US population, SNAP participation has grown from 6.1 percent in 2000 to a high of 15.1 percent in 2013, falling back to 12.9 percent in 2017.

Figure 3, reproduced from a paper I coauthored with Hilary Hoynes and Leslie McGranahan,[7] shows a stylized version of the relationship among a family's income, benefits, and food spending, for a family of a fixed size. The horizontal axis shows a family's net income, or the amount of disposable income that is available for food purchase under the assumptions of the SNAP benefit formula. The vertical axis represents dollars and measures dollars in both SNAP benefits and food spending. The maximum SNAP benefit, shown as the dashed horizontal line, represents the minimum guaranteed budget for food. The maximum SNAP benefit is typically set to be equal to the value of the Thrifty Food Plan—a low-cost but nutritionally adequate diet the Department of Agriculture (USDA) established—but can be altered by congressional action. For example, the American Recovery and Reinvestment Act of 2009 temporarily raised the maximum benefit by 13.6 percent, which would push up the line on the graph.

The upward-sloping line represents a family's total food spending. As income increases, typically so does spending on food (and all other normal goods). As depicted in the figure, the majority of families spend more on food than the maximum SNAP benefit level.[8]

SNAP is designed to fill the gap between the cash resources that are available to a family to purchase food and the minimum guaranteed budget for food. A family with no net income receives the maximum benefit amount, and benefits are calculated as if the family will contribute none of its own cash to out-of-pocket food purchases. Thus, in the figure, the family's total food spending is shown being equal to the maximum benefit amount for a family with no other income sources.

Table 1. SNAP Maximum Income and Benefits by Household Size, FY2018

Household Size	Net Monthly Income (100 Percent of Poverty Line)	Maximum Monthly SNAP Benefit
1	$1,005	$192
2	$1,354	$352
3	$1,702	$504
4	$2,050	$640
5	$2,399	$760
6	$2,747	$913
7	$3,095	$1,009
Each Additional Person	$349	$146

Source: US Department of Agriculture, Food and Nutrition Service, "Supplemental Nutrition Assistance Program: Eligibility," https://www.fns.usda.gov/snap/eligibility.

As a family's income increases, they are expected to be able to spend more of their own cash on food purchases, and SNAP benefits are reduced accordingly, as illustrated by the downward-sloping line. The slope of the SNAP benefits line is the benefit reduction rate, which Congress currently sets at 0.3—that is, for every additional dollar in net income, SNAP benefits are reduced by 30 cents. Therefore, the benefit formula can be described mathematically as follows:

$$(1)\ SNAP = Max\_Benefit - 0.3*(Net\_Income)$$

Note that the amount the family spends on food out of its own cash income is represented by the vertical distance between the SNAP benefits line and the food spending line. In practice, due to differences in prevailing food prices and their own tastes and preferences, some families spend more than the amount represented by the stylized food spending line, and some families spend less.

The actual SNAP benefit formula is somewhat more complicated than what is depicted in this stylized figure because benefits are based on net income—that is, total income minus deductions Congress specifies. Net income is calculated as total earned income plus unearned income minus the following deductions: a standard deduction, a deduction of 20 percent of earned income, an excess shelter cost deduction, a deduction for child-care costs associated with working and training, and a medical cost deduction that is available to only the elderly and disabled. In practice, because of the mechanics of these deductions, the benefit reduction rate out of gross income is somewhat lower than 0.3. Important policy decisions for Congress include whether the maximum benefit, benefit reduction rate, and net income calculations are set appropriately.

Table 1 presents maximum monthly SNAP benefits (excluding Alaska and Hawaii, which have higher schedules) by household size for FY2017. To be eligible for benefits, a household of four must have net income—total income minus the allowable deductions specified in the benefit formula—less than or equal to $2,025 per month. The maximum monthly SNAP benefit a family of four can receive is $649; for a single person, it is $194. These maximum benefits correspond to dollar levels between 20 percent and 33 percent of the federal poverty line.

Characteristics of SNAP Participants

Table 2, updated from Hoynes and Schanzenbach,[9] presents summary characteristics over time for SNAP recipient units calculated from administrative data from the USDA's Quality Control files. In 2015, about 43 percent of SNAP recipient units included children, down from about 60 percent in 1996. The share of individuals on SNAP that are children has also fallen somewhat over time, from 47 percent in 2005 to 41 percent in 2015. The share of the caseload that is female-headed households with children has also been falling, from 39 percent in 1996 to 24 percent in 2015. About 20 percent contain an elderly individual, and another 20 percent contain a disabled individual—both shares that have been relatively stable. The share of households without children, elderly, or disabled persons—a proxy for the able-bodied adults without dependents (ABAWD) population—has increased from 15 percent in 1996 to 25 percent in 2015.

About 32 percent of households earned income in 2015, a rate that has consistently climbed across the years and is 9 percentage points higher than in 1996. On the other hand, some 22 percent of recipient households report having no cash income, more than double the rate reported in 1996. The

Table 2. Characteristics of SNAP Households

	1996	2000	2005	2010	2015
% with Children	60	54	54	49	43
% Female Heads with Children	39	35	32	26	24
% with Elderly Members	16	21	17	16	20
% with Disabled Members	20	28	23	20	20
% with Households Without Elderly, Child, or Disabled	15	11	16	24	25
% Individuals < 18	47	47	47	44	41
% with Gross Monthly Income < Poverty Line	91	89	88	85	82
% with No Cash Income	10	8	14	20	22
% with Any Earnings	23	27	29	30	32
% Receiving Maximum Benefit	25	20	30	38	41
Multiple Program Participation: % with Income from					
AFDC/TANF	37	26	15	8	6
General Assistance	6	5	6	4	3
SSI	24	32	26	21	20
Social Security	19	25	23	21	24
Unemployment Insurance	2	2	2	7	1
Veterans' Benefits	1	1	1	1	0

Source: Hilary W. Hoynes and Diane Whitmore Schanzenbach, "U.S. Food and Nutrition Programs," in *Economics of Means-Tested Transfer Programs in the United States, Volume I*, ed. Robert A. Moffitt (Chicago: University of Chicago Press, 2016). Author's calculations for FY2015 adapted from US Department of Agriculture, Food and Nutrition Service, "Quality Control Database, Fiscal Year 2015."

share receiving the maximum benefit—because they have zero net income after allowable deductions—was 41 percent of households in 2015, up from 25 percent in 1996.

It is also useful to examine simultaneous participation in multiple safety-net programs, especially in light of concerns about a reduction in safety-net supports and cumulative work disincentives.[10] Although before welfare reform 37 percent of the caseload received income from Temporary Assistance for Needy Families (TANF), this share fell to 6 percent by 2015. About one in five SNAP participants had income from Social Security or Supplemental Security Income (SSI), a rate that has remained relatively

Table 3. Effective Tax Rates in SNAP

	1996	2000	2005	2010	2015
Earned Income	18	15	16	15	15
Unearned Income	19	17	17	17	16

Note: These are calculated only for households without elderly members.
Source: Hilary W. Hoynes and Diane Whitmore Schanzenbach, "U.S. Food and Nutrition Programs," in *Economics of Means-Tested Transfer Programs in the United States, Volume I*, ed. Robert A. Moffitt (Chicago: University of Chicago Press, 2016); and James P. Ziliak, "Effective Tax Rates and Guarantees in the Food Stamp Program," University of Kentucky, April 2008, http://gattonweb.uky.edu/Faculty/ziliak/ERS_FSP_Rates&Guarantees_042308.pdf.

stable over time. Few food stamp recipients have income from unemployment insurance (1 percent), although this share increased noticeably during the Great Recession. SNAP recipients' participation in general assistance (3 percent) or veterans' payments (less than 0.5 percent) is also quite low.

Robert Moffitt[11] uses the Survey of Income and Program Participation to study multiple program participation across a wider range of programs that are not available in the SNAP administrative data. He finds that (in 2008) 30 percent of nondisabled, nonelderly SNAP families received aid from the Special Supplemental Nutrition Program for Women, Infants, and Children; more than half received the EITC; and 21 percent received subsidized housing. Laura Wheaton, Victoria Lynch, and Martha Johnson[12] estimate eligibility for SNAP and Medicaid, finding that, because Medicaid has relatively generous eligibility thresholds, almost all children nationwide who were eligible for SNAP were also eligible for Medicaid. Among SNAP-eligible adults, 61 percent of parents and 26 percent of nonparents were also eligible for Medicaid.

There is some concern among policymakers that SNAP recipients who participate in multiple programs face high marginal tax rates, providing strong disincentives to work. In practice, however, average tax rates are lower in 2015 than they were in 1996 and are in the range of 15–16 percent. Table 3, reproduced and updated from Hoynes and Schanzenbach and James Ziliak, presents the effective tax rates (nonelderly) SNAP recipients face.[13] To calculate these tax rates, first the marginal tax rates on SNAP benefits on households' observed income amounts are calculated, and then these tax rates are averaged across households. The effective tax rate on earned income was 15 percent in 2015, down slightly from 18 percent in 1996.

Table 4. Characteristics of SNAP Households, by Employment Status (2015)

	Households Without Earnings	Households with Earnings
Share of Households	54	46
Share of Individuals	43	57
Average Benefits	334	323
Share of Total Benefits	54	46
Share with Children	46	76
Share of Female Heads with Children	31	38
Average Gross Monthly Income, Percentage Poverty	12	78

Note: Includes only SNAP households without an elderly or disabled member.
Source: Author's calculations for FY2015 adapted from US Department of Agriculture, Food and Nutrition Service, "Quality Control Database, Fiscal Year 2015."

The tax rate on unearned income is marginally higher at 16 percent in 2015. This is the tax rate in SNAP only and does not reflect the cumulative tax rate experienced across multiple programs. For example, among SNAP recipients with children and low earnings, the negative marginal tax rates in the EITC will offset SNAP's effective tax rates. On the other hand, those with higher earnings in the EITC's phaseout range would experience cumulative tax rates exceeding the SNAP effective tax rate.

Table 4 separates the caseload by whether participating households have earnings. The table is restricted to households without elderly or disabled members, who are not expected to work. Just over half of households have no earnings, while 46 percent of households had earnings. Households with earnings are on average larger, so 57 percent of individuals in the sample are in households with earnings.

A large share of SNAP households with earnings have children (76 percent), and 38 percent of these are headed by an unmarried woman. Households with earnings are financially better off, with average total income at 78 percent of the poverty level, compared with only 12 percent for nonearning households. Average benefit levels are nearly the same in households with and without earnings, with average monthly benefits of $323 and $334, respectively. In total, 46 percent of SNAP benefits paid to households without a disabled or elderly member are paid to households with earnings.

Table 5. Employment and Income Among Households over Time

	1996	2000	2005	2010	2015
Share of Participating Households with Children	78	79	74	64	60
Among Households with Children:					
Any Earnings	35	49	51	52	61
No Cash Income	6	8	12	14	16
Among Households Without Children:					
Any Earnings	17	20	23	23	26
No Cash Income	47	42	49	54	61

Note: Includes only SNAP households without an elderly or disabled member.
Source: Author's calculations for FY2015 adapted from US Department of Agriculture, Food and Nutrition Service, "Quality Control Database, Fiscal Year 2015."

There is concern about the increasing number of childless, nondisabled adults participating in SNAP. Table 5 shows how employment and income characteristics have changed over time among households without disabled or elderly (age 60 or older) individuals. Among such households with children present, the share with earnings reached 61 percent in 2015—a substantial increase from the 35 percent that had earnings in 1996. On the other hand, 16 percent of these households report no cash income, up from 6 percent in 1996.

However, households without a disabled or elderly member and without children have much worse outcomes. Only 26 percent of these households reported earnings in 2015, compared with 17 percent in 1996. A majority (61 percent) of these households report no cash income at all, up from 47 percent in 1996. Over time, households without children, elderly, or disabled members have become a larger share of the total caseload. In 2015, such cases represented 25 percent of households overall and 40 percent of households without elderly or disabled members.

Table 6 reports more detailed characteristics of SNAP households that contain no children or disabled members and only contain members age 18–49—a proxy measure of ABAWD-only households. In 2015, these households comprise 7 percent of individuals on SNAP. Such households receive average monthly benefits of $183—11 percent of total SNAP benefits paid

Table 6. Characteristics of SNAP Households with Only Nondisabled Adults Age 18–49 (2015)

	ABAWD-Only Households
Share of Individuals	7
Average Monthly Benefits	$183
Share of Total Benefits	11
Share with Earnings	25
Average Gross Monthly Income, Percentage Poverty	22.5
Share of Female Heads	44
Share by Age Group:	
18–25	24
26–34	33
35–49	44

Source: Author's calculations for FY2015 adapted from US Department of Agriculture, Food and Nutrition Service, "Quality Control Database, Fiscal Year 2015."

to all households. One-quarter of ABAWD-only households report earnings. These individuals have low income levels, with average monthly income (excluding SNAP) at 22.5 percent of the poverty level. Women comprise 44 percent of individuals living in ABAWD-only households, and 56 percent are between age 18 and 34 while 44 percent are between age 35 and 49.

The SNAP take-up rate, calculated as the fraction of the eligible population that participates in the program, is fairly high—83 percent in 2014.[14] Among the working poor, the take-up rate is 70 percent. Take-up rates also vary substantially across states, with higher rates in the Midwest (94 percent) and lower rates in the Southwest and West (74 and 73 percent, respectively). Take-up rates have risen steadily since 2002; after dropping from 75 percent in 1994 to 59 percent in 2000 (after federal welfare reform), they climbed to 67 percent in 2006 and 83 percent in 2014.[15]

SNAP serves a diverse caseload. The overwhelming majority of individuals who participate (78.4 percent in 2015) are children, elderly, disabled, or working adults. Program participants' characteristics have shown signs toward polarization over the past 20 years. On one hand, an increasing share of households is combining benefit receipt with employment, and an increasing but modest share has incomes above the poverty line. On the other hand, the share of the caseload reporting no monthly cash income of any type has more than doubled over the past two decades, and the share of participating households without an elderly, disabled, or child member has also been growing.

Impacts of SNAP

SNAP provides many benefits to both individuals and society. The program plays an important role in the macroeconomy, providing an automatic stimulus in times of economic downturn. In addition, by improving families' purchasing power for groceries, SNAP reduces food insecurity and, particularly for children, has been shown to improve health and academic outcomes. At the same time, since SNAP provides unearned income to recipients, it may also have work disincentive effects. The benefits must be carefully weighed against the disincentive effects and budget constraints to design a program that best serves the nation. In this section, I provide an overview of what is known about the impacts of SNAP to lay out the trade-offs involved.

Macroeconomic Benefits of SNAP. SNAP benefits the macroeconomy by providing an effective countercyclical economic stimulus and ensuring consumption among recipients. Figure 4 plots annual per capita SNAP benefit expenditures from 1980 to 2016—that is, inflation-adjusted total benefits divided by the total US population in each year, along with the annual unemployment rate. Real per capita spending on SNAP was relatively stable in the 1980s, increased in the early 1990s, and then fell again through the early 2000s. Between 2001 and 2012, real spending per capita increased steadily and has come down 17 percent between 2012 and 2016 as the unemployment rate in the US economy declined from more than 8 percent to about 4.5 percent. Overall, the program shows a countercyclical pattern, with spending increasing in the recessions in the early 1990s and early 2000s, and particularly during the Great Recession from 2008 to 2012.

By design, SNAP can quickly adapt to economic downturns. As more households become eligible for the program (e.g., due to job loss), they can quickly enroll, with total program outlays automatically increasing with need. This has an important stimulus impact on the economy.

Figure 4. Real per Capita SNAP Benefits and Unemployment Rate

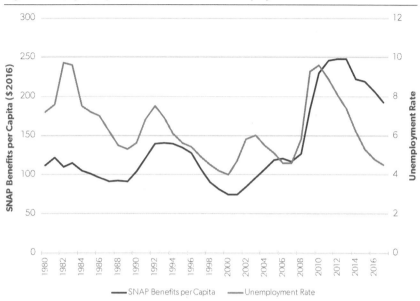

Note: This figure was estimated with data available in July 2017.
Source: Author's calculations using data from the US Department of Agriculture, Food and Nutrition Service and the Bureau of Labor Statistics.

Recipients quickly spend SNAP funds, providing a relatively rapid fiscal stimulus to the local economy, including the retail, wholesale, and transportation systems that deliver the food purchased. The USDA estimates that every $5 in new SNAP benefits generates as much as $9 of economic activity. This translates into almost 10,000 jobs from a billion dollars in total SNAP spending.[16] Alan Blinder and Mark Zandi found that the temporary SNAP increase Congress authorized during the Great Recession had a fiscal stimulus impact larger than any other potential spending increase or tax cut policy.[17]

Challenges to Estimating Impacts of SNAP. A fundamental challenge for measuring SNAP's impact is that there are few ways to separately estimate the cause and effect of participation. Some studies compare participants to nonparticipants, attempting to attribute differences between groups to SNAP's impact. Many researchers have highlighted the shortcomings of this approach.[18] The issue is that selection into participation in these programs is nonrandom, and SNAP participants tend to be more disadvantaged than nonparticipants.

As a result, statistical comparisons between participants and nonparticipants are likely to understate the program's impact—potentially even yielding a wrong-signed impact—and are likely to be misleading. To illustrate the problem, Marianne Bitler compares detailed health data by program participation status and shows that SNAP recipients have worse health than nonparticipants do.[19] SNAP recipients have worse diets and nutritional intake, higher rates of being underweight or obese, and worse child health and adult health than all non-recipients or income-eligible non-recipients.

A growing literature focuses on the causal impact of SNAP participation. Arguably the most convincing evidence comes from two research designs, each of which has been leveraged to provide evidence on both sides of the equation—measuring the protective benefits of participation and also quantifying modest work disincentive effects.

The first set of studies relies on the relatively long program introduction period, using program implementation variation across counties. This allows for an event study or difference-in-differences approach to evaluate access to SNAP, essentially using untreated counties as controls for treated counties. The second set of studies uses variation in SNAP access driven by removing legal immigrants from the program as part of the 1996 welfare reform law. Nationally, immigrants' eligibility was restored in 2003, but some individual states restored eligibility before this date, giving variation used to identify the impacts.[20]

SNAP Benefits to Participants. We think of the primary benefit of SNAP as its short-term impact on ensuring consumption levels for families that temporarily experience economic setbacks. By increasing resources available to purchase food, SNAP increases food spending, lifts millions of people out of poverty, and reduces food insecurity. A recent study finds that by shoring up purchasing power, SNAP participation also diminishes other financial hardships such as falling behind on housing or utility expenses or forgoing necessary medical care.[21]

Recent research has documented benefits of SNAP beyond short-term, "in the moment" reductions in poverty and food insecurity. SNAP also prevents lasting negative effects of inadequate resource availability during childhood; improves children's health in the short, medium, and long run; and improves economic outcomes in the long run.

A series of papers that I coauthored with Hoynes and Douglas Almond studied birth cohorts that had differential access to SNAP—then called the Food Stamp Program—in utero and during their childhoods. The program was phased in across different counties over a decade, which provides the opportunity to statistically isolate the program's impact by comparing children born at different times and living in different counties in the same states during the rollout period.

Almond, Hoynes, and Schanzenbach find that access to the program improved infant health.[22] In particular, when a pregnant woman had access to the program during her third trimester, the baby was born with a higher birth weight and was less likely to be born with a birth weight below the clinical threshold of low birth weight. The improvements were largest among the lowest birth-weight babies and in counties with the highest poverty rates. This would be expected to have sustained downstream benefits, as several studies have shown that birth weight has persistent effects into adulthood on health, education, and earnings.[23]

Hoynes, Almond, and Schanzenbach directly investigate the impact of access to the program on a host of adult economic and health outcomes for individuals who had differential access to the Food Stamp Program during their childhoods in the 1960s and 1970s.[24] They found that adult health—measured as an index comprising obesity, high blood pressure, diabetes, and other measures associated with metabolic syndrome—was markedly improved if the individual had access to the safety net during childhood. In particular, food stamp access had the largest long-term health impact during early childhood, from the prenatal period through age 3–5.

Food stamp access increased the high school graduation rate by 18 percentage points. Looking at a broader range of economic and education outcomes, among women (but surprisingly not among men), food stamp access not only improved an index of adult economic outcomes, including higher earnings and educational attainment, but also reduced the likelihood of relying on the safety net during adulthood. This last finding suggests that the correlation in welfare use across generations within families does not reflect the causal impact of safety-net programs. Instead of SNAP in households with young children being a "welfare trap," it appears to be the opposite. Providing benefits to children at important stages of their development likely allows them to invest in the skills that will help them escape poverty when they grow up.

These results are consistent with a growing literature in economics and medicine that has documented the importance of early life events on adult outcomes such as earnings and mortality. Early life access to food and other resources has been shown to affect health in adulthood. Evidence from diverse settings such as children exposed to war, disease, severe weather, or famine suggests deprivation in childhood can cause adults' diminished employment prospects and chronic health conditions. On the other hand, safety-net spending such as cash assistance, survivors' benefits, and Medicaid has been shown to increase earnings, education, and health.[25]

Immigrants' eligibility for SNAP varied across states and over time, beginning with the 1996 welfare reform and extending through subsequent legislation in the early 2000s. Chloe East uses this variation to identify the impact of gaining access to SNAP and finds that parental access to SNAP during pregnancy improves the child's health at birth, as measured by birth weight and an indicator for low birth weight.[26] She also examines the impact on medium-run health, finding that a child's SNAP access before age 5 improves the child's parent-reported health at age 6–16. She also finds suggestive evidence that SNAP reduces school absences, doctor visits, and hospitalizations.

Measuring Predicted Work Disincentives. The benefits described above must be weighed against the costs. In addition to the program's budgetary costs, potential work disincentive effects should be considered. In the classic economic model of labor supply, individuals' labor supply—that is, whether and how many hours they work—is a function of the hourly wage they could receive by working, how much unearned income they have, and how they prefer to allocate their time between labor supply and leisure consumption. This model predicts how labor supply will change when the parameters individuals face are changed.

For example, imagine a woman who works 35 hours per week for $8 per hour, for a total weekly income of $280. Say she receives a raise, so her new hourly rate is $10. The labor supply response to this pay raise is ambiguous.

One type of person will continue working 35 hours per week, now earning $350 per week, and will enjoy consuming goods with her additional earnings. Another type will actually work more hours because now the cost of every employment hour that she is offered but does not work—the so-called price of leisure—has increased, and whenever the relative price of a normal good goes up, some people may consume less of it. The third type will reduce her hours; for example, if she drops her weekly hours to 28, she still earns the same $280 per week but now is able to enjoy seven more hours of leisure time. An individual's preferences about the trade-off between cash income and leisure solve the uncertainty over which of the three options an individual will choose.

The labor supply model is unambiguous, though, about its predictions about the labor supply impact of unearned income. Anytime an individual is given unearned income such as SNAP, the model predicts that the individual will reduce his or her labor supply. Why? Because the individual has more resources and thus is expected to purchase more of all normal goods, and leisure is a normal good.

The question then becomes empirical: In practice, how large is the predicted labor supply reduction? The answer depends on the magnitude of the unearned income, the worker's preferred trade-off between labor and leisure, and any labor market rigidities. The sum of unearned income is certainly important: While unearned income at any magnitude is predicted to reduce labor supply, winning the lottery would be expected to reduce labor supply by more than getting a $10 birthday gift from grandma. In addition, labor market norms may dampen the impact in practice.

For example, say an employer offers either full-time employment at 40 hours per week or part-time employment at 20 hours per week. When given the option between these two discrete choices, even a sizable increase in unearned income may not reduce labor supply. The model also predicts that single earners may respond differently than married couples, with the secondary earner in a married couple predicted to more strongly respond to the incentive than a single or primary earner.

To date, there is only one well-identified study of labor supply responses to SNAP in the era after welfare reform and EITC expansion. East uses variation across states and over time in immigrants' eligibility for SNAP to measure how benefit eligibility affects employment and hours worked.[27]

She models labor supply reductions in response to SNAP eligibility. Single women reduce their employment rates by 2 to 5 percentage points on a base rate of 65 to 70 percent. While married men's employment rates are not affected, married men do reduce their weekly hours of work; on average, they work about 1.5 fewer hours per week when eligible for SNAP and are 4 to 4.5 percentage points less likely to work full time (on a base rate of 72 percent). The labor supply of unmarried men does not have detectable impacts.

Hoynes and Schanzenbach also estimate how food stamps affect labor supply, using county variation in the rollout of food stamps in the 1960s and 1970s to identify the impact.[28] Their research finds that the overall sample does not significantly affect labor supply, but among single-parent households with a female head—a group much more likely to participate in the program—they find a significant reduction among participants of 505 annual hours, or approximately 10 hours per week. They find that access to the Food Stamp Program does not significantly affect earnings or family income, although the estimates are imprecise. These findings are limited because they are measured before welfare reform and the mid-1990s EITC expansions, a time when women—especially unmarried mothers—had less labor force attachment than they do today.

Reforms to SNAP: Balancing Protection and Incentives

As currently structured, SNAP is an efficient and effective program. It provides economic protection to families during times of economic crisis, serves as an investment in children's long-term well-being, and is an automatic macroeconomic stabilizer. The limited existing empirical evidence suggests that the work disincentive effects are modest. Nonetheless, potential reforms to SNAP are worth considering.

Should the Program Be Block Granted? As discussed above, a crucial role of SNAP is to serve as an automatic fiscal stabilizer in times of economic downturn. Its current structure allows the program to expand quickly, providing benefits to families that become eligible for the program due to job loss or other economic shocks. SNAP benefits are targeted at low-income families that spend the resources quickly, and typically in their local communities, so it is also an effective fiscal stimulus. According to models Alan Blinder and Mark Zandi developed, during the height of the Great Recession, every dollar in SNAP spending was estimated to yield $1.74 in increased economic activity.[29] In more normal economic times, they estimate that the multiplier is $1.24—estimated to have the highest return of any stimulus spending program.

Block granting the program would fundamentally undermine the program's stabilizing impact on the macroeconomy. If the program does not automatically expand during economic downturns, some families made eligible during downturns may not be able to receive benefits. Even though Congress could allocate additional resources in times of economic need, this would necessarily come with delays, reducing the ability to quickly stimulate the economy.

Is the Program Correctly Targeted? Historically, three tests have been applied for SNAP eligibility. The first is an asset test, intending to exclude potential participants who are income poor but who hold high levels of wealth. The second is the net income test—that is, households are eligible for the program only if their net income after allowable deductions yielded a positive SNAP payment amount according to the SNAP benefit formula. The third is the gross income test, requiring that a participating household's income from all sources—before allowable deductions—be less than or equal to 130 percent of the poverty threshold.

Allowable deductions may bring a household's net income down substantially due to earnings, eligible childcare costs, excess shelter costs, and so on. Thus, some households meet the net income test but fail the gross income test. When the gross income test is enforced, such families are not eligible for SNAP benefits. Broad-based categorical eligibility (BBCE) in essence waives both the gross income and asset tests. The CBO estimates that eliminating BBCE for the nonelderly and reducing the gross income cutoff from 130 percent to 67 percent of the poverty threshold would save $87.6 billion between 2017 and 2026.

The gross income test and the asset test should be separately discussed because they affect different types of households. Waiving the gross income test allows households with moderately higher levels of income and high levels of allowable deductions to participate in the program. As shown in Table 6, SNAP families with gross incomes above 130 percent of the poverty threshold make up approximately 4 percent of households and receive 1.3 percent of total SNAP payments, and they are disproportionately families with children (68 percent), earnings (97 percent), or both. Preserving such families' access to SNAP through waiving the gross income test reduces the benefit tax rate that they would otherwise face, promotes work, and provides needed support to these families. On the other hand, reinstating the gross income test—or making it more stringent by lowering the ceiling to 67 percent of the poverty line—would harm families that combine work and benefits.

The SNAP asset test limits eligibility to households with $2,250 or less in countable assets (excluding the value of vehicles); the limit is higher for households with an elderly or disabled member. Caroline Ratcliffe et al. estimate that the asset test reduces the population eligible for SNAP by 14 percent—although if households with high asset levels are less likely to participate in SNAP, the impact on the caseload may be smaller than this.[30] Low-income households with assets above the test limit tend to have assets substantially above the limits, with median liquid asset levels of $36,000, and are more likely to include elderly members. Eliminating waivers to the asset test in SNAP could reduce participation, although the increased administrative cost burden associated with collecting asset data would offset potential savings.

Is Work Adequately Rewarded in the Benefit Formula? Overall, the SNAP program is designed to support work. Among SNAP households without elderly or disabled members, at least one adult is employed in 61 percent of households with children and in 26 percent of households without children. The benefit formula includes incentives designed to encourage work by making households financially better in response to work. In theory, receiving unearned income is expected to reduce an individual's work effort. However, the empirical evidence suggests that this impact is small in SNAP. For example, Dottie Rosenbaum reports that among those who were employed when they enrolled in SNAP, 96 percent of SNAP recipients continue to work after joining the program.[31]

The benefit formula encourages work through its deduction for earned income. For every dollar earned by the household, it can deduct 20 cents in the calculation of net income used in the benefit formula. This is intended to offset some of the additional costs a household incurs when working (e.g., commuting costs). However, one concern is that a 20 percent deduction is not enough to offset the increased costs associated with working. For example, if employment reduces the amount of time available for food preparation, SNAP recipients might instead replace their own cooking time with purchasing more expensive prepared ingredients and foods, such as frozen dinners. Raising the earned-income deduction would increase not only the incentive to work but also the SNAP benefits paid to working households.

If the earned-income deduction were increased from 20 percent to 30 percent of earned income, it would increase monthly benefits by $40 on average for households with earnings. The CBO predicts that this would increase program spending by $2.7 billion per year.[32] This would further increase the incentives to work among SNAP recipients and increase food purchasing power for families with workers.

Are Work Requirements Adequately Supported? Overall, an increasing share of the SNAP caseload combines benefit receipt with employment. In normal economic times, benefits are contingent on employment for ABAWDs. In 2015, approximately 25 percent of all SNAP households fell into this category. Typically located in one-person households, ABAWDs are eligible for modest benefits, with a maximum benefit amount of just under $200 per month and average benefits of approximately $160 per month ($5.30 per day).

If an individual's only resources come from SNAP, the maximum benefit level allows them to consume at a level equal to 20 percent of the poverty threshold. In most of the United States, SNAP is the only safety-net program available to this population.[33] Many of those subject to the time limit face substantial barriers to employment, including low levels of education and criminal records.[34]

Under normal circumstances, ABAWDs face strict time-limit requirements. They may receive SNAP benefits for only three months in a three-year period, unless they are either employed for at least 20 hours per week or engaged in a workfare or training activity (not including job search). States are not required to offer those individuals subject to the time limit a job or training program, and the law limits the characteristics of training programs that a state can provide. As a result, the requirements can be mismatched to the needs of the population to be served. The rule is also administratively complex and one of the most error-prone aspects of SNAP.[35]

States are permitted to apply for temporary waivers to the time-limit rules in areas that demonstrate having insufficient jobs available. States qualify for a waiver in all or part of a state under the following conditions: They have eligibility for extended unemployment insurance benefits, there was a recent unemployment rate above 10 percent, there was a recent 24-month period during which the average unemployment rate was elevated 20 percent above the national unemployment rate during the same time, or the area is designated as a Labor Surplus Area by the US Department of Labor. Waivers are typically granted for one year. Due to the weak economic recovery in some areas, some areas have had a time-limit waiver in place continuously for more than seven years.

The option to pursue temporary waivers to the three-month time limit in unfavorable economic conditions is an important design feature of SNAP, enabling the program to respond quickly to sharp economic downturns and provide automatic countercyclical government spending. There can be legitimate debate about whether the waiver criteria have been set at too permissive a level, though. President Donald Trump's 2017 budget proposed a strict tightening, limiting the availability of ABAWD waivers to counties with an unemployment rate above 10 percent and saving $21.5 billion in costs over a 10-year period. Such a threshold is extreme; since unemployment rates tend to be higher among populations with low education levels—the same population SNAP typically serves—the unemployment rate potential SNAP participants face would be substantially higher than 10 percent. On the other hand, tightening the eligibility standards somewhat may be warranted.

A related problem is that the rule's narrow definition of allowable work limits states' flexibility on how to engage their caseload in work activities when time limits are not waived. As a result, when waivers are not in place, the rules may undermine states' abilities to craft work requirements that are better tailored to their needs—including local economic conditions and available education and job-training programs. If reforms to the waiver criteria are adopted, then the definition of allowable work should be expanded in tandem (e.g., by counting job-search efforts or work programs that are fewer than 20 hours per week). Alternatively, a more robust investment in the SNAP employment and training program would help states move more participants into the workforce.

Make Federal Investments in Reducing Fraud and Error. SNAP has low levels of fraud and error. Two recent innovations that have successfully further improved the fidelity of the program merit expansion.

First, the National Accuracy Clearinghouse (NAC) now monitors for dual SNAP enrollment across multiple states. Dual enrollment may occur, for example, if parents living in different states and sharing custody each claim the same children on their SNAP application or if a participating family moves across state lines and enrolls in SNAP in the new state but fails to discontinue enrollment from the prior state.

The NAC established a shared cross-state database of SNAP eligibility, updated daily, to monitor dual enrollment. A recent demonstration project in southeastern states identified approximately 2,000 cases per month of dual enrollment, and the NAC reduced these numbers substantially. If implemented nationwide, the NAC is predicted to save $114 million per year in erroneous payments. The NAC should be scaled nationally to improve the program's integrity.

Second, providing access to the "work number" service, which provides real-time data on employment and wages, can be used for data verification. Currently, states must purchase the service. (Although since the federal government matches the state's administrative costs, it already pays for half the total cost of accessing the service.) Not all states currently participate, but federal support for the service would expand its use. In addition, some states pay separately for access to the service for their Medicaid programs. Federal support for purchasing the service could streamline this, reducing total costs to the programs. The service may help improve fraud and error rates of other means-tested programs such as the school meals programs.

Conclusions

For 50 years, SNAP has been an important fiscal stabilizer and safety-net program that enhances households' food purchasing power. Its impact grew during the Great Recession, as rates of unemployment and food insecurity soared. With a new farm bill on the horizon, policymakers are evaluating the program's effectiveness and considering potential reforms to strengthen it.

Overall, the program currently works quite well. The design and targeting of the program is effective and efficient. The current structure that allows the program to expand and contract with macroeconomic conditions serves as a highly effective automatic stabilizer, and proposals to instead block grant the program would severely undermine this important role of the program.

Ultimately, the foundation of economic well-being is built on steady employment and wage growth. While a functioning safety net is vital for when families face temporary economic setbacks, preserving and expanding employment among SNAP participants are key to promote participants' longer-run success. In response to earlier reforms to the cash welfare system and expanding the EITC, an increasing share of participants is employed. SNAP must continue to support and reward work.

Proposals to reduce eligibility to families with lower levels of income relative to poverty will, perversely, threaten to undermine the progress that has been made regarding employment rates by increasing tax rates on work and instituting benefit cliffs. Continuing to allow households with incomes above 130 percent of the poverty threshold that also have high deductions through the net income calculation to participate in SNAP helps working families. At the same time, a moderate increase to the earned-income disregard will strengthen the incentive to work for all SNAP recipients.

On the other hand, a sizable fraction of the caseload is not employed. This is especially true among ABAWDs. Modifications to the rules governing time limits for childless adults would allow states the flexibility to more effectively engage nonworkers in employment opportunities—for example, by better tailoring employment and training programs to local economies' needs and using other strategies outlined in a recent report by Brent Orrell, Harry Holzer, and Robert Doar.[36]

Smart investments will help ensure program integrity and save money. Any future farm bill legislation should promote national participation in the NAC and the work number service. Together, these proposed reforms can strengthen SNAP by promoting work, improving the program's integrity, and shoring up the program's effectiveness as a safety net.

Notes

1. Renée Johnson and Jim Monke, *What Is the Farm Bill?*, Congressional Research Service, February 8, 2017, https://fas.org/sgp/crs/misc/RS22131.pdf.

2. Patricia M. Anderson, Kristin F. Butcher, and Diane Whitmore Schanzenbach, "Changes in Safety Net Use During the Great Recession," *American Economic Review* 105, no. 5 (2015): 161–65, https://www.aeaweb.org/articles?id=10.1257/aer.p20151056.

3. Judith Bartfeld et al., *SNAP Matters: How Food Stamps Affect Health and Well-Being* (Palo Alto, CA: Stanford University Press, 2015).

4. Laura Wheaton and Victoria Tran, *The Antipoverty Effects of the Supplemental Nutrition Assistance Program*, Urban Institute, February 15, 2018, https://www.urban.org/research/publication/antipoverty-effects-supplemental-nutrition-assistance-program.

5. Marianne P. Bitler and Hilary W. Hoynes, "The State of the Social Safety Net in the Post-Welfare Reform Era," *Brookings Papers on Economic Activity* 2 (October 2010), https://www.brookings.edu/bpea-articles/the-state-of-the-social-safety-net-in-the-post-welfare-reform-era-with-comments-and-discussion.

6. Dottie Rosenbaum, "SNAP Marks Four Years of Falling Caseloads," Center on Budget and Policy Priorities, March 16, 2017, https://www.cbpp.org/blog/snap-marks-four-years-of-falling-caseloads.

7. Hilary W. Hoynes, Leslie McGranahan, and Diane Whitmore Schanzenbach, "SNAP and Food Consumption," in *SNAP Matters: How Food Stamps Affect Health and Well-Being*, eds. Judith Bartfeld et al. (Palo Alto, CA: Stanford University Press, 2015).

8. Hoynes, McGranahan, and Schanzenbach, "SNAP and Food Consumption."

9. Hilary W. Hoynes and Diane Whitmore Schanzenbach, "U.S. Food and Nutrition Programs," in *Economics of Means-Tested Transfer Programs in the United States, Volume I*, ed. Robert A. Moffitt (Chicago: University of Chicago Press, 2016).

10. Congressional Budget Office, "The Supplemental Nutrition Assistance Program," April 2012, https://www.cbo.gov/publication/ 43173; and Casey B. Mulligan, *The Redistribution Recession: How Labor Market Distortions Contracted the Economy* (New York: Oxford University Press, 2012).

11. Robert A. Moffitt, "Multiple Program Participation and SNAP," in *SNAP Matters: How Food Stamps Affect Health and Well-Being*, eds. Judith Bartfeld et al. (Redwood City, CA: Stanford University Press, 2015).

12. Laura Wheaton, Victoria Lynch, and Martha C. Johnson, "The Overlap in SNAP and Medicaid/CHIP Eligibility, 2013," Urban Institute, January 9, 2017, https://www.urban.org/research/publication/overlap-snap-and-medicaidchip-eligibility-2013.

13. Hoynes and Schanzenbach, "U.S. Food and Nutrition Programs"; and James P. Ziliak, "Effective Tax Rates and Guarantees in the Food Stamp Program," University of Kentucky, April 2008, http://gattonweb.uky.edu/Faculty/ziliak/ERS_FSP_Rates&Guarantees_ 042308.pdf.

14. Kelsey F. Gray and Karen Cunnyngham, "Trends in Supplemental Nutrition Assistance Program Participation Rates: Fiscal Year 2010 to Fiscal Year 2013," US Department of Agriculture, June 2016, https://www.fns.usda.gov/snap/trends-supplemental-nutrition-assistance-program-participation-rates-fiscal-year-2010-fiscal-year.

15. Karen Cunnyngham, "Trends in Food Stamp Program Participation Rates: 1994

to 2000," Mathematica Policy Research, June 2002, https://www.fns.usda.gov/snap/trends-food-stamp-program-participation-rates-1994-2000; Karen Cunnyngham, "State Trends in Supplemental Nutrition Assistance Program Eligibility and Participation Among Elderly Individuals," Mathematica Policy Research, September 2010, https://www.mathematica-mpr.com/our-publications-and-findings/publications/state-trends-in-supplemental-nutrition-assistance-program-eligibility-and-participation-among; and Gray and Cunnyngham, "Trends in Supplemental Nutrition."

16. Kenneth Hanson, "The Food Assistance National Input-Output Multiplier (FANIOM) Model and Stimulus Effects of SNAP," US Department of Agriculture, October 2010, https://www.ers.usda.gov/publications/pub-details/?pubid=44749.

17. Alan S. Blinder and Mark Zandi, "The Financial Crisis: Lessons for the Next One," Center on Budget and Policy Priorities, October 15, 2015, https://www.cbpp.org/research/economy/the-financial-crisis-lessons-for-the-next-one.

18. Marianne Bitler, "Health and Nutrition Effects of SNAP: Selection into the Program and a Review of the Literature," in SNAP Matters: How Food Stamps Affect Health and Well-Being, eds. Judith Bartfeld et al. (Palo Alto, CA: Stanford University Press, 2015); Marianne Bitler and Janet Currie, "Does WIC Work? The Effects of WIC on Pregnancy and Birth Outcomes," Journal of Policy Analysis and Management 24, no. 1 (June 2004): 73–91, https://www.princeton.edu/~jcurrie/publications/Does_WIC_Work.pdf; and Jens Ludwig and Matthew Miller, "Interpreting the WIC Debate," Journal of Policy Analysis and Management 24, no. 4 (2005): 691–701, http://home.uchicago.edu/ludwigj/papers/JPAM_WIC_2005.pdf.

19. Bitler, "Health and Nutrition Effects of SNAP."

20. Other studies have relied on within-family or within-individual variation in SNAP participation but are subject to the concern that changes in unobserved variables are simultaneously driving SNAP participation and changes in the outcome of interest. These are reviewed in Janet Currie, "U.S. Food and Nutrition Programs," in Means-Tested Transfer Programs in the United States, ed. Ronald A. Moffitt (Chicago: University of Chicago Press, 2003): 291–363; and Hoynes and Schanzenbach, "U.S. Food and Nutrition Programs." In addition, randomized experiments could in principle capture the effect of changes to SNAP. Two notable recent randomized trials are in the field. The Healthy Incentives Pilot tested the impact of providing financial rebates for the purchase of fruits and vegetables. See Susan Bartlett et al., Evaluation of the Healthy Incentives Pilot (HIP): Final Report, US Department of Agriculture, September 2014. The Summer Electronic Benefit Transfer for Children program measured the impact of providing additional food support resources to children during summer months when school is not in session. See Anne Gordon et al., "Delivering Summer Electronic Benefit Transfers for Children Through the Supplemental Nutrition Assistance Program or the Special Supplemental Nutrition Program for Women, Infants, and Children: Benefit Use and Impacts on Food Security and Foods Consumed," Journal of the Academy of Nutrition and Dietetics 117, no. 3 (December 2016): 367–75.

21. H. Luke Shaefer and Italo A. Gutierrez, "The Supplemental Nutrition Assistance Program and Material Hardships Among Low-Income Households with Children," Social Service Review 87, no. 4 (2013): 753–79, http://www.journals.uchicago.edu/doi/abs/10.1086/673999?journalCode=ssr.

22. Douglas Almond, Hilary W. Hoynes, and Diane Whitmore Schanzenbach, "Inside

the War on Poverty: The Impact of Food Stamps on Birth Outcomes," *Review of Economics and Statistics* 93, no. 2 (May 2011): 387–403, http://www.mitpressjournals.org/doi/abs/10.1162/REST_a_00089.

23. See Douglas Almond and Janet Currie, "Killing Me Softly: The Fetal Origins Hypothesis," *Journal of Economic Perspectives* 25, no. 3 (2011): 153–72, https://www.aeaweb.org/articles?id=10.1257/jep.25.3.153; Dalton Conley, Kate W. Strully, and Neil G. Bennett, *The Starting Gate: Birth Weight and Life Chances* (Berkeley and Los Angeles, CA: University of California Press, 2003); and Sandra E. Black, Paul J. Devereux, and Kjell G. Salvanes, "From the Cradle to the Labor Market? The Effect of Birth Weight on Adult Outcomes," *Quarterly Journal of Economics* 122, no. 1 (2007): 409–39, http://www.econ.ucla.edu/people/papers/Black/Black491.pdf.

24. Hilary W. Hoynes, Diane Whitmore Schanzenbach, and Douglas Almond, "Long Run Impacts of Childhood Access to the Safety Net," *American Economic Review* 106, no. 4 (2016): 903–34, http://www.nber.org/papers/w18535.

25. Almond and Currie, "Killing Me Softly"; Anna Aizer et al., "The Long-Run Impact of Cash Transfers to Poor Families," *American Economic Review* 106, no. 4 (2016): 935–71, https://www.aeaweb.org/articles?id=10.1257%2Faer.20140529; and David W. Brown, Amanda E. Kowalski, and Ithai Z. Lurie, "Medicaid as an Investment in Children: What Is the Long-Term Impact on Tax Receipts?," National Bureau of Economic Research, January 2015, http://www.nber.org/papers/w20835.

26. Chloe N. East, "The Effect of Food Stamps on Children's Health: Evidence from Immigrants' Changing Eligibility," University of California, Davis, 2015, http://www.sole-jole.org/17153.pdf.

27. Chloe N. East, "The Labor Supply Response to Food Stamp Access," University of California, Davis, 2015.

28. Hilary W. Hoynes and Diane Whitmore Schanzenbach, "Work Incentives and the Food Stamp Program," *Journal of Public Economics* 96, no. 1 (2012): 151–62, http://www.nber.org/papers/w16198.

29. Blinder and Zandi, "The Financial Crisis: Lessons for the Next One."

30. Caroline Ratcliffe et al., *Asset Limits, SNAP Participation, and Financial Stability*, Urban Institute, June 29, 2016, https://www.urban.org/research/publication/asset-limits-snap-participation-and-financial-stability.

31. Dottie Rosenbaum, "The Relationship Between SNAP and Work Among Low-Income Households," Center on Budget and Policy Priorities, January 30, 2013, http://www.cbpp.org/research/the-relationship-between-snap-and-work-among-low-income-households.

32. Congressional Budget Office, "The Supplemental Nutrition Assistance Program."

33. Rosenbaum, "The Relationship Between SNAP and Work."

34. Ed Bolen and Stacy Dean, "Waivers Add Key State Flexibility to SNAP's Three-Month Time Limit," Center on Budget and Policy Priorities, March 24, 2017, https://www.cbpp.org/research/food-assistance/waivers-add-key-state-flexibility-to-snaps-three-month-time-limit.

35. Bolen and Dean, "Waivers Add Key State Flexibility."

36. Brent Orrell, Harry J. Holzer, and Robert Doar, *Getting Men Back to Work: Solutions from the Right and Left*, American Enterprise Institute, April 20, 2017, http://www.aei.org/publication/getting-men-back-to-work-solutions-from-the-right-and-left/.

3

International Food Aid and Food Assistance Programs and the Next Farm Bill

ERIN C. LENTZ, STEPHANIE MERCIER,
AND CHRISTOPHER B. BARRETT

Food aid is a scarce but important resource. The United States is, by far, the world's largest food aid donor. In recent years, it has contributed more than 40 percent of the global food aid that helps feed the hungry.[1]

For more than 60 years, United States food aid programs have helped save or improve the lives of hundreds of millions of people. The size and design of these programs matter to intended recipient populations. The farm bill shapes the design of the largest of these programs, so that legislation matters fundamentally for the scope and efficiency of global food assistance programming.

Since 2014, total US government (USG) spending on international food assistance (IFA) has averaged roughly $2.4 billion a year.[2] Nonetheless, in inflation-adjusted terms, annual average expenditures on USG IFA programs authorized through the regular farm bill[3] process fell by 76 percent from the 1960s to 2010–14.[4] However, the global need for aid continues to be substantial. The United Nations Food and Agriculture Organization estimates that roughly 800 million people are undernourished—and billions more suffer from micronutrient deficiencies.

Simple arithmetic indicates that USG IFA expenditures are woefully insufficient to significantly reduce global food insecurity in aggregate terms. These limited resources need to be targeted strategically to obtain the largest effects on hunger and malnutrition. The biggest impacts come from relief operations in response to conflict and natural disasters, which occur frequently and annually cost an estimated 42 million human life years, mostly in low- and middle-income countries.[5]

The number of refugees and displaced persons worldwide is now the highest on record. And for the first time ever, in 2017 the United Nations declared four nations—Nigeria, Somalia, South Sudan, and Yemen—in famine or near-famine conditions and proclaimed it "the largest humanitarian crisis" since the UN's creation in 1945. Yet, the UN's World Food Programme (WFP), the world's largest operational food assistance agency, is chronically underfunded relative to the emergency needs it is charged with addressing. Thus, in recent years, WFP has often had to cut or reduce food rations provided to refugees in multiple countries.[6]

Over the past two decades, the USG has appropriately focused IFA increasingly on addressing humanitarian emergencies and child nutrition, where the impacts are greatest.[7] The statutory justification for IFA was narrowed in the 2008 Farm Bill, focusing more tightly on humanitarian response and abandoning the surplus disposal and trade promotion objectives that defined US food aid for much of the second half of the 20th century.

Until 1990, a majority of IFA consisted of shipments under Title I of Public Law 480, which delivered food commodities to foreign governments under concessional lending arrangements to support nonemergency programs. Since 2000, however, shipments under Title I have been negligible (less than 5 percent of total USG aid), and the program has not received new funding since fiscal year 2006.[8]

Title II of Public Law 480 shipments are provided as outright grants of US-sourced commodities to nongovernmental organizations (NGOs) and multilateral organizations (primarily WFP) to support both emergency and longer-term development programs. Historically, Title II programming accounted for approximately one-third of total USG food aid shipments.[9] Title II's share increased to more than three-quarters of US food aid shipments between 2000 and 2010 and has remained at or above two-thirds in recent years.

At the same time, the United States Agency for International Development's (USAID) Emergency Food Security Program (EFSP)—a cash-based program funded through a different appropriations process unconnected to the farm bill—has expanded dramatically to offer food assistance in forms other than commodities procured in and shipped from the US.[10]

The upcoming farm bill offers an opportunity to reinforce the positive changes that have enhanced the humanitarian impact of ever-scarcer resources for USG IFA in recent years. These opportunities can be informed by a growing body of research on food aid that is extraordinarily clear in its broad conclusions about how to stretch IFA budgets to reach more people. Current statutory restrictions imposed on US international food aid programs waste taxpayer money at great human cost. For example, Alex Nikulkov et al. estimate that eliminating major constraints on US food aid policy, including cargo preference and domestic procurement requirements, could reduce child mortality in northern Kenya by 16 percent during severe drought episodes.[11]

Relative to the reformed food assistance programs operated by other countries and NGOs, the costs of US food aid are excessive, delivery of assistance is slow, and the programs have not kept pace with global emergency needs. And there is no measurable evidence that American agriculture, maritime employment, or military readiness benefits in any appreciable way from these statutory restrictions. No debate remains among serious scholars who have studied the issue: Significant US food aid reform is long overdue.[12]

The 2014 Farm Bill continued a pattern of slow progress in relaxing the constraints that impede the effectiveness of the USG's increasingly limited IFA programs. Three main opportunities still exist to further advance program efficiency and impact: (1) relaxing cargo preference requirements on shipments of agricultural commodities procured in the US for food aid purposes, (2) expanding access to cash-based instruments rather than commodities so that programs need not rely solely on food delivery to targeted beneficiaries, and (3) relaxing procurement requirements that compel commodity purchase in the US.

We focus on those three areas in the discussion that follows. Meanwhile, the core funding for IFA is under continued threat. In both 2017 and 2018, the Trump administration has proposed steep cuts in these programs' budgets, including completely eliminating the McGovern-Dole International Food for Education and Child Nutrition Program. This suggests that the challenges facing IFA are not solely structural reform in the farm bill authorization process but also preservation in the appropriations process. One lesson from the 2014 Farm Bill is that Congress might not fund structural improvements ushered in with the farm bill, sometimes making apparent gains illusory.

Cargo Preference Rules

The United States' first formal international food aid program was established under the Agricultural Trade Development and Assistance Act (Public Law 480) in July 1954. Less than two months later, the act was encumbered by a requirement that at least 50 percent of all USG food aid shipments be carried to their overseas destinations by US-flagged vessels. The same requirement was then applied to other US food aid programs as soon as they were instituted—the Food for Progress Program in 1986 and the McGovern-Dole International Food for Education and Child Nutrition Program in 2002. The requirement was increased to 75 percent under a provision of the Food Security Act of 1985 and lowered back to 50 percent under a provision of a 2012 omnibus surface transportation bill, as a budgetary offset.

Although these programs are authorized by the House and Senate Agriculture Committees through the farm bill process, the statutes governing cargo preference requirements fall under a different set of congressional committees, the Commerce Committee in the Senate and the Transportation and Infrastructure Committee in the House. This jurisdictional complication would make it more difficult to amend this provision as part of the upcoming farm bill. However, such modifications have appeared in past legislation crafted by the House and Senate Agriculture Committees, such as language exempting agricultural commodity export transactions assisted through US export credit guarantee programs from cargo preference law, which was included in the Agricultural Trade Act of 1978 (Public Law 95-501).

The stated goal of this policy, which has become known as the cargo preference rule, is to ensure that US-flagged vessels continue to carry goods procured by USG agencies. The reasoning is that this preferential treatment incentivizes owners of US-flagged vessels to stay in business, and in the event of an extended overseas US military engagement, the US-flagged ships and their trained crews would be available to carry military cargo.

This policy applies to US food aid, shipments of US military material such as tanks and ammunition, and goods procured for international use through transactions assisted by other US agencies such as the Export-Import Bank and the Overseas Private Investment Corporation. According to 2011 data compiled by the US Maritime Administration (MARAD), which oversees enforcement of cargo preference, about 86 percent of all cargo shipped under this requirement (by volume) was military equipment, about 11 percent was food aid, and about 3 percent was cargo "impelled" by other civilian agencies.[13]

These mandates have not stemmed the long-term decline of the US-flagged civilian fleet, which, due to a variety of factors, is no longer cost competitive with commercial shipping capacity available elsewhere in the world. According to a MARAD survey conducted in 2011, the daily operating costs of US-flagged ships averaged 270 percent more than their foreign counterparts.[14] In general, US-flagged ships are older, smaller, and slower than foreign competitors, as the needs of commercial shippers continue to diverge from those of the military. In 1955, US-flagged ships carried 25 percent of US foreign trade; today, that share has plummeted to 1 percent. The size of the fleet in terms of vessels has also declined substantially over the same period, from 1,075 vessels in 1995 to 175 in December 2016.[15]

The food aid component of cargo preference has been particularly ineffective in meeting the policy's stated objectives because in recent years the majority of shipments has been moved on vessels deemed by the USG not to be "militarily useful." Even more striking, the additional costs associated with adhering to cargo preference rules, stemming from higher freight rates charged by US-flagged vessels, now fall entirely on US food aid program recipients. This is a relatively new development. In 2012 and 2015, Congress repealed two provisions requiring MARAD to reimburse separate aspects of the higher costs to the agencies operating the food aid program.[16]

Relevant Programs. Cargo preference as a formal US policy began in 1904, when the requirement was applied to all supplies carried overseas by the various US military branches under the Military Cargo Preference Act of 1904. Shipments of material (including food) provided as international assistance made under the Marshall Plan to Western Europe in the aftermath of World War II were not formally subjected to statutory cargo preference rules. However, the Foreign Assistance Act of 1948, which authorized the plan, did require that 50 percent of gross tonnage be shipped on US-flagged vessels "to the extent that such vessels are available at market rates."[17] Subsequently, the Cargo Preference Act of 1954, an amendment to the Merchant Marine Act of 1936, made it clear that shipments made under any US food aid program should be considered "government-impelled cargo" for the purposes of this requirement.

Regulations governing cargo preference for international shipments include restrictions on what vessels qualify for preference cargo. For the purposes of carrying US food aid, a vessel must have been registered under the US flag for at least three years, be owned by a US-based company, and employ crew members who are all US citizens. There is no requirement that the ship be built in a US shipyard.

The Merchant Marine Act of 1920, also known as the Jones Act, governs waterborne shipment of goods within the United States. Unlike cargo preference, it requires that any vessels carrying goods between US states and territories (including Alaska and Hawaii) be not only US flagged but also built in US shipyards. As of 2016, the Jones Act fleet had an estimated 32,000 vessels, most of them barges and tugs operating on inland or coastal waterways such as rivers and canals.[18] Only 97 oceangoing ships qualify for both Jones Act and cargo preference shipments, about 55 percent of the private US-flagged fleet as reported in MARAD statistics.[19]

In addition to cargo preference rules, under the Maritime Security Program (MSP), the US government also provides specific subsidies for up to 60 US-flagged vessels that are determined to be militarily useful.[20] In fiscal year 2017, each ship on the MSP registry will receive a payment of just under $5 million to offset the higher cost of operating US-flagged ships. Note that the MSP annual payment has increased from $3.1 million at the end of 2015.[21] As of December 1, 2016, the owners of 58 ships were receiving MSP payments.[22]

The MSP fleet is the third option for carrying US military cargo in the event of a military surge. First, the US Department of Defense (DOD) owns 14 ships capable of carrying munitions and dry cargo under the Military Sealift Command (MSC).[23] These vessels are berthed at US ports and must be maintained so that they can be fully operational and crewed within 5–10 days if activated. The second option consists of 46 vessels owned by the US Department of Transportation in the Ready Reserve Fleet (RRF). Both groups of ships are maintained and manned under contract with civilian maritime operators.

The consensus of three studies on cargo preference published in 2015—from the US Government Accountability Office (GAO),[24] a team from the Center for Public Service at George Mason University,[25] and Stephanie Mercier and Vincent Smith[26]—is that the limited number of ships in the

US-flagged fleet is not the source of potential bottlenecks in a military surge scenario. Instead, the issue is the number of trained US mariners available to crew the MSC and RRF vessels described above.

In addition, the evidence indicates that the food aid component of cargo preference does relatively little to buttress the viability of the civilian US-flagged vessels from the point of view of the US military (MSP ships) or in sustaining the supply of trained US mariners. MSP ships carried only 18 percent of all food aid preference cargo between 2011 and 2013.[27] Most of the remainder was carried by non-MSP ships, which are US-flagged vessels not deemed to be militarily useful because of their age, size, or vessel type.

The recent GAO report estimated that in 2014 the number of qualified US mariners available for a surge fleet was nearly 55,000, based on information from the US Coast Guard.[28] Regarding impacts on US mariners, Frank Kendall, at the time the under secretary of defense for acquisition, technology, and logistics, asserted in a 2013 letter sent to Rep. Edward Royce (R-CA), then chairman of the House Foreign Affairs Committee, that reforms to food aid programs that might reduce food aid shipments would affect only 8–11 US-flagged vessels, employing between 360 and 495 mariners.[29] Consequently, less than 1 percent of the total pool of 55,000 mariners would even potentially be affected by a reduction in food aid shipments subject to cargo preference restrictions, either because commodity food aid shipments sourced from the United States declined overall or because the cargo preference requirement was relaxed.

The minimal military benefit associated with food aid cargo preference comes at a significant cost. Several studies have estimated the financial impact of the cargo preference requirement on the operation of US food aid programs. The studies were conducted over periods of time when different cargo preference rules were in effect (i.e., 75 percent versus 50 percent cargo preference), except the 2015 GAO study, in which the authors excluded bulk shipments from their analysis.

Thus, the studies have consistent but not identical results. They demonstrate that cargo preference restricts competition, increasing the market power of the owners of US-flagged vessels. As a result, the USG pays consistently higher freight rates on those shipments relative to comparable shipments carried on foreign-flagged ships that are not constrained by cargo preference.

Estimates of the annual impact of this pricing power ranged from $140 million using 2006 data (with the 75 percent cargo preference requirement in effect) to about $50 million annually using data from 2012–15 (mostly collected under the 50 percent cargo preference regime).[30] Over the past few years, the entirety of this additional cost has been borne by the food aid programs themselves. The compelling implication is that US food aid programs feed at least 1.8 million fewer hungry people than would be the case if contracts for shipping US food aid were awarded on a competitive basis.[31]

Recommendations, Opportunities, and Challenges. Ending cargo preference requirements for food aid would make the increasingly scarce funds for food aid programs go further. In addition, ending these mandates would have minimal adverse impact on the component of the US-flagged ocean-going fleet that might actually be called on during an extended US military deployment overseas.

Even during the peak 2003 period, when many US military units were dispatched to Iraq while others were still engaged in combat in Afghanistan, cargo volume necessitated activating only 35 RRF vessels. None of the civilian US-flagged ships, either MSP or non-MSP, were pulled off their regular routes.[32] Only during a Stage III deployment, which occurs when the US military has to fight in more than one major theater war at the same time or is forced to operate in a larger crisis, would calling in ships from the US-flagged civilian fleet be required.[33] The non-MSP ships, which have carried the majority of food aid shipments in recent years, would be the last vessels called on in such a situation.[34] They have never been mobilized in this way in the 60-plus years since the cargo preference law took effect.

Supporters of cargo preference increasingly cite an alternative rationale for retaining cargo preference for food aid. They maintain that cargo preferences ensure employment for trained mariners who might be needed to serve in a military surge. Deploying MSC or RRF vessels to carry military cargo does require civilian mariners to operate these vessels.

When the RRF ships were taken out of mothballs during the beginning of the Second Gulf War in early 2003, the GAO report indicated that 1,024 civilian mariners were assigned to operate those ships. According to the MARAD administrator's testimony to the House Armed Services Committee in 2014, the average age of RRF vessels was 40 years at that time.[35]

Anecdotal reports suggest that the technology embodied in the equipment on many of these ships was so obsolete that many mariners found it difficult to operate them.

The bulk of profits accruing through agricultural cargo preferences goes to vessel owners, not to workers. The industry does not provide the data necessary to make credible estimates of the likely employment effects of relaxing current restrictions on US food aid. However, the small number—up to 495—of mariners who hypothetically could be affected by food aid reforms could be readily absorbed by one of the more than 32,000 US-flagged coastal or inland freight vessels operating under the Jones Act.[36]

Furthermore, most cargo preference vessels are ultimately owned by foreign corporations. US divisions of three foreign shipping lines—the A.P. Moller–Maersk Group from Denmark, Neptune Orient Lines from Singapore, and Hapag-Lloyd of Germany—accounted for 45 percent of all food aid carried by US-flagged ships from 2012 through mid-2015.[37] In other words, several companies that profit from anticompetitive statutory restrictions on US food aid are not even American.

Advocates for cargo preference, which include the US maritime industry, the unions representing the seamen and officers who operate them, and their supporters in Congress and the executive branch, seem unwilling or unable to contemplate alternatives to cargo preference rules that might also ensure an adequate supply of trained mariners. In his 2014 testimony, Paul Jaenichen presented the attitude of mariners unions, which is that without berths on oceangoing ships their members would have no incentive to maintain certification in their professional skills.[38]

This assertion begs the question. What if the US government, either through the DOD or Department of Transportation, established a program that actually provided such mariners with a financial incentive to keep their certification current? Such a program could follow the model of the National Guard and Reserve, under which individuals who have civilian jobs nonetheless train and serve in military units that can be deployed in the event of war, in exchange for regular pay based on their rank and education level, insurance, education benefits under the GI Bill, and even retirement pay. Such a program already exists for deck and engineering officers in the Strategic Sealift Officer Program, but not for mariners filling non-officer berths.

Even though MARAD estimates that 3,886 US mariners would be needed to man the full reserve sealift fleet (both MSC and RRF vessels), they maintain that the real number is 13,034 mariners because they assume the civilian US-flagged ships would maintain their regular operations during such a Stage III scenario. Part of the reason MARAD's estimate is so high is that some mariners may decline to accept deployment to a surge fleet because their civilian position would not be protected while they are absent.

Members of the National Guard and Reserves already have such protection under the Uniformed Services Employment and Reemployment Rights Act, which provides that persons taking time off to perform military service cannot be disadvantaged in their civilian careers because of that service.[39] Extending such protection to mariners deployed under similar circumstances would seem consistent with the role they would be asked to play to ensure the national security of the United States.

Cash for Programming

Food security programming requires cash. Even a program that simply distributes food to targeted hungry individuals incurs administrative, distribution, and storage costs.

The Food Security Act of 1985 introduced monetization—allowing for the overseas sale of US food aid purchased in and shipped from the US—as a way to help NGOs cover such costs. Over time, legislation expanded the acceptable uses of monetization proceeds beyond administrative costs to include funding broad development initiatives. The 1996 Farm Bill set a 15 percent *minimum* for the volume of nonemergency food aid that must be monetized.

Monetization is wasteful for at least two reasons.[40] First, in open monetization, each taxpayer dollar spent purchasing US food and international freight services earns only 70–75 cents when sold abroad for use in recipient countries. By its very nature, monetization loses money; the GAO estimated that the inefficiency of the monetization process reduced funding available for development projects by more than $70 million a year.[41]

Second, ill-conceived monetization transactions can also destabilize commodity markets in those countries. A multi-country study from 2013 found that food aid deliveries from donor countries, including for monetization purposes, are far more likely to hurt food price levels and volatility than are local food aid purchases.[42] These market effects undermine the farmers, traders, and processors whose financial well-being and commercial viability the US government aims to promote through many of the same programs that monetization finances.

The law requires assessments of the likely impact of food aid monetization on local markets—known as Bellmon analyses. However, the GAO found that neither the US Department of Agriculture (USDA) nor USAID conduct effective market assessments or post-monetization evaluations, and given that they often monetize large volumes, they cannot credibly guarantee not to disrupt local food markets, which raises concerns in the World Trade Organization (on which, more below).[43]

The net result is that monetization often undoes with one hand whatever good work is done with the other hand through the programs the proceeds are designed to support. That is why most other donor countries and some of the major NGOs involved in distributing US food aid have chosen to curtail their use of monetization in recent years.

Relevant Programs. USAID meets the current 15 percent statutory minimum on monetization through a single large ($16 million), closed monetization arrangement with the government of Bangladesh. This marks a sharp decrease from recent years. In fiscal year 2011, $157 million of Title II nonemergency food aid was monetized in multiple countries.[44]

The 90 percent decrease in Title II monetization to the statutory minimum was made possible because the 2014 Farm Bill increased the percentage of Title II resources that can be requested as cash under Section 202(e). This cash now covers much of the non-commodity costs associated with food aid deliveries, effectively removing the need for operational agencies to monetize food aid above the statutory minimum.

More precisely, the 2014 Farm Bill raised the maximum share of 202(e) funds that USAID could make available to NGOs undertaking Title II programs from 13 percent to 20 percent. It also expanded the activities and expenses that Section 202(e) funds are authorized to cover. Section 202(e) funds can now fund development activities previously funded through monetization and enhance any existing Title II program, including emergency programs, through Impact Funds.

These changes have enabled USAID to pay directly for the costs associated with nonemergency programs, sharply reduce monetization in Title II programs, and channel essential cash resources to emergencies such as the Ebola crisis in West Africa.[45] As a result, more people are reached per Title II dollar expended, and greater programmatic flexibility is available to fill critical food assistance gaps. The shift has also enabled USAID to prioritize Title II in-kind food deliveries for nutrition interventions where local markets provide less reliable means of inexpensively sourcing high-quality commodities.

Nevertheless, the statutory minimum requirement for monetization necessarily generates inefficiencies. Moreover, activities under the USDA's Food for Progress Program are financed almost entirely through monetized food aid commodity shipments, roughly $150 million annually. A 2011 GAO study reported that cost recovery in monetization was only 58 cents on the dollar for this program.[46]

Monetization also continues in part due to a "hard earmark"/"safe box" provision introduced in the 2008 Farm Bill (and revised in the 2014 Farm Bill) that between 20 and 30 percent of Title II funding, and no less than $350 million, be available for nonemergency, development food aid. This rule was intended to ensure that food aid would be reliably available to support NGO development programming, at a time when funding for agricultural development efforts elsewhere in USAID was at historically low levels.

Although most nonemergency food aid projects are beneficial, they typically have less impact in nutritional, development, and humanitarian terms than emergency food aid.[47] Further, in emergencies, timely response matters. The populations affected by disasters and war are at all-time highs globally. Currently, there is insufficient food aid available to address food insecurity associated with those emergencies, so resources should be provided where the bang for the food aid buck is greatest and where funds are most needed.

For example, had Typhoon Haiyan struck the Philippines two months earlier in 2013, before the end of fiscal year 2013 rather than at the start of fiscal year 2014, the US government would have been unable to tap Title II resources to respond because the nonemergency minimum was binding late in the fiscal year. In that case, lucky timing precluded an embarrassing encumbrance on humanitarian response. But it underscored for astute observers how current restrictions could restrict humanitarian response to an August or September disaster, in the final months of the USG fiscal year. Effective disaster response requires flexibility in funding. Until the hard earmark/safe box provision was introduced with the 2008 Farm Bill, the USAID administrator had the authority to use as much of the total Title II budget for emergency needs as necessary to respond to humanitarian disasters and exercised that authority in each of the previous 20-plus years to address underfunded disasters. This authority may have diverted funds from other effective nonemergency food aid projects that build rural roads, provide school lunches, or enhance smallholder farmers' productivity. But saving lives and preventing disaster victims' collapse into poverty traps are the best uses of food aid, especially now that new resources for such projects are available under the Feed the Future initiative established in 2010.

Recommendations, Opportunities, and Challenges. Perhaps the most important food aid reform included in the 2014 Farm Bill was the increase in 202(e) funding, which enabled a sharp reduction in Title II monetization and greater flexibility in Public Law 480 Title II deployment. The clear lesson is to make cash available and obviate the wasteful shipment of food commodities that get sold at a significant loss, often disrupting local markets in the process.

This outcome argues in favor of providing cash to support USDA Food for Progress projects in place of reliance on food aid monetization. This could advance the same policy objective of strengthening the agriculture sectors in developing countries at lower cost and risk. Meanwhile, ending the statutory minimum on monetization and the hard earmark/safe box provision on Title II nonemergency food aid, while maintaining or increasing the maximum level of 202(e) funding, can reinforce the proven positive effects of replacing monetization with cash.

US Sourcing and Procurement Flexibility

Worldwide, the gap between food aid needs and available funding has been growing in recent decades. In March 2017, the UN's under-secretary-general and emergency relief coordinator announced the need for $4.4 billion within three months to stave off famine in Nigeria, Somalia, South Sudan, and Yemen.[48] Emergencies are more common than they were 15 years ago and often more complex or protracted. The 2015 *State of Food Insecurity in the World* report argued, "Protracted crises have become the new norm, while acute short-term crises are now the exception."[49]

Countries in protracted crisis face rates of undernourishment more than double the rates of undernourishment in other developing countries: 39 percent compared to 15 percent.[50] Globally, this has put pressure on humanitarian and emergency funding, resulting in a practical and moral imperative to use funds in the most efficient manner possible.[51]

The successful use of cash-based distributions following the 2004 Asian tsunami generated interest in alternative approaches, including cash and vouchers, local and regional purchases of food (LRP), and prepositioning food aid closer to places likely to be in need. A growing body of evidence indicates that these tools tend to be faster and cheaper than transoceanic food aid.[52]

Donors such as Australia, Canada, and the European Union have "untied" their food assistance, meaning assistance does not need to be purchased within their borders. This flexibility has expanded their programs' reach. For example, Canadian food assistance dollars go twice as far as US food aid dollars because Canadian programs can leverage lower-cost food assistance options such as LRP, cash, and vouchers for the entirety of their IFA.[53]

Both the George W. Bush and Obama administrations advocated for a variety of food aid reforms, including increased flexibility to use different food assistance tools.[54] The Obama administration's 2014 proposed budget allowed for up to 45 percent of Title II funds to be untied from domestic sourcing requirements. USAID estimated that, in total, the Obama administration's proposed changes would have allowed them to reach between two and four million more people per year.[55]

As other donors have untied their assistance, they have raised concerns during World Trade Organization negotiations, during the Uruguay and Doha rounds, that food aid may displace commercial products.[56] This is of particular concern regarding monetization, which is more likely to displace commercial products because it is sold in markets to generate cash rather than delivered to needy individuals.[57] Untying food aid would more clearly decouple food assistance from domestic commercial interests, and ending monetization would indicate a commitment to not displacing commercial sales in low-income countries.

Relevant Programs. The current lack of flexibility to use the most appropriate food assistance tool, be it transoceanic food aid, prepositioned food aid, cash, vouchers, or LRP foods, decreases the timeliness of delivery and increases costs. Flexible funding would enable USAID, the USDA, and their implementing partners to leverage the most appropriate combination of food assistance tools, meaning that US food assistance could reach more people faster or at a lower cost.

The 2002, 2008, and 2014 Farm Bills made modest steps toward increasing flexibility. First, the 2002 Farm Bill introduced funds for prepositioning of food aid, discussed below. Second, the 2008 Farm Bill authorized $60 million for the USDA to run a local and regional procurement pilot project (LRPPP) and expanded the number of overseas prepositioning sites. The LRPPP allocated funds to NGOs and the WFP to purchase food locally or regionally. Under the 2014 Farm Bill, funds were authorized for LRP, but no funds were appropriated in 2014, 2015, or 2016.[58]

Funding from other sources, such as the EFSP, has expanded the use of LRP, cash, and vouchers for food assistance programming. EFSP, funded through the International Disaster Assistance and Overseas Contingency Operations accounts and intended to complement Title II emergency food aid, has grown from $244 million in fiscal year 2010 to more than $1.9 billion in fiscal year 2017.[59]

The Bill Emerson Humanitarian Trust (BEHT) is a reserve of resources to help meet needs resulting from unanticipated humanitarian crises. In 2008, the BEHT moved to holding cash rather than commodities. It was last used in fiscal year 2014 to support responses in South Sudan and currently holds about $281 million.[60]

Transoceanic Food Aid and Domestic Sourcing. The most common form of food assistance is transoceanic food aid, food purchased in the US and then shipped abroad. Since 2000, Title II programs have accounted for 73 percent of all US food aid funds, and all Title II in-kind food aid must be sourced in the US.[61]

Food aid sourced from the US tends to be the slowest of all food assistance tools. Transoceanic food aid deliveries can take between three and six months to reach their destination.[62] USAID notes that, to reach their destinations, on average, bulk commodities, such as cereals, require about three months, whereas processed foods, such as vegetable oils and blended foods, require six months.[63]

Prepositioning. Prepositioning was first authorized in the 2002 Farm Bill. It allows USAID to tap into up to 100,000 metric tons of food aid for emergency deliveries. Prepositioned food aid is currently stored at one of five global locations, including US Gulf ports.[64] In emergencies, USAID can also redirect food aid vessels that were headed to a prepositioning site to a location in crisis, called diversion. The GAO found that on average diversions saved two months while prepositioned food aid saved between one and two months relative to standard food aid deliveries.[65] Prepositioning of Title II food aid has increased from 6 percent in 2007 to 22 percent in 2012.[66]

Prepositioning is not without its downside. A 2014 GAO report noted that prepositioning is more expensive than procuring food on demand. For example, the 2014 Farm Bill allows for international warehouse costs of up to $15 million. Beyond storage expenditures, prepositioning requires additional fumigation costs and second-leg shipping (e.g., from storage to the final destination).

In 2014, USAID commissioned an outside study to evaluate the additional costs associated with prepositioned commodities. Based on data for prepositioning shipments made in 2012–13, that study found that such commodities, primarily bagged sorghum, corn-soy blend, vegetable oil, and split yellow peas, cost on average about $56 per ton more than commodities delivered directly from the United States.[67]

Local and Regional Procurement. Local and regional procurement affords significant time savings, and often cost savings, relative to in-kind transoceanic food aid. In a nine-country study of the LRP pilot from the 2008 Farm Bill, Erin Lentz, Simone Passarelli, and Christopher Barrett found that procuring cereals locally or regionally saved 53 percent relative to purchasing grains in the US, while procuring legumes and pulses locally and regionally saved 25 percent.[68] However, the authors also reported that procuring vegetable oil in Latin America was not less expensive than purchasing US vegetable oil.

This suggests that the program's location, which is closely linked to shipping costs, and the type of product influence the relative costs of US and local sourcing. Thus, the evidence indicates that the further a recipient country is from the US and the less processed (and therefore bulkier) the product, the likelier it is that LRP is significantly cheaper than in-kind shipments from the US.

Aurelie Harou et al. found substantial cost savings using local procurement in a side-by-side comparison of LRP and in-kind food delivered to school feeding programs in Burkina Faso.[69] On average, procuring school rations locally was 38 percent cheaper. Local rations were also more nutrient dense, with more protein and fat, both badly needed by the children targeted in the program.

According to Lentz, Passarelli, and Barrett, transoceanic in-kind food aid also reaches individuals about 14 weeks more slowly than other forms of food assistance.[70] Recent evidence on the first 1,000 days of life—from conception to a child reaching the age of 2—shows that adequate nutrition during this window is vitally important for life outcomes. Children who are well nourished and healthy during the first 1,000 days have higher educational attainment, increased income, healthier lives, and healthier offspring than those who are not.[71] Fourteen weeks is about 10 percent of the first 1,000 days; delays of assistance during this crucial period can have lifelong consequences, making the human costs of slower delivery of transoceanic food aid clear.[72]

Cash and Vouchers. Cash and vouchers are two other widely used forms of food assistance. Cash transfers can be conditional, meaning that beneficiaries have to undertake some action (e.g., send children to school or engage in a local work project) to receive the transfer, or unconditional, meaning that beneficiaries have complete control over when and on what the transfers are used. Vouchers are coupons or credit that can be redeemed to acquire food by recipients at certain times, usually through preapproved vendors. Use of cash and vouchers is growing rapidly.

In general, cash-based interventions have been found to have a much lower cost on both a per-person and per-ton basis than in-kind food aid shipped from the donor country. In Ethiopia, WFP estimated that delivering cash was 25 to 35 percent more efficient than delivering food.[73] An evaluation of food assistance responses during the 2011–12 crisis in Somalia found that 85 percent of cash transfer and voucher budgets went to recipients, while only 35 percent of the value of the resources expended to provide in-kind food aid went to recipients.[74] Amy Margolies and John Hoddinott find that, in a four-country study examining Ecuador, Niger, Uganda, and Yemen, if everyone received cash rather than food, 18 percent more people could be reached.[75]

Cash and vouchers also tend to be much faster than in-kind food aid.[76] As mobile money becomes more commonplace in developing countries, distributing cash transfers will likely become even faster.[77]

Recommendations, Opportunities, and Challenges. The evidence is clear. Increasing flexibility of food assistance sourcing in the next farm bill would shorten delivery times and ensure that more of every taxpayer dollar goes to those who need it most. Transoceanic in-kind food aid is the slowest form of food assistance and often the most expensive. Ending requirements that food aid must be sourced in the US could allow the US to reach an additional 4–10 million people, at no additional cost.[78] With savings of between 18 and 53 percent on some products,[79] this is perhaps the single-most effective change that could be made to current US food assistance policies.

Incremental improvements to programming include (1) directly appropriating funds for LRP and expanding the size of the program and (2) increasing USAID's ability to use Title II funds as global need requires by ending the hard earmark/safe box and expanding use of 202(e) funds. These changes would allow USAID to use more funding for emergency response to reach more people.

Prepositioning allows for some time savings but is more expensive than transoceanic food aid. Based on available evidence, in nearly all cases, LRP, cash, and vouchers are cheaper and faster than prepositioning and in-kind food aid sourced from the US. Therefore, expanding flexibility to allow for funding these food assistance modalities should be the priority.

A 2015 High Level Panel on Humanitarian Cash Transfers argued that the best available evidence clearly indicates that cash transfers are often, but not always, "first best." There are instances when noncash forms of transfers may be preferred, such as in some conflict environments, when markets are unstable, when inflation is a concern, or when people have limited mobility or access to markets.[80]

While much of the earlier debate about food assistance took the form of "cash versus food," the different types of food assistance are best considered not in competition with one another but as synergistic and complementary tools.[81] While cash tends to be the lowest-cost and fastest form of food assistance, in some situations, it may not be appropriate. Food assistance programming needs the flexibility to enable cooperating sponsors to sequence different forms of assistance or combine them in complementary ways.

Concerns that cooperating sponsors would not be able to choose among and effectively use food assistance tools appropriate to the local situation have proved, thus far, to be unfounded.[82] Many NGOs have developed the capacity to manage more flexibility in food assistance programming.[83] Researchers, practitioners, and donors have identified a series of best practices to identify the best food assistance tools for local needs.[84] For example, response analysis can help agencies and donors identify which food assistance tool is most appropriate given a local market context.[85]

Nonetheless, as the GAO notes, there is a need for careful data collection from both cash and food-based assistance programs to better facilitate comparing the efficacy of different transfers and to monitor any potential market-related impacts of transfers.[86] Thus, the primary barrier to reaching more people in need more quickly is one of flexibility of funding, not of capacity.

Conclusion

The Global Food Security Act (GFSA), enacted in July 2016, calls for a whole-of-government approach to addressing global food insecurity, primarily by focusing on smallholder farmers and women.[87] The GFSA also seeks to "ensure the effective use of United States taxpayer dollars to further [GFSA] objectives."[88] As a primary tool for the USG's response to immediate food insecurity, particularly in emergencies, US food aid and food assistance is an important complement to the GFSA. Ending statutory restrictions on food aid to allow for greater flexibility will allow current levels of Title II funds to reach more people, more quickly.

Improving flexibility can be accomplished in three ways. First, the farm bill should end cargo preference requirements for food aid and protect the positions of merchant mariners through other means. To maintain the availability of trained mariners, employment protections similar to those offered by the National Guard and Reserves ought to be established.

Second, effective disaster response requires flexibility in funding. Increasing the share of Title II funding under Section 202(e) that is available to support food assistance programming and decreasing the hard earmark/safe box for nonemergency Title II Public Law 480 will allow more funds to reach people in emergencies, arguably those who are most in need.

Third, requirements that food aid be sourced in the US (i.e., "tied" food aid) should be ended. Locally procured food, cash, and vouchers are nearly always less costly and faster relative to food aid procured from the US. Cash also provides individuals with the dignity of choice.

The net economic and humanitarian losses caused by the inflexibility of US food aid programs are substantial. Every tax dollar spent on US food aid yields only 35–40 cents in food commodities delivered to those in need. In recent years, American taxpayers have spent more Food for Peace Act funds on shipping and handling than on food.[89] By way of comparison, Canada has no such restrictions and more extensively uses LRP, cash, and vouchers; Canadian taxpayers deliver almost 70 cents worth of food to those who need help from every food aid dollar spent.[90]

Further, there are real human costs from the wasteful mandates embedded in the current US food aid legislation. It costs roughly $125 per child life year saved to manage the acute malnutrition that routinely arises in the wake of natural disasters and conflict.[91] Using conservative, back-of-the-envelope estimates derived from the research cited above, the $350–$400 million per year wasted on cargo preference, monetization, and US-sourcing requirements, when cash-based alternatives would be cheaper, effectively costs at least three million child life years every year. Given global life expectancy at birth of roughly 70 years, a conservative estimate is that we put at risk 40,000–45,000 children's lives annually because of antiquated food aid policies.

Opponents of reform deploy several myths about food aid to discourage changes to the status quo. First, the special interests served by cargo preference claim cargo preference advances military readiness. But, as described above, that myth has been conclusively rebutted by multiple recent rigorously conducted studies, which find that the overwhelming majority of the agricultural cargo preference fleet is out-of-date and fails to satisfy the DOD standards for militarily usefulness.[92] The DOD and Homeland Security's clear support in recent years for food aid reforms indicates that cargo preference makes no important contribution to military readiness.[93]

Advocates of cargo preference also claim that cargo preference supports employment for trained mariners who might need to be deployed to operate ships carrying military cargo. The 2012 reforms that reduced food aid cargo preference coverage from 75 percent to 50 percent do not appear to have led to a single vessel ceasing ocean freight service nor to the loss of any mariner jobs. Further, direct subsidy payments or employment protections, similar to those offered to members of the National Guard, would be far more efficient than this indirect subsidy, which costs taxpayers an estimated $100,000 per mariner position.[94]

Another myth used to maintain the status quo is that food aid purchased in the United States helps American farmers. No careful study supports such a claim. Commodity prices are set by global markets, not by USG purchases of food aid, which are dwarfed by the scale of the commercial market. Food aid procurement has no effect on the prices farmers receive, even for the commodities for which US food aid programs absorb 5 percent or more of domestic production (such as sorghum, lentils, dried beans, or peas).[95] The basic reason is that US food aid is a drop in the ocean of the global agricultural market. US food aid programs procure hundreds of millions of dollars' worth of commodities in a US agricultural industry that generates close to $100 billion in annual net farm income in recent years and is tightly integrated into a nearly $4 trillion global agricultural economy.

Some opponents of food aid reform claim that purchasing food abroad under cash-based programs compromises food safety and quality. This conjecture is also untrue. A recent study in Burkina Faso found that the quality and safety of locally procured commodities was equal to or better than that of commodities shipped from the United States.[96] Spoilage is commonplace in transoceanic shipments, for which replacement deliveries may be impossible or prohibitively expensive.[97] Consumer satisfaction surveys among food aid recipients in multiple countries likewise find no advantage from commodities shipped from the US over those locally procured; if anything, local products are favored and found to be of higher quality.[98]

A final myth is that cash-based food aid programs are somehow more vulnerable to theft and corruption. In some extreme cases, either cash-based or in-kind food transfers may be at risk of theft, corruption, and fraud. However, as Laura Gordon notes, well-designed, modern cash-based programs are often at less risk than in-kind food donations.[99] Cash transfers can take advantage of technologies, such as electronic payments, that can minimize fraud and diversion and improve accountability. Such technologies are infeasible for in-kind deliveries.[100] High loss rates of food shipments have been commonplace, especially in programs that serve conflict-affected populations.[101] To avoid this issue, USAID, for example, relies almost exclusively on cash-based assistance provided under the EFSP to serve Syrian refugees.

US food aid is a highly visible symbol of Americans' commitment to assist the downtrodden wherever they are in the world. But US food aid programs can do better. The shortcomings of US international food aid programs directly result from statutory restrictions, many of which can be addressed in a farm bill reauthorization. In responding to food emergencies around the world and to the distressingly high level of food insecurity faced by the world's poor, the USAID administrator and secretary of agriculture need flexibility to employ current best practices, as is currently provided through the International Disaster Assistance account but not through US international food aid programs.

The upcoming farm bill has the opportunity to eliminate (1) food aid cargo preferences; (2) the hard earmark/safe box, which protects less critical nonemergency food aid over emergency assistance; and (3) the restriction against cash-based IFA, while reinforcing cash availability through enhanced 202(e) funding. It is time to reform food assistance programs to stop wasting taxpayer dollars and putting people's lives at risk unnecessarily.[102]

Notes

1. World Food Programme, "Contributions to WFP in 2015," accessed August 29, 2017, http://www.wfp.org/funding/year/2015.

2. Randy Schnepf, *U.S. International Food Aid Programs: Background and Issues*, Congressional Research Service, September 14, 2016, https://fas.org/sgp/crs/misc/R41072.pdf.

3. Titles I, III, and V of Public Law 480; Food for Progress; and the McGovern-Dole International Food for Education and Child Nutrition Program are all run by the United States Department of Agriculture Foreign Agricultural Service. Public Law 480 Title II is run by the United States Agency for International Development.

4. Schnepf, *U.S. International Food Aid Programs.*

5. UN Office for Disaster Risk Reduction, *Global Assessment Report on Disaster Risk Reduction: Making Development Sustainable: The Future of Disaster Risk Management,* 2015, http://www.preventionweb.net/english/hyogo/gar/2015/en/gar-pdf/GAR2015_EN.pdf.

6. UN High Commissioner for Refugees, *World at War: Global Trends, Forced Displacement in 2014,* 2015, http://www.unhcr.org/en-us/statistics/country/556725e69/unhcr-global-trends-2014.html.

7. Christopher B. Barrett and Daniel G. Maxwell, *Food Aid After Fifty Years: Recasting Its Role* (London: Routledge, 2005).

8. Schnepf, *U.S. International Food Aid Programs.*

9. Barrett and Maxwell, *Food Aid After Fifty Years.*

10. Schnepf, *U.S. International Food Aid Programs.*

11. Alex Nikulkov et al., "Assessing the Impact of U.S. Food Assistance Delivery Policies on Child Mortality in Northern Kenya," *PLOS ONE* 11, no. 12 (December 20, 2016), http://journals.plos.org/plosone/article?id=10.1371/journal.pone.0168432.

12. Barrett and Maxwell, *Food Aid After Fifty Years;* Elizabeth R. Bageant, Christopher B. Barrett, and Erin C. Lentz, "Food Aid and Cargo Preference," *Applied Economic Perspectives and Policy* 32, no. 4 (2010): 624–41; Kimberly Ann Elliot and William McKitterick, "Food Aid for the 21st Century: Saving More Money, Time, and Lives," Center for Global Development, June 2013, http://www.cgdev.org/sites/default/files/archive/doc/full_text/CGDBriefs/3120442/food-aid-for-the-21st-century.html; Erin C. Lentz and Christopher B. Barrett, "The Negligible Welfare Effects of the International Food Aid Provisions in the 2014 Farm Bill," *Choices* 29, no. 3 (2014), http://www.choicesmagazine.org/choices-magazine/theme-articles/3rd-quarter-2014/the-negligible-welfare-effects-of-the-internationalfood-aid-provisions-in-the-2014-farm-bill; Stephanie Mercier and Vincent H. Smith, *Military Readiness and Food Aid Cargo Preference: Many Costs and Few Benefits,* American Enterprise Institute, September 28, 2015, http://www.aei.org/publication/military-readinessand-food-aid-cargo-preference-many-costs-and-few-benefits/; Phillip J. Thomas and Wayne H. Ferris, "Food Aid Reforms Will Not Significantly Affect Shipping Industry or Surge Fleet," George Mason University, Centers on the Public Service, June 2015; and Nikulkov et al., "Assessing the Impact of U.S. Food Assistance Delivery Policies on Child Mortality in Northern Kenya."

13. John Frittelli, *Cargo Preferences for U.S.-Flag Shipping,* Congressional Research Service, October 29, 2015, https://fas.org/sgp/crs/misc/R44254.pdf.

14. Note that these cost estimates were based on unaudited information from shipping companies. US Department of Transportation, US Maritime Administration, "Comparison of US and Foreign-Flagged Operating Costs," September 2011.

15. US Department of Transportation, US Maritime Administration, "U.S. Flag Privately Owned Merchant Fleet, 1946–Present," 2016, https://www.marad.dot.gov/wp-content/uploads/pdf/US-Fleet-Summary-Table-1946-2016.pdf.

16. Moving Ahead for Progress in the 21st Century Act, Pub. L. No. 112-141; and the Bipartisan Budget Act of 2015, Pub. L. No. 114-74.

17. Foreign Assistance Act of 1948, Pub. L. No. 87-195, http://marshallfoundation.org/library/wp-content/uploads/sites/16/2014/06/Foreign_Assistance_Act_of_1948.pdf.

18. Max Schlubach, *Logistics in Focus: U.S. Waterways,* Brown Brothers

Harriman Company, 2016, https://www.bbh.com/blob/17578/6a121b48eb1647ab-76337fab48e3001b/logistics-in-focus--u-s--waterways-pdf-data.pdf.

19. US Department of Transportation, US Maritime Administration, "U.S. Flag Privately Owned Merchant Fleet, 1946-Present."

20. US Maritime Security Act, established in 1996 (46 App. USC 1101 et seq.), was reauthorized initially as part of the National Defense Authorization Act of 2003 for 10 years. The authority was extended as part of the National Defense Authorization Act of 2013 through 2025. Maritime Security Act of 1996 (46 App. USC 1101 et seq.).

21. Consolidated Appropriations Act, Pub. L. No. 114-113.

22. US Department of Transportation, US Maritime Administration, "United States Flag Privately Owned Merchant Fleet Report," accessed December 1, 2016, https://www.marad.dot.gov/copy-of-ds_usflag-fleet20161201/.

23. The Military Sealift Command also maintains several other types of ships, including fleet oilers, special mission, prepositioning, and expeditionary fast transport classes.

24. US Government Accountability Office, "International Food Assistance: Cargo Preference Increases Food Aid Shipping Costs, and Benefits Are Unclear," August 2015, https://www.gao.gov/assets/680/672181.pdf.

25. Thomas and Ferris, "Food Aid Reforms Will Not Significantly Affect Shipping Industry or Surge Fleet."

26. Mercier and Smith, *Military Readiness and Food Aid Cargo Preference.*

27. Thomas and Ferris, "Food Aid Reforms Will Not Significantly Affect Shipping Industry or Surge Fleet."

28. US Government Accountability Office, "International Food Assistance: Cargo Preference Increases Food Aid Shipping Costs, and Benefits Are Unclear."

29. Frank Kendall, "Letter to the Chairman of the House Foreign Affairs Committee," June 18, 2013.

30. The 2015 GAO analysis that excluded bulk shipments yielded an estimate of about $31 million annually. US Government Accountability Office, "International Food Assistance: Cargo Preference Increases Food Aid Shipping Costs, and Benefits Are Unclear." See also Bageant, Barrett, and Lentz, "Food Aid and Cargo Preference"; Mercier and Smith, *Military Readiness and Food Aid Cargo Preference*; and US Government Accountability Office, "International Food Assistance: Cargo Preference Increases Food Aid Shipping Costs, and Benefits Are Unclear."

31. This estimate is calculated using the $50 million annual cost of cargo preference from Mercier and Smith and an average cost of $27 per beneficiary from Elliott and McKitterick. Mercier and Smith, *Military Readiness and Food Aid Cargo Preference*; and Elliot and William McKitterick, "Food Aid for the 21st Century: Saving More Money, Time, and Lives."

32. US Government Accountability Office, "International Food Assistance: Cargo Preference Increases Food Aid Shipping Costs, and Benefits Are Unclear."

33. US Government Accountability Office, "Military Airlift: DOD Needs to Take Steps to Manage Workload Distributed to the Civilian Reserve Air Fleet," June 2013, https://www.gao.gov/assets/660/655338.pdf.

34. Albert J. Herberger, Kenneth C. Gaulden, and Rolf Marshall, *Global Reach: Revolutionizing the Use of Commercial Vessels and Intermodal Systems for Military Sealift, 1990–2012*

(Annapolis, MD: Naval Institute Press, 2016).

35. Paul N. Jaenichen, "Logistics and Sealift Force Requirements and Force Structure Assessment," testimony before the Subcommittee on Seapower and Projection Forces, Committee on Armed Services, US House of Representatives, July 30, 2014, http://docs.house.gov/meetings/AS/AS28/20140730/102432/HHRG-113-AS28-Wstate-JaenichenP-20140730.pdf.

36. US Department of Transportation, US Maritime Administration, "U.S.-Flag Waterborne Domestic Trade and Related Programs," http://www.marad.dot.gov/ships-and-shipping/domestic-shipping/.

37. Mercier and Smith, *Military Readiness and Food Aid Cargo Preference.*

38. Jaenichen, "Logistics and Sealift Force Requirements and Force Structure Assessment."

39. Uniformed Services Employment and Reemployment Rights Act of 1994, 38 USC § 4301 (1994).

40. Christopher B. Barrett and Erin C. Lentz, *U.S. Monetization Policy: Recommendations for Improvement*, Chicago Council on Global Affairs Policy, December 2009, http://barrett.dyson.cornell.edu/Papers/Chicago%20Council%20-%20Policy%20Development%20Study%20on%20Monetization%20-%20December%202009.pdf; and US Government Accountability Office, "International Food Assistance: Funding Development Projects Through the Purchase, Shipment, and Sale of U.S. Commodities Is Inefficient and Can Cause Adverse Market Impacts," June 2011, http://www.gao.gov/assets/330/320013.pdf.

41. US Government Accountability Office, "International Food Assistance: Funding Development Projects."

42. Teevrat Garg et al., "Market Prices and Food Aid Local and Regional Procurement and Distribution: A Multi-Country Analysis," *World Development* 49, no. 9 (2013): 19–29, http://barrett.dyson.cornell.edu/Papers/Gargetal_Resubmit2.pdf.

43. US Government Accountability Office, "International Food Assistance: Funding Development Projects."

44. US Agency for International Development, "Food for Peace Act, Section 202(e) Funding Report: Fiscal Year 2015"; and US Agency for International Development, "Quick Facts," accessed January 20, 2017, https://www.usaid.gov/what-we-do/agricultureand-food-security/food-assistance/quick-facts.

45. US Agency for International Development, "Food for Peace Emergency Program: Impact Funds Case Study," accessed January 20, 2017, https://www.usaid.gov/sites/default/files/documents/1866/202e%20stories%20FY%202014%20-%20Food%20for%20Peace.pdf.

46. Government Accountability Office, "International Food Assistance: Funding Development Projects."

47. Barrett and Maxwell, *Food Aid After Fifty Years.*

48. For sample media coverage, see Associated Press, "UN Humanitarian Chief Warns of Famine Crisis, Urges Global Action," CBC News, March 11, 2017, http://www.cbc.ca/news/world/un-famine-starvation-warning-1.4020901.

49. Food and Agriculture Organization, *The State of Food Insecurity in the World: Meeting the 2015 International Hunger Targets: Taking Stock of Uneven Progress*, 2015, 38, http://www.fao.org/3/a4ef2d16-70a7-460a-a9ac-2a65a533269a/i4646e.pdf.

50. Food and Agriculture Organization, *The State of Food Insecurity in the World.*

51. Overseas Development Institute, "Doing Cash Differently: How Cash Transfers Can Transform Humanitarian Aid: Report to the High Level Pane on Humanitarian Cash Transfers," September 2015, https://www.odi.org/sites/odi.org.uk/files/odi-assets/publications-opinion-files/9828.pdf; and World Food Programme, "Annual Performance Report for 2015," May 25, 2016, http://documents.wfp.org/stellent/groups/public/documents/eb/wfp282360.pdf.

52. Erin C. Lentz, Simone Passarelli, and Christopher B. Barrett, "The Timeliness and Cost Effectiveness of the Local and Regional Procurement of Food Aid," *World Development* 49 (September 2013): 9–18, http://www.sciencedirect.com/science/article/pii/S0305750X13000235; Lentz and Barrett, "The Negligible Welfare Effects of the International Food Aid Provisions in the 2014 Farm Bill"; and Amy Margolies and John Hoddinott, "Costing Alternative Transfer Modalities," *Journal of Development Effectiveness* 7, no. 1 (December 2014): 1–16.

53. Lentz and Barrett, "The Negligible Welfare Effects of the International Food Aid Provisions in the 2014 Farm Bill."

54. Schnepf, *U.S. International Food Aid Programs: Background and Issues.*

55. Schnepf, *U.S. International Food Aid Programs: Background and Issues.*

56. Schnepf, *U.S. International Food Aid Programs: Background and Issues.*

57. Christopher B. Barrett and Daniel G. Maxwell, "Towards a Global Food Aid Compact," *Food Policy* 31, no. 2 (2006): 105–18.

58. For fiscal years 2016 and 2017, the USDA was allowed to use up to $5 million of funding provided to the McGovern-Dole program for locally procured foods. US Department of Agriculture, "Local and Regional Food Aid Procurement Program, Report to the United States Congress, Fiscal Year 2017," accessed June 7, 2018, https://www.fas.usda.gov/sites/default/files/2018-02/lrp_report_fy_2017.pdf.

59. Schnepf, *U.S. International Food Aid Programs: Background and Issues*; and US Agency for International Development, "USAID FY 2017 Emergency Food Security Program Report to Congress Appendix C," accessed June 7, 2018, https://www.usaid.gov/sites/default/files/documents/1867/PA00SW3C.pdf.

60. Schnepf, *U.S. International Food Aid Programs: Background and Issues.*

61. Schnepf, *U.S. International Food Aid Programs: Background and Issues.*

62. Barrett and Maxwell, *Food Aid After Fifty Years*; Lentz, Passarelli, and Barrett, "The Timeliness and Cost Effectiveness of the Local and Regional Procurement of Food Aid"; and US Agency for International Development, "Quick Facts," accessed January 20, 2017, https://www.usaid.gov/what-we-do/agriculture-and-food-security/food-assistance/quick-facts.

63. US Agency for International Development, "Quick Facts."

64. US Agency for International Development, "Quick Facts."

65. US Government Accountability Office, "International Food Aid: Prepositioning Speeds Delivery of Emergency Aid, but Additional Monitoring of Time Frames and Costs Is Needed," March 5, 2014, https://www.gao.gov/products/GAO-14-277.

66. US Government Accountability Office, "International Food Aid."

67. Gregory Olson (USAID/Office of Food for Peace), in discussion with the author, January 2017.

68. Lentz, Passarelli, and Barrett, "The Timeliness and Cost Effectiveness of the Local and Regional Procurement of Food Aid."

69. Aurelie Harou et al., "Tradeoffs or Synergies? Assessing Local and Regional Food Aid Procurement Through Case Studies in Burkina Faso and Guatemala," *World Development* 49 (2013): 44–57.

70. Lentz, Passarelli, and Barrett, "The Timeliness and Cost Effectiveness of the Local and Regional Procurement of Food Aid."

71. Robert E. Black et al., "Maternal and Child Undernutrition and Overweight in Low-Income and Middle-Income Countries," *Lancet* 382, no. 9890 (2013): 427–51.

72. Lentz and Barrett, "The Negligible Welfare Effects of the International Food Aid Provisions in the 2014 Farm Bill."

73. Overseas Development Institute, "Doing Cash Differently."

74. Kerren Hedlund et al., "Final Evaluation of the Unconditional Cash and Voucher Response to the 2011–12 Crisis in Southern and Central Somalia," United Nation's Children's Fund, 2012, https://www.unicef.org/somalia/SOM_resources_cashevalfinep.pdf.

75. Margolies and Hoddinott, "Costing Alternative Transfer Modalities."

76. Joanna Upton and Erin Lentz, "Expanding the Food Assistance Toolbox" in *Uniting on Food Assistance: The Case for Transatlantic Cooperation*, eds. Christopher B. Barrett, Julia Steets, and Andrea Binder (London: Routledge, 2012); and Lentz, Passarelli, and Barrett, "The Timeliness and Cost Effectiveness of the Local and Regional Procurement of Food Aid."

77. Overseas Development Institute, "Doing Cash Differently."

78. Elliot and McKitterick, "Food Aid for the 21st Century."

79. Lentz, Passarelli, and Barrett, "The Timeliness and Cost Effectiveness of the Local and Regional Procurement of Food Aid"; and Margolies and Hoddinott, "Costing Alternative Transfer Modalities."

80. Upton and Lentz, "Expanding the Food Assistance Toolbox"; Sarah Bailey and Paul Harvey, "State of Evidence on Humanitarian Cash Transfers: Background Note for the High Level Panel on Humanitarian Cash Transfers," Overseas Development Institute, March 2015, https://www.odi.org/sites/odi.org.uk/files/odi-assets/publications-opinion-files/9591.pdf; and Laura Gordon, "Risk and Humanitarian Cash Transfer Programming: Background Note for the High Level Panel on Humanitarian Cash Transfers," Overseas Development Institute, May 2015, https://www.odi.org/sites/odi.org.uk/files/odi-assets/publications-opinion-files/9727.pdf.

81. Stephanie Mercier, "New and Unique Provisions in the Agricultural Act of 2014," Agree, March 2014, http://www.foodandagpolicy.org/sites/default/files/Farm%20Bill%20 2014_Mercier.pdf.

82. Overseas Development Institute, "Doing Cash Differently"; and Cash Learning Partnership, "An Agenda for Cash: Part of CaLP's '100 Days of Cash' Initiative," May 2016, http://www.cashlearning.org/downloads/100daysofcash-agendaforcash---final.pdf.

83. Cash Learning Partnership, "An Agenda for Cash."

84. Christopher B. Barrett et al., "Market Information and Food Insecurity Response Analysis," *Food Security* 1 (2009): 151–68, https://www.researchgate.net/publication/225394825_Market_information_and_food_insecurity_response_analysis; Overseas Development Institute, "Doing Cash Differently"; and Cash Learning Partnership, "An

Agenda for Cash."

85. Barrett et al., "Market Information and Food Insecurity Response Analysis."

86. Government Accountability Office, "International Cash-Based Food Assistance: USAID Has Established Processes to Monitor Cash and Voucher Projects, but Data Limitations Impede Evaluation," 2016.

87. The Global Food Security Act of 2016, Pub. L. No. 114-195.

88. The Global Food Security Act of 2016, Pub. L. No. 114-195, § 3a(9).

89. US Agency for International Development, *Food for Peace: Behind the Numbers*; and US Government Accountability Office, "International Food Assistance: Cargo Preference Increases Food Aid Shipping Costs, and Benefits Are Unclear."

90. Lentz and Barrett, "The Negligible Welfare Effects of the International Food Aid Provisions in the 2014 Farm Bill."

91. Zulfiqar A. Bhutta et al., "Evidence-Based Interventions for Improvement of Maternal and Child Nutrition: What Can Be Done and at What Cost?," *Lancet* 382, no. 9890 (2013): 452–77.

92. Bageant, Barrett, and Lentz, "Food Aid and Cargo Preference"; US Government Accountability Office, "International Food Assistance: Cargo Preference Increases Food Aid Shipping Costs, and Benefits Are Unclear"; Mercier and Smith, *Military Readiness and Food Aid Cargo Preference*; and Thomas and Ferris, "Food Aid Reforms Will Not Significantly Affect Shipping Industry or Surge Fleet."

93. Frank Kendall, letter to Eliot L. Engel, June 18, 2013, https://www.documentcloud.org/documents/814075-pentagon-letter-on-food-aid-reform.html; and Brian de Vallance, letter to Jay Rockefeller, April 17, 2014, http://www.scribd.com/doc/220264499/DHS-Coast-Guard-Letter.

94. Bageant, Barrett, and Lentz, "Food Aid and Cargo Preference."

95. Mercier and Smith, *Military Readiness and Food Aid Cargo Preference*.

96. Harou et al., "Tradeoffs or Synergies?"

97. US Government Accountability Office, "International Food Assistance: Better Nutrition and Quality Control Can Further Improve U.S. Food Aid," May 2011, http://www.gao.gov/assets/320/318210.pdf.

98. William J. Violette et al., "Recipients' Satisfaction with Locally Procured Food Aid Rations: Comparative Evidence from a Three Country Matched Survey," *World Development* 49 (2013): 30–43.

99. Gordon, "Risk and Humanitarian Cash Transfer Programming."

100. Gordon, "Risk and Humanitarian Cash Transfer Programming."

101. Daniel Maxwell et al., "Facing Famine: Somali Experiences in the Famine of 2011," *Food Policy* 65 (2016): 63–73.

102. The "Conclusion" section draws on Barrett's testimony before House Foreign Affairs Committee. Christopher B. Barrett, testimony before Committee on Foreign Affairs, US House of Representatives, October 7, 2015, http://docs.house.gov/meetings/FA/FA00/20151007/104039/HHRG-114-FA00-Wstate-BarrettC-20151007.pdf.

Section II

Agricultural Research and Development and Technological Innovation

4

Waste Not, Want Not: Transactional Politics, Research and Development Funding, and the US Farm Bill

PHILIP G. PARDEY AND VINCENT H. SMITH

Doling out taxpayer dollars via the farm bill is transactional politics in its finest form, pitting the self-interests of agricultural lobbies against society's community-wide well-being. Many of the farm programs we know today have their roots in Franklin D. Roosevelt's 1930s New Deal legislation, which were emergency measures put in place to address the farm income implications of severely depressed farm prices during the Great Depression and as Dust Bowl droughts were ravaging parts of the United States. The Agriculture Adjustment Act of 1933 established the precedent for using federal resources to prop up farm prices and farm incomes, and the subsequent 1938 Farm Bill committed substantial federal funds for farm subsidy payments.[1]

The 1933 Farm Bill represented an explicit, radical expansion and shift in the spending priorities of the US Department of Agriculture (USDA), arguably the most dramatic change since President Abraham Lincoln signed an act to establish the Department of Agriculture in 1862 as the Civil War unfolded. The charge for the new fledgling federal department was "to acquire and to diffuse among the people of the United States useful information on subjects connected with agriculture in the most general and comprehensive sense of that word, and to procure, propagate, and distribute among the people new and valuable seeds and plants."[2]

The original research and innovation-centric vision of the USDA has been heavily diluted over the past 150 years. Figure 1 shows the USDA annual budget (in 2009 dollars) for 1889–2015 and the share of that budget allocated to research and development (R&D). In the early 1890s, expenditures

Figure 1. USDA Spending Priorities: From Promoting Productivity to Political Payments, 1889–2014

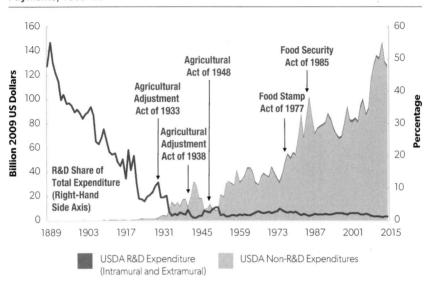

Note: Research spending represents intramural and extramural food and agricultural (exclusive of forestry) R&D spending by the USDA. Spending totals were deflated to 2009 prices using the implicit gross domestic product (GDP) deflator from Louis Johnston and Samuel H. Williamson. See Louis Johnston and Samuel H. Williamson, "What Was the U.S. GDP Then?," MeasuringWorth, 2017, www.measuringworth.com/usgdp/. The major contents of the various legislative initiatives identified in Figure 1 were as follows. The 1933 Agricultural Adjustment Act introduced programs to support prices for major commodities, with costs to be financed by a processor tax, and it introduced the Soil Bank paid land retirement program. Subsequently, the price support provisions of the 1933 act were found to be unconstitutional. Thus, the 1938 Agricultural Adjustment Act established mandatory price support for corn, cotton, and wheat financed by federal subsidies, marketing quotas, and the federal crop insurance program. The 1948 Agricultural Act expanded mandatory price supports at relatively high prices. (Parity prices based on inflation adjust prices received for covered commodities between 1910 and 1914, the so-called golden age of agriculture.) The 1977 Food Stamp Act substantially expanded the scope of the original Food Stamp Program introduced in 1964. Eligible families would now receive food stamps at zero cost. The 1985 Food Security Act introduced the Conservation Reserve Program (essentially an updated version of the Soil Bank Program introduced in the 1930s, revived in the 1950s, and ended in the 1960s). The 1985 act reflected an accommodation between the growing influence of the environmental lobby and the farm lobby. It marked the reintroduction and subsequent expansion in successive farm bills of substantial subsidies for conservation programs.

Source: USDA spending was compiled from the US Treasury Department and the USDA reports. See US Treasury Department, Office of the Secretary, "Combined Statement of the Receipts and Disbursements Balances, etc., of the United States"; and US Department of Agriculture, *Budget Summary*, www.obpa.usda.gov/budsum/fy17budsum.pdf. R&D spending was compiled from the International Science and Technology Practice and Policy (InSTePP) Innovation Accounts version 3.5. See Philip G. Pardey and Jason M. Beddow, "Revitalizing Agricultural Research and Development to Sustain US Competitiveness," Farm Journal Foundation, February 28, 2017, www.farmersfeedingtheworld.org/assets/7/6/revitalizingagresearch_print.pdf.

on R&D accounted for more than half of total USDA spending. By 1929, at the onset of the Great Depression, that share had declined to about 11 percent as the USDA's extension, education, food safety, and other regulatory functions expanded.[3] However, subsequent to the passage of the 1933 and 1938 Agricultural Adjustment Acts, the share of the USDA budget allocated to research spending dropped sharply, averaging 4.6 percent in the 1930s. In the 1940s, R&D's share declined further to an average of around 2 percent, peaking at about 4 percent in 1952. Nevertheless, following the 1948 Agricultural Act, which introduced price supports at relatively high levels for some major commodities (e.g., wheat and corn), R&D's share dropped back to as little as 2 percent.

The USDA's budget rose sharply after the mid-1970s as the department's mission further expanded. In 1977, the Food Stamp Program, which is now known as the Supplemental Nutrition Assistance Program (SNAP), underwent major reforms, and participation in the program jumped substantially. Then, through the 1985 Food Security Act, which in effect reintroduced a Soil Bank (now called the Conservation Reserve Program) and subsequent farm bills, spending on conservation programs was increased. The result was a further diminution of the share of USDA resources allocated to R&D, the department's original raison d'être, to an average of less than 1.5 percent of its budget over the past decade.

The 19th and 20th centuries each had pivotal moments in terms of how federal funds would be spent on US agriculture. At some point, it will be time to revisit and realign USDA spending priorities to deal with 21st-century realities. With increasing concerns about trade deficits, the rate of growth of agricultural exports, the impact of US direct subsidies to farmers on US trade relations with other countries, access to overseas markets, and a decline in US agricultural productivity, is this the time to consider reallocating resources toward publicly funded R&D? Or does the near "rounding error" that, at about $20 billion a year, farm subsidies represent in an overall federal government budget of $3.65 trillion (about 0.5 percent) once again spare that part of farm bill spending from any serious scrutiny?

Slicing Up the Farm Bill Pie

Historically, much of the federal government's public funding for agricultural R&D has been directly authorized through the farm bill, which includes a plethora of policy initiatives. Those initiatives range from nutrition assistance programs, such as SNAP and the Special Supplemental Nutrition Program for Women, Infants, and Children (WIC), to direct farm subsidies, subsidized federal agricultural insurance, and conservation programs.

From a budget perspective, federal spending on farm bill initiatives can be divided between programs that are not focused on agriculture and programs that directly focus on the farm and farming operations.

Total federal spending on USDA programs was around $151 billion in fiscal year 2017 (Figure 2). The bulk of this spending, more than 85 percent, is for nonagricultural programs (about $129 billion in 2017).

Most of these funds are allocated to the major nutrition assistance programs, including SNAP and WIC. These initiatives are a major component of the US federal antipoverty, low-income household economic safety net and in 2017 served more than 42 million people who live in households with incomes below the federal poverty line (13 percent of the US total population). Rural housing and rural development programs for infrastructure and nonfarm-based economic development account for less than 0.5 percent of the total USDA budget (about $440 million a year). About $1.4 billion a year is allocated for emergency food aid programs, and a similar amount is allocated to extension and outreach education programs. Other funds are allocated for USDA personnel and administration costs.

The remaining $22.7 billion in the USDA's annual budget is spent on farm subsidies ($20.4 billion in 2017) and publicly funded agricultural R&D (about $2.4 billion in 2017) (Figure 2, Panel B). The farm subsidy portion of the annual federal farm bill budgets is almost completely allocated among three major programs: the federal crop insurance program (on average approximately $7 billion), two major direct farm subsidy programs called Agricultural Risk Coverage and Price Loss Coverage (totaling $8.6 billion), and conservation programs ($4.7 billion). Approximately $600 million of federal money is spent on a suite of four livestock-oriented disaster aid programs.

Figure 2. Farm Bill Spending, 2017

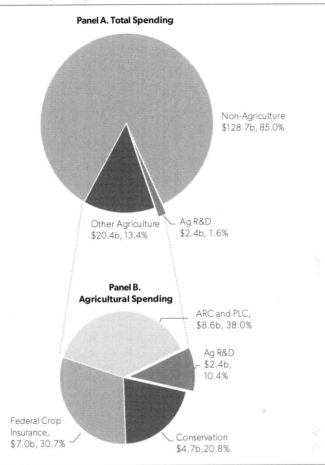

Panel A. Total Spending

Non-Agriculture
$128.7b, 85.0%

Other Agriculture
$20.4b, 13.4%

Ag R&D
$2.4b, 1.6%

**Panel B.
Agricultural Spending**

ARC and PLC,
$8.6b, 38.0%

Ag R&D
$2.4b,
10.4%

Federal Crop
Insurance,
$7.0b, 30.7%

Conservation
$4.7b, 20.8%

Note: Data are forecast fiscal year 2017 expenditures or outlays except for federal crop insurance, which is budget authority given the considerable year-to-year variation. In this figure, "ARC" stands for the Agricultural Risk Coverage, and "PLC" stands for Price Loss Coverage programs.
Source: US Department of Agriculture, *Budget Summary*, www.obpa.usda.gov/budsum/fy17budsum.pdf; US Department of Agriculture, National Institute for Food and Agriculture, "2018 President's Budget," October 2017, 19–31, https://nifa.usda.gov/archivedbudget-information; and Congressional Budget Office, "June 2017 Baseline for Farm Programs," August 2017, 3–26, www.cbo.gov/sites/default/files/recurringdata/51317-2017-06-usda.pdf.

The evidence about the value to society of crop insurance subsidies is unambiguous. Numerous analyses have demonstrated that, from an economic efficiency perspective, the US crop insurance program represents a waste of scarce economic resources. For example, by giving farmers incentives to adopt more risky production practices, such subsidies have encouraged them to use relatively inefficient production methods.[4] They have also had complex environmental effects, many of which are adverse.[5] For example, crop insurance subsidies have incentivized farmers to plant crops on fragile lands previously used for grazing, with adverse effects on soil erosion and wildlife habitat. Further, subsidy payments largely flow to landowners and owners of farm businesses with relatively high incomes and average levels of wealth that are substantial.[6]

Farmers benefit from the crop insurance program through premium subsidies that enhance their average incomes, estimated by the Congressional Budget Office to average about $5.5 billion annually over the next 10 years.[7] However, the sector that arguably benefits most from the program, to the extent of about $2.4 billion a year in income from federal subsidies, consists of crop insurance companies and independent crop insurance agents. Effectively, that industry exists largely because of the federal crop insurance subsidies provided to farmers.[8] It is noteworthy that federal spending on subsidies to crop insurance companies is similar to spending on agricultural R&D.

A similar case can be made for waste with respect to the $8.6 billion a year currently being spent on two programs, Agricultural Risk Coverage and Price Loss Coverage, which now serve as major sources of direct subsidies. These payments also flow mainly to the wealthiest and largest farm operations and enhance farm incomes in a sector that, by any reasonable measure, is on average in good financial condition.[9]

Conservation programs are often classified into two broad categories: working-lands programs, through which farmers are paid to adopt or continue farming practices that reduce pollution and less adversely affect environmental amenities, and land retirement programs, through which farmers receive federal funds when they remove land from crop production and place it into conservation uses. Some of these programs, as Erik Lichtenberg points out in Chapter 6 of Volume II, do generate environmental benefits of value to society as a whole, but some do not, and many are poorly targeted.[10] Working-lands initiatives such as the Conservation Stewardship Program (CSP), which are budgeted at an annual average of about $1.8 billion over the next 10 years, are especially questionable. The reason is that the CSP is designed largely to pay farmers to continue using practices they have already adopted for other reasons.

Public investments in agricultural R&D are the one farm-oriented set of farm bill–authorized outlays that have consistently generated broad-based social benefits for both innovative farmers and consumers.[11] However, public spending on agricultural R&D has atrophied since the late 1990s. The question is why, given that agricultural R&D is one of the rare places in the agriculture-oriented programs authorized by the farm bill in which federal funds generate high social rates of return and are substantially underfunded.

The answer is relatively straightforward. Much like teachers unions that primarily (albeit, not exclusively) exist to serve the interests of their members (teachers, not students), farm and agribusiness interest groups primarily exist to serve the interests of their members (farmers and agribusinesses, not consumers). They lobby Congress most heavily for programs that generate the most, and most immediate, benefits for their members.

The benefits that flow from public agricultural R&D investments are (1) diffuse and shared with consumers and (2) occur only after a relatively long delay, and typically not in the short term. By contrast, the benefits that flow from direct subsidy programs such as Price Loss Coverage, Agricultural Risk Coverage, federal crop insurance, and most conservation programs flow almost completely to a small set of farm owners and landowners and arrive almost immediately. (The annual check shows up in the mail.) If the choice is between spending a federal dollar on publicly funded R&D or more direct subsidies, farm interest groups will likely prefer the latter and therefore lobby more intensively for more direct subsidies. A third concern for the farm lobbies is also that because USDA agencies have increasingly responded to pressures from other interest groups, they have shifted a larger share of authorized R&D funds to research areas such as human nutrition and the environment that have less (and likely little) impact on agricultural productivity.

US Agricultural R&D Realities

The global agricultural R&D landscape is changing rapidly, and the US is losing ground as US policymakers have scaled back their support while policymakers in agriculturally important economies elsewhere in the world have opted to ramp up their pace of investment in agricultural innovation.

Figure 3. US Versus Rest-of-World Public Agricultural R&D Spending, 1960 and 2011

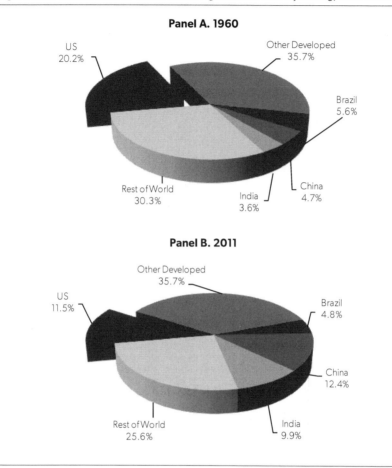

Panel A. 1960

US
20.2%

Other Developed
35.7%

Brazil
5.6%

China
4.7%

India
3.6%

Rest of World
30.3%

Panel B. 2011

Other Developed
35.7%

US
11.5%

Brazil
4.8%

China
12.4%

India
9.9%

Rest of World
25.6%

Source: Philip G. Pardey et al., "Agricultural R&D Is on the Move," *Nature* 15, no. 537 (September 2016): 301–03.

R&D Spending Trends. In 1960, the US accounted for 20 percent of global investments in public agricultural R&D, most of which were carried out by agencies such as the USDA and the land-grant universities. Fast forward to 2011—the latest year of available global data—and the picture is different (Figure 3). The US share of the global public-sector total has fallen to just 11.5 percent, second to the 12.4 percent share of global R&D contributed by China. In fact, collectively, China, India, and Brazil—three agriculturally

Figure 4. China, India, and Brazil Outspend the US on Public Agricultural Research

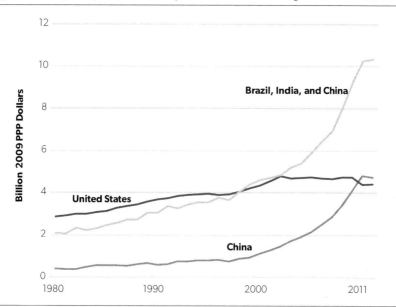

Note: "PPP" indicates purchasing power parity rate of currency exchange.
Source: Developed from data summarized in Philip G. Pardey et al., "Agricultural R&D Is on the Move," *Nature* 15, no. 537 (September 2016): 301–03.

large, middle-income countries—overtook US spending in 1998 and by 2011 together spent $2.35 on public agricultural research for every $1 invested in US public agricultural R&D (Figure 4).

How did this happen? Since at least the middle of the 20th century, real (inflation-adjusted) spending on US public agricultural research has grown at an ever-declining rate (Figure 5). Even more significantly, starting around 2002 the US began cutting back, not just slowing down, the rate of growth of spending on public agricultural R&D investments. By 2015, aggregate US spending had retreated to the inflation-adjusted levels that prevailed in 1992. In marked contrast to the US retreat from investments in public agricultural R&D, Brazil, India, and in particular China have been doubling down on their investments in public agricultural R&D, especially in the decades after 1990.

Do these changing cross-country research relativities matter? Certainly, and in potentially profound ways. The US agricultural economy now heavily relies

Figure 5. Whittling Away at US Public Agricultural R&D Investments

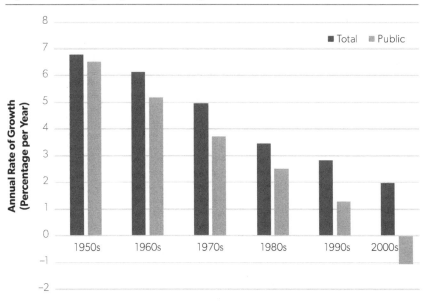

Note: Annual average growth rates for each period are derived by a log-linear regression method. The 2000s include data for 2000–14. Growth rates represent real growth rates as agricultural R&D series were deflated using the implicit GDP deflator from Louis Johnston and Samuel H. Williamson, "What Was the U.S. GDP Then?," MeasuringWorth, 2017, https://www.measuringworth.com/usgdp/.
Source: Philip G. Pardey et al., "Agricultural R&D Is on the Move," *Nature* 15, no. 537 (September 2016): 301–03; and US Department of Agriculture, Current Research Information System, unpublished annual data files, 1970–2015.

on exports, shipping abroad more than 20 percent of its total agricultural production (by volume) in recent years.[12] For three commodities (cotton, walnuts, and almonds), at least two-thirds of US production is exported, and for six commodities (nonfat dry and powder milk, wheat, soybeans, grapes, and rice), more than one-third of production is exported.[13] Gaining and then sustaining international markets is inextricably linked to the quality and unit cost of production of US agricultural output relative to agricultural competitors elsewhere in the world. Improving product quality and lowering production costs is driven by improvements in agricultural productivity that in turn rely heavily on investments in agricultural R&D.[14] As the US slips further behind regarding investments in agricultural R&D, so too will it undercut its competitive advantage, the more so if other countries continue to sustain or even further ramp up their investments in productivity-promoting R&D.

Public Versus Private R&D. Why not leave it to the private sector? One oft-told line of argument suggests that the private sector will fill the R&D void left by scaling back public research. Certainly the private sector has increased its presence in agricultural innovation markets, now spending more than $2 (specifically $2.35 in 2014) on food and agricultural R&D for every public dollar invested in research.[15] But there are limits to what the private sector will find economical to do.

Consider, for example, the US health sector, where large public-sector investments in health research administered by federal agencies such as the National Institutes of Health (NIH) and National Science Foundation (NSF) provide the basic and applied science that is socially valuable in areas such as pharmaceuticals, medical devices, and cancer treatments but which private-sector health care–oriented firms find hard to make privately profitable. Patient and persistent support for public science provides the essential scientific building blocks for the more developmental, nearer-market, and typically shorter-term research that is more readily commercialized, and which the private sector does best. This public-private division of scientific labor helps solve the "market failure" problem that bedevils R&D by funding valuable growth preserving and promoting R&D that would not happen if left entirely to the private (inclusive of farmers) sector.[16] Moreover, the public science helps drive forward the private R&D it enables.

Just as the US has lost its preeminent global position regarding investments in public agricultural R&D, so too it is ceding ground on the private research front. In 1980, private agricultural R&D conducted in the US accounted for 33 percent of the world total. By 2011, that share had slipped by nearly a quarter. This shift also reflects an increase in domestic spending on private agricultural R&D elsewhere in the world, along with recent decisions by some multinational agribusiness firms headquartered in the United States (and other high-income countries) to shift some of their R&D investments to locations in the agriculturally large and growing middle-income countries.[17] For example, China now outspends the US in both public *and* private agricultural R&D (Figure 6).[18]

Does It Pay to Invest Public Dollars in Agricultural R&D? Most of the farm bill dollars dedicated to agriculture simply slice up the agricultural pie, redistributing dollars from taxpayers to farmers, insurance intermediaries,

Figure 6. China Versus the US, 1980 and 2013

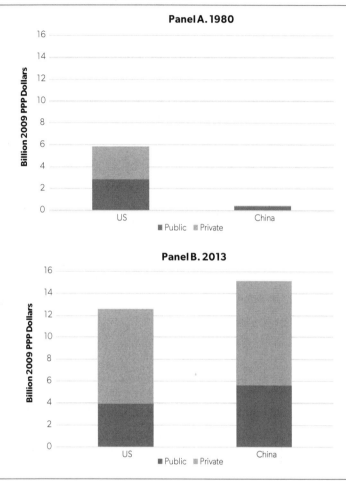

Source: Yuan Chai et al., "Passing the Agricultural R&D Buck? The United States and China" (working paper, International Science and Technology Practice and Policy Center, University of Minnesota and China Center for Agricultural Policy, Peking University, forthcoming).

and various agribusinesses.[19] In stark contrast, farm bill dollars dedicated to food and agricultural R&D expand the overall size of the agricultural pie to benefit not only innovative farmers and agribusinesses but also taxpaying consumers who foot the bill. R&D-induced productivity growth lowers the cost of production (to the benefit of innovative farmers and other agribusinesses) and lowers the price of food (to the benefit of all consumers, especially low-income consumers who spend a sizable share of their meager household incomes on food purchases). In the jargon of economists, there are both economic efficiency *and* poverty-targeted distributional or equity benefits from investing in food and agricultural R&D—a rare win-win outcome.

The overall economic gains from investing in agricultural R&D are especially large. Research is intrinsically risky. However, in practice, the big (and not-so-big) R&D winners pay for those that do not pan out commercially. In line with the compelling evidence gleaned from a large body of literature, Julian Alston et al.[20] (in their Table 4) estimated that every dollar invested in US food and agricultural R&D on average generates $32 of benefits. Importantly, recent evidence also shows that the returns to more recent research investments are as large as the returns to distant past research.[21] In other words, the payoffs to agricultural R&D are as high as they have ever been.

Who Foots the Public Agricultural R&D Bill? Research by USDA agencies has long relied on federal funding allocated through the farm bill. However, over time, USDA agencies have shrunk as a share of the total pool of public funds directed to agricultural R&D. The state agricultural experiment stations (SAESs)—typically colocated on the campuses of the land-grant universities—now conduct the lion's share of US public agricultural R&D: 73 percent in 2015, substantially larger than their 61 percent share in 1950.

The sources of financial support for SAES research are more diversified and have changed dramatically over time. The state government share of funding for SAES research fell dramatically: from 69 percent in 1970 to just 37 percent in 2015 (Figure 7, Panel A). Federal funding picked up much of the shortfall and now accounts for 40 percent of overall SAES funding, almost double its share in 1970. Subtly, but importantly, farm bill funding that the USDA made available to the SAESs declined as a share of total federal funding to the SAESs over the past several decades. The decline was substantial, from around three-quarters of total federal funding to the SAESs in the mid-1970s to just 39 percent in 2011 (Figure 7, Panel A). The increase in federal funding to the SAESs—from a 28 percent share of total SAES funding in 1975 to 40 percent in 2015—stemmed from a substantial increase in (mainly competitive, grant-allocated) funds coming from agencies such as the NIH, NSF, Department of Energy, Department of Defense, and United States Agency for International Development. A modest rebound

Figure 7. Shifting State Versus Federal Government Support for SAES Research

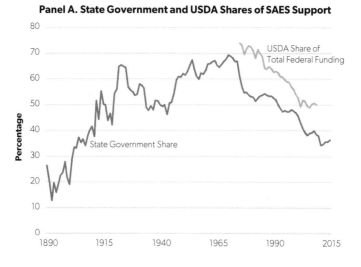

Panel A. State Government and USDA Shares of SAES Support

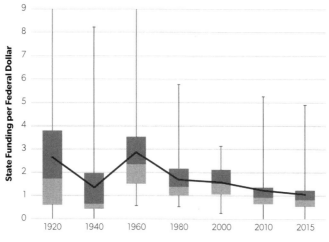

Panel B. Ratio of State to Federal Government Funding for SAESs

Note: In Panel A, "USDA Share of Total Federal Funding" is the share of USDA funding in total federal funds provided to SAESs. In Panel B, the black line plots are respective ratio averages for the SAESs. Dark and light gray meet at respective ratio medians. The upper bound of the box indicates the 75th percentile, while the lower bound indicates the 25th percentile. The upper bound of the whisker indicates maximum value, and the lower bound indicates the minimum value observed across the SAESs. For plotting purposes, upper bounds were truncated in 1920 and 1960.

Source: Updated InStePP Innovation Accounts (US agricultural R&D spending series) version 3.5. See Philip G. Pardey and Jason M. Beddow, "Revitalizing Agricultural Research and Development to Sustain US Competitiveness," Farm Journal Foundation, February 28, 2017, http://www.farmersfeedingtheworld.org/assets/7/6/revitalizingagresearch_print.pdf.

in National Institute of Food and Agricultural Research (NIFA) funding in more recent years has seen the USDA share of total federal funding rise to 50 percent in 2009 (the last year data were available to credibly estimate this share), but it is still well below historical norms.

Coincident with the reduction in state-government and USDA-sourced federal funding, SAES research priorities also shifted. Most notably, there was a sizable and sustained reduction in research aimed at preserving or promoting farm productivity.[22] Instead, the SAES research agenda has increasingly focused on food safety, food security, and environmental concerns, programs of research that have little if any impact on enhancing or maintaining farm-level productivity. No doubt these other areas of research have social value, but their expansion has been at the expense of, not in addition to, productivity-related R&D, putting at increasing risk the competitiveness of US agriculture in highly contested international markets.

What Is to Be Done?

In short, the familiar adage "waste not, want not" applies directly to federal spending on agricultural R&D as opposed to farm subsidies. From a society-wide perspective, the economically sensible strategy is to cut back on wasteful farm bill spending and instead significantly increase funding for public investments in agricultural R&D.[23] This realignment of spending priorities can readily be accommodated while also reducing overall farm bill outlays. Shifting farm bill policy from a "spending" and "income transfer" program to an "investment" strategy is much more than mere political rhetoric.

For example, crop insurance subsidies, at a minimum, waste more than $2 billion of society's resources every year in deadweight costs.[24] More than 80 percent of price support program payments have consistently been distributed to the largest 20 percent of farm businesses owned by households with levels of wealth that are many times larger than the average American household.[25] In contrast, investments in US agricultural R&D yield a 32-fold increase in economic benefits (to producers and consumers) for every taxpayer dollar invested.[26] With global population growth projected to result in two billion more mouths to feed by 2050, ensuring US agriculture remains internationally competitive to meet the anticipated massive growth in global food, feed, and fiber demand is self-evidently a strategic economic and national security imperative given the expanded market opportunities this presents, coupled with increased political instabilities from failing to address food shortages around the world.[27]

While the economic payoffs to agricultural R&D are profound, they take considerable time to materialize. Developing and deploying new crop varieties and animal breeds require decades of research effort. This gives a genuine sense of urgency to realigning farm bill spending priorities, particularly if we are serious about shifting the present production and productivity trajectories of US agriculture to better address emerging global food security and US competiveness concerns over the decades ahead.

Increased farm bill funding for food and agricultural R&D can also be done in ways that improve the effectiveness and accountability of public research. Accountable block grants to SAES institutions would inject some longer-term stability into the funding of intrinsically longer-term research processes, albeit periodically reviewed, reassessed, and, if required, reallocated funding. An increase in programmatic (or block) funding, with decisions on how best to allocate that funding being taken closer to the (typically more informed) research action, would reinvigorate forms of funding that were the hallmark of success of the SAESs during the past century. It would also better align funding timelines to the longer timelines it takes to actually do the funded research. As part of a larger farm bill commitment to agricultural research, further expanding NIFA's competitive funding program, the Agriculture and Food Research Initiative (AFRI), would also ensure the growth of a balanced portfolio of less volatile (5–10 year) programmatic (block) funding and more variable and contestable (3–5 year) AFRI project funding.

More federal funds are one important way of refinancing US public agricultural R&D. But farm bill legislation can also reshape and revitalize the incentives for others to coinvest in publicly performed agricultural R&D. Matching federal funds with state government funds has long been a feature of SAES financing modalities.

However, funds provided through the 1887 Hatch Act, the 1937 Bankhead-Jones Farm Tenant Act, and other acts as subsequently amended require a state match and have shrunk as a share of total (and federal) funding to the SAESs. Thus, for instance, in 2015 state governments committed just $1.07 on average for every dollar of federal funding made available for

SAES research, well below the $2.87 of state funding per federal dollar in 1960 (Figure 7, Panel B). Expanding the amount of state matching require-ments—either by increasing the amount of USDA-sourced funds subject to a matching requirement or increasing the required rate of state match for every federal dollar—is one likely effective strategy.

State governments are not the only source of additional SAES support. Innovative farmers and agribusinesses also benefit from public agricultural R&D, so putting efficient public financing principals into practice—whereby research costs are borne in proportion to research benefits—would argue in favor of Title VII farm bill statutes that incentivize farms and agribusinesses to also increase their support for SAES research.

US farmers already engage in collective action to fund activities that benefit agricultural producers. In recent years, these collective "checkoff" arrangements have garnered annual funding of around $1 billion, and although some of the funds support R&D—typically less than 20 percent, but it varies substantially across various marketing programs—most of these funds are used for short-term promotional activities.[28] Legislation that provides enabling (not obligatory) incentives for the industry to impose a research-levy scheme—where the funds are focused specifically on R&D and managed outside existing US checkoff programs in ways that optimize the innovative "bang for the buck"—would be a straightforward way to enable (and induce) producers to collectively cofinance the research that benefits their enterprises. The federally matched, research-levy scheme the Australian government introduced decades ago is an example of a successful and now significant source of funding for public research carried out by universities and other government institutions in that country.[29]

Giving producers incentives to implement such a research levy would likely require more than arguments about the effectiveness of collective action. To make such a program palatable to grower groups, one option (used to great effect in the Australian scheme) is for the government to offer matching funds (up to some predetermined limit), thus splitting the R&D burden between the research-levy program and general tax revenues. Includ-ing other industries that benefit from agricultural R&D in the scheme (such as input suppliers and food processors) would allow for even more agricul-tural R&D and, if implemented wisely, substantially correct the persistent underinvestment problem that has long bedeviled US agricultural R&D.[30]

The Foundation for Food and Agriculture Research (FFAR) provided in the Agricultural Act of 2014 is a potentially game-changing institutional innovation that is beginning to find its operational legs. Congress awarded the FFAR $200 million of startup funds to underwrite public agricultural R&D, with the requirement that the farm bill funds be dispensed via a one-to-one match with nonfederal funds. The arguments above speak in favor of renewing this venture-capital form of funding for public agricultural R&D. Expanding or even perhaps shifting this funding model to a matched research-levy approach could substantially expand the base of support for public agricultural R&D in the US while splitting the bill for that research among the taxpayers, farmers, and agribusinesses who benefit most from it.

Notes

1. Douglas E. Bowers, Wayne D. Rasmussen, and Gladys L. Baker, *History of Agricultural Price Support and Adjustment Programs, 1933–84*, US Department of Agriculture, Economic Research Service, 1984, https://www.ers.usda.gov/publications/pub-details/?pubid=41994; and Bruce L. Gardner, *American Agriculture in the Twentieth Century: How It Flourished and What It Cost* (Cambridge, MA: Harvard University Press, 2002).

2. Wayne D. Rasmussen and Gladys L. Baker, *The Department of Agriculture* (New York: Praeger, 1972), 6.

3. Rasmussen and Baker, *The Department of Agriculture*. For example, food safety activities increased with the 1906 passage of the Food and Drugs Act and the Meat Inspection Act—the latter attributable in part to the outcry stemming from Upton Sinclair's 1906 novel, *The Jungle*—while extension activities were given a boost with the passage of the Smith-Lever Act in 1914.

4. Barry K. Goodwin and Vincent H. Smith, *The Economics of Crop Insurance and Disaster Aid* (Washington, DC: AEI Press, 1995); Bruce A. Babcock and David A. Hennessy, "Input Demand Under Yield and Revenue Insurance," *American Journal of Agricultural Economics* 78, no. 2 (1996): 416–27, https://www.jstor.org/stable/1243713; Vincent H. Smith and Joseph W. Glauber, "Agricultural Insurance in Developed Countries," *Applied Economic Perspectives and Policy* 34, no. 3 (2012): 363–90, https://academic.oup.com/aepp/article-abstract/34/3/363/8759?; Barry K. Goodwin and Vincent H. Smith, "What Harm Is Done by Subsidizing Crop Insurance?," *American Journal of Agricultural Economics* 95, no. 2 (2013): 489–97, https://academic.oup.com/ajae/article-abstract/95/2/489/71210?; and Brian Davern Wright, "Multiple Peril Crop Insurance," *Choices* 29, no. 3 (2014): 1–5, http://www.choicesmagazine.org/UserFiles/file/cmsarticle_388.pdf.

5. Vincent H. Smith and Barry K. Goodwin, "The Environmental Consequences of Subsidized Risk Management and Disaster Assistance Programs," *Annual Review of Resource Economics* 5, no. 1 (2013): 35–60, http://www.annualreviews.org/doi/abs/10.1146/

annurevresource-110811-114505.

6. Bruce A. Babcock, "The Concentration of U.S. Agricultural Subsidies," *Iowa Ag Review* 7, no. 4 (2001): 8–9, www.card.iastate.edu/iowa_ag_review/fall_01/IAR.pdf; Michael J. Roberts and Nigel Key, "Who Benefits from Government Farm Payments?," *Choices* 3 (2003): 7–14, http://www.choicesmagazine.org/2003-3/2003-3-02.htm; and Anton Bekkerman, Eric J. Belasco, and Vincent H. Smith, "Does Size Matter? Distribution of Crop Insurance Subsidies and Government Program Payments Across U.S. Farms" (working paper, Montana State University Initiative for Regulation and Applied Economics Research, Bozeman, MT, September 2017), https://www.agri-pulse.com/ext/resources/pdfs/Smith-distributions-paper-october-2017.pdf.

7. Congressional Budget Office, "June 2017 Baseline for Farm Programs," August 2017, www.cbo.gov/sites/default/files/recurringdata/51317-2017-06-usda.pdf.

8. Smith and Glauber, "Agricultural Insurance in Developed Countries"; Wright, "Multiple Peril Crop Insurance"; and Vincent H. Smith, Joseph W. Glauber, and Barry K. Goodwin, *Time to Reform the US Federal Agricultural Insurance Program*, American Enterprise Institute, October 15, 2017, https://www.aei.org/publication/time-to-reform-the-us-federal-agricultural-insurance-program/.

9. Vincent H. Smith et al., *Agricultural Policy in Disarray: Reforming the Farm Bill—An Overview*, American Enterprise Institute, October 13, 2017; and Bruce A. Babcock, *Covering Losses with Price Loss Coverage, Agricultural Risk Coverage, and the Stacked Income Protection Plan*, American Enterprise Institute, October 13, 2017, https://www.aei.org/publication/time-to-reform-the-usfederal-agricultural-insurance-program/.

10. Erik Lichtenberg, *The Farm Bill, Conservation, and the Environment*, American Enterprise Institute, November 13, 2017, http://www.aei.org/publication/the-farm-bill-conservation-and-the-environment/.

11. Xudong Rao, Terrance M. Hurley, and Philip G. Pardey, "Are Agricultural R&D Returns Declining and Development Dependent?" (working paper, InSTePP Center, University of Minnesota, St. Paul, MN, 2017); and Xudong Rao, Terrance M. Hurley, and Philip G. Pardey, "Recalibrating the Reported Returns to Agricultural R&D: What If We All Heeded Griliches?" (working paper, InSTePP Center, University of Minnesota, St. Paul, MN, 2017).

12. US Department of Agriculture, Economic Research Service, "How Important Are Exports to the U.S. Agricultural Sector?," 2017, www.ers.usda.gov/faqs/#Q12.

13. Walt Gardiner, "U.S. Agriculture Exports: Recent Trends and Commodity Exposure to International Trade," US Food and Drug Administration, Office of Regulatory Policy, 2016, www.fca.gov/Download/EconomicReports/5%20USAgricultureExports-RecentTrendsAndCommodityExposure.pdf.

14. Philip G. Pardey and Jason M. Beddow, *Agricultural Innovation: The United States in a Changing Global Reality*, Chicago Council on Global Affairs, 2013, https://www.thechicagocouncil.org/sites/default/files/Agricultural_Innovation_Final%281%29.pdf.

15. Kyuseon Lee et al., "Private R&D Investment in the U.S. Food and Agricultural Sectors, 1950–2014" (working paper, InSTePP Center, University of Minnesota, St. Paul, MN, 2017), http://ageconsearch.umn.edu/record/259112?ln=en.

16. Failing to comprehend the nature of the market failure problem in agricultural R&D has a long history. As Rasmussen and Baker observed, "The chairman of the House

Committee on Agriculture, J. W. Covert of New York, displayed his complete misunderstanding of the role the Department could play in scientific research when he claimed on February 18, 1881: 'The controlling idea involved in the creation of the department is that our wide domain should be tested, to ascertain what can be most successfully produced in its various sections. Experiments in this direction cannot be profitably conducted forever. Sooner or later the work of the department should be closed, and meanwhile I cannot see why the farmer should not, like other men engaged in other pursuits, learn to experiment for himself and act for himself without reference to governmental aid.'" Rasmussen and Baker, *The Department of Agriculture.*

17. Philip G. Pardey and Jason M. Beddow, "Revitalizing Agricultural Research and Development to Sustain US Competitiveness," Farm Journal Foundation, February 28, 2017, http://www.farmersfeedingtheworld.org/assets/7/6/revitalizingagresearch_print.pdf.

18. Y. Chai et al., "Passing the Agricultural R&D Buck? The United States and China" (working paper, InSTePP Center, University of Minnesota, St. Paul, MN, and Chinese Center for Agricultural Policy, Peking University, Beijing, 2017).

19. Smith, Glauber, and Goodwin, *Time to Reform the US Federal Agricultural Insurance Program*; and Smith et al., *Agricultural Policy in Disarray: Reforming the Farm Bill—An Overview.*

20. Julian M. Alston et al., "The Economic Returns to U.S. Public Agricultural Research," *American Journal of Agricultural Economics* 93, no. 5 (2011): 1257–77.

21. Rao, Hurley, and Pardey, "Are Agricultural R&D Returns Declining and Development Dependent?"

22. Philip G. Pardey, Julian M. Alston, and Connie Chan-Kang, *Public Food and Agricultural Research in the United States: The Rise and Decline of Public Investments, and Policies for Renewal,* AGree, 2013, http://foodandagpolicy.org/content/public-food-and-agricultural-research-united-statesthe-rise-and-decline-public-investments-a.

23. As Pardey et al. noted, "Although no one really knows much quantitatively about the nature of diminishing returns to public agricultural research investments, it seems safe to say that the total U.S. public agricultural research enterprise could double in size without exceeding the national economic optimum—and certainly in the 'longer run,' after allowing appropriate time for building up the stocks of human and physical capital inputs to take efficient advantage of increases in operating funds." Pardey et al., *Public Food and Agricultural Research in the United States.*

24. Smith, Glauber, and Goodwin, *Time to Reform the US Federal Agricultural Insurance Program.*

25. Bekkerman, Belasco, and Smith, "Does Size Matter?"

26. Alston et al., "The Economic Returns to U.S. Public Agricultural Research," 1257–77.

27. Marc F. Bellemare, "Rising Food Prices, Food Price Volatility, and Social Unrest," *American Journal of Agricultural Economics* 97, no. 1 (2015): 1–21, https://academic.oup.com/ajae/article/97/1/1/135390/Rising-Food-Prices-Food-Price-Volatility-and.

28. Julian M. Alston, Richard S. Gray, and Katarzyna Bolek, *Farmer-Funded R&D: Institutional Innovations for Enhancing Agricultural Research Investments,* Canadian Agricultural Innovation and Regulation Network, March 27, 2012; and Hyunok Lee et al., *Mandated Marketing Programs for California Commodities,* Giannini Foundation, 1996.

29. Alston, Gray, and Bolek, *Farmer-Funded R&D*; and John C. Kerin, *The Way I Saw It; The Way It Was: The Making of National Agricultural and Natural Resource Management Policy* (Melbourne: Analysis and Policy Observatory, 2017).

30. Pardey, Alston, and Chan-Kang, *Public Food and Agricultural Research in the United States*.

5

The Impact of Genetic Modification Technologies on Agricultural Productivity: Evidence from a Comparison of US and EU Crop Yields

GARY W. BRESTER AND JOSEPH A. ATWOOD

Genetically modified (GM) crops are plants in which DNA has been altered in a way that does not occur naturally through plant breeding.[1] Genetic engineering transfers selected individual genes within or across plant species to produce plants with targeted characteristics. Golden rice, for example, is a GM plant that produces more vitamin A (which can reduce blindness in susceptible human populations) than conventional rice. For other crops, genetic engineering produces plants that are resistant to insects, viruses, and certain herbicides. The technology can greatly reduce or eliminate the need to use insecticides and fungicides to control insects and viruses, while herbicide-resistant traits increase the efficacy of weed control.

Over the past 20 years, genetic engineering has most often been used to produce crop varieties that resist the effects of glyphosate herbicides. A non-glyphosate-resistant crop (and all weeds) will die if sprayed with a glyphosate. However, a glyphosate-resistant GM crop will not die when sprayed with a glyphosate, while other plants (i.e., weeds) will die. The GM approach to weed control is much more effective than the traditional use of selective and nonselective herbicides. In some cases, several GM traits (e.g., insect or virus resistance) have been "stacked" into a single crop variety.

GM seed varieties were first introduced in the United States in 1996 and are currently available for corn, cotton, soybeans, sugar beets, canola, and alfalfa. Although GM adoption rates were initially modest, 100 percent of US sugar beets, almost 100 percent of Canadian canola, and more than

90 percent of US corn, cotton, and soybeans were planted with GM seed in 2016.[2]

The high adoption rates might appear surprising given that GM seed varieties are two to four times more expensive than conventional seed varieties. Agricultural producers, however, generally adopt practices that increase profits through per-unit cost reductions or increased yields. Cost savings associated with GM crop varieties have accrued through reductions in the use of agricultural chemicals, mechanical tillage, labor, and, perhaps, increased yields. Nonetheless, the European Union has prohibited the use of these technologies.

A recent *New York Times* article by Danny Hakim titled "Doubts About the Promised Bounty of Genetically Modified Crops" discussed the impact of GM crops in the United States and Canada by comparing crop yield outcomes in those countries with outcomes in the European Union, which has banned GM technologies.[3] Hakim asserts that although the United States has been using GM crops for two decades, yield trends between the two regions have not changed. Several other reports appear to echo similar concerns about an apparent lack of GM technology benefits.[4] However, those assertions run counter to research that indicates GM technologies can increase yields through increased plant populations and reduced rotational impacts at the lower end of yield distributions,[5] as well as improved pest control.[6]

Various issues regarding GM technologies have been extensively debated since their introduction in the United States 20 years ago. However, the impacts of agricultural technological change have a long research history as many other innovations have been the subject of similar assessments.[7] For example, Zvi Griliches investigated the impacts of research expenditures on the development of hybrid corn (a plant modification that occurs through the selective movement of DNA material contained in pollen across plants within a species) and related innovations.[8] He estimated that the social rate of return on public and private funds used to develop hybrid corn technologies was substantial. Yujiro Hayami and Vernon Ruttan also examined the impact of technology on agricultural productivity. They argued that a continuous sequence of innovations can yield increased agricultural output even in regions where agricultural production is not the focus of the research that led to the innovations.[9]

The issue of yield outcomes resulting from GM crop technologies is complex, especially when comparisons are made across countries and regions. Hakim used data from the United Nations Food and Agricultural Organization (FAO) to claim that there has been no difference in per-acre yield trends among the United States (corn and sugar beets), Canada (canola), and the European Union since the introduction of GM crops. However, the "promised" benefits of GM crops could have little to do with yield increases.

For example, E. D. Perry, G. Moschini, and D. A. Hennessy observe that GM technologies have reduced mechanical tillage operations with resulting reductions in CO_2 emissions, soil compaction, soil erosion, and production costs.[10] While GM corn varieties have reduced the use of many production inputs (agricultural chemicals, labor, etc.), most weed and insect problems were effectively controlled before the use of GM seeds—albeit, with the use of more toxic chemicals, labor, and machinery inputs.[11]

Consequently, perhaps the primary result of GM technologies is a reduction in input usage and lower per-unit production costs.[12] Nonetheless, it seems reasonable that if a technology increases the efficacy of weed and pest control and reduces soil compaction, yields should respond positively.

Hakim's Approach

Hakim compares corn (and other crops) yield trends between the United States and Western Europe using data from the FAO between 1985 and 2014 (the most recent year available).[13] Western Europe consists of seven countries: Austria, Belgium, France, Germany, Luxembourg, the Netherlands, and Switzerland. Although the original data are in hectograms per hectare, we have converted the data to bushels per acre, an adjustment that does not affect the analysis.[14] Figure 1 shows Western Europe and US corn yields and regression-fitted linear trend lines for 1985–2014.

Hakim's visual interpretation of the data is that Western Europe and US yield trend lines are not different from one another. Quantitatively, we regress corn yields for each region onto a linear time trend and find that the slope of the Western Europe regression-fitted trend line is 1.69 and the slope of the US trend line is 1.79. In this case, the visual comparison of the data matches the statistical comparison. A standard chi-squared test cannot reject

Figure 1. US and Western EU Corn Yields, 1985–2014

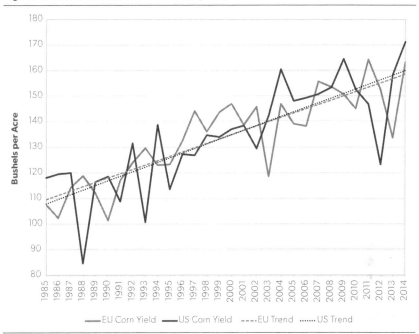

Source: Gary W. Brester and Joseph A. Atwood, "A Non-Linear Examination of the 'Doubts' Regarding Genetically Modified Crop Yields," Montana State University Institute of Regulation and Applied Economic Analysis, November 2017, http:// www.montana.edu/econ/documents/nonlinearexamgmoyieldsbrester111517.pdf.

the null hypothesis that the two slope coefficients are the same. Although the slope of the US yield trend line is slightly larger, it is not statistically different from the slope of the EU trend line. Hakim notes that this outcome has been echoed by others:

> Jack Heinemann, a professor [biologist] at the University of Canterbury in New Zealand, did a pioneering 2013 study comparing trans-Atlantic yield trends, using United Nations data. Western Europe, he said, "hasn't been penalized in any way for not making genetic engineering one of its biotechnology choices."[15]

A similar conclusion appears in a National Academies of Sciences report that notes a lack of evidence that GM crops have contributed to increased yield growth.[16] Rather, the report attributes continued yield increases to other factors such as improved conventional seeds and management practices.[17] It is not clear, however, how improved conventional seed technologies could be responsible for increased yields when less than 10 percent of corn, cotton, and soybean acreages are currently planted with non-GM varieties. Nonetheless, if conventional technologies continue to be transferable between the United States and the European Union, then yield trends should be similar between the two regions.

Trend Analyses

The first problem with Hakim's corn yield comparisons involves his selected time period. Certainly, the starting point for any trend analysis is often ambiguous. Although GM seed research was conducted throughout the 1980s, GM corn technology was not commercially available until 1996. In addition, the adoption rate was, initially, modest. It was not until 2005 that 50 percent of corn acreage was planted to a GM variety.[18] Consequently, GM varieties probably did not substantially influence average annual US corn yields until a relatively large share of acreage was planted with those varieties.

Nonetheless, estimating trends over short time periods (in this case, 10 years since 2005 when 50 percent of acreage was planted to GM varieties) is also fraught with potential errors. Indeed, the choice of the initial year can change trend differences from being inconsequential to substantial. For example, by using 1988 as a starting point in Figure 1 (a year in which the western EU countries had relatively high yields and the United States had relatively low yields) rather than 1985, regression results indicate that the Western Europe yield trend line slope is 1.6 and the US trend line slope is 2.1. Although the United States has a larger yield trend relative to the western EU for this period, the limited number of observations causes relatively imprecise estimates. Consequently, the two results are not statistically different from each other. As the time period for trend analyses is lengthened, however, the influence of starting (or ending) points is reduced.

A second problem occurs when comparing regions that have different production opportunities, agricultural policies, weather, and scale. For example, Hakim compares Western Europe yields to those of the entire

United States. The western EU countries represent the best growing conditions relative to the rest of the European Union.

During the past decade, US corn acreage expanded from 70 million acres in 2005 to almost 87 million acres in 2016.[19] Much of this expansion was caused by higher corn prices and the availability of GM seed technologies. Consequently, corn production has extended into areas that previously were not prime corn production land. Jayson Lusk, Jesse Tack, and Nathan Hendricks note that because of weather and soil type heterogeneity, the impact of GM technologies on average US corn yields may be understated.[20] Hence, if one is to consider yields for the entire United States, it seems reasonable to consider yields for the entire EU region.

A Closer Look at the Data

FAO Statistical Database (FAOSTAT) data do not currently include yield estimates beyond 2014. However, the US Department of Agriculture Foreign Agricultural Service's Production Supply and Disposition (FAS PSD) website provides crop yield data for most countries and regions including the United States and the European Union between 1961 and 2016.[21] Parenthetically, the FAOSTAT data and FAS PSD data are almost identical for those years in which overlap occurs. Figure 2 presents corn yields for the entire EU and the United States between 1961 and 2016 using FAS PSD data.

Linear Corn Yield Trends. Before considering the potential for nonlinear yield trends, we first estimate linear trend lines for US and EU corn yields. The results show that the annual linear yield trend for corn is 1.83 bushels in the United States and 1.35 bushels in the European Union. Unlike the estimates based on Hakim's much shorter time series, these two estimates are statistically different from each other. The US corn yield trend has almost a 0.5 bushel per acre advantage over the EU yield trend for the 56-year period. That is, over 56 years, the difference between US and EU corn yields has increased by about 28 bushels an acre.

Given that more than 90 million acres of corn are planted each year in the United States, the difference results in a net gain of more than 2.5 billion

Figure 2. US and EU Corn Yields, 1961–2016

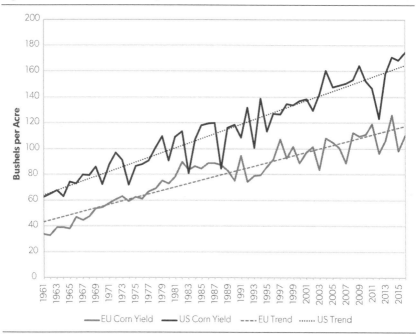

Source: Gary W. Brester et al., "An Examination of the Influence of Genetic Modification Technologies on U.S. and EU Crop Yields," *Journal of Agricultural and Resource Economics*, forthcoming.

bushels in the United States compared to the gain that would have accrued had US corn yields increased at the EU linear growth rate. The linear trend line for the United States predicts a 2016 yield of 165 bushels per acre. If yields in the US had grown at the same rate as EU yields, recent US corn crops, on average, would have been 17 percent lower than actual levels.

The question at hand, however, is to what extent can the differences in corn (and other crop) yield growth rates between the US and the EU be attributed to GM crop technologies. To examine this question, we estimated a second regression that allows for a shift in the rate of growth of US and EU corn yields beginning in 1996 (the year GM technologies were introduced in the United States). The results indicate that GM technologies have not altered the US corn yield trend. That is, it has continued on its long-term upward linear path.

However, this does not mean that GM technologies have not affected US corn yields. Increasing yield trends are the result of adopting new technologies. Without yield-enhancing technologies, there would be, at best, no increase in yields. And at worst, the absence of new technologies needed to offset new or increased pest and weed pressures could result in negative yield trends.

In contrast to the United States, the EU corn yield trend has flattened since 1996. The estimates show that since the introduction of GM technologies in the United States, the EU corn yield trend has been 0.87 bushels per acre annually, which is 0.96 bushels less than the US yield. While the EU per-acre yield trend was only about 0.5 bushels less than the US trend before 1996, the slope of the EU trend line indicates that EU corn yields have increased at a substantially slower rate (almost a bushel per year less since 1996 with an aggregate net adverse effect over the 20-year period of about 18 bushels per acre).

The widening difference between US and EU corn yields could be attributable to non-GM factors such as changes in agricultural policy, environmental issues, or relative factor prices. For example, the European Union instituted regulations that reduced the use of nitrogen fertilizers in the late 1980s while reducing various agricultural support programs.[22] Hence, total nitrogen fertilizer use declined by about 30 percent in the early 1990s from record levels in the late 1980s. This is an important consideration given that corn production generally requires high nitrogen fertilizer inputs. US nitrogen fertilizer use has been relatively constant since the early 1980s, while nitrogen use in the European Union has been relatively constant since the early 1990s. Consequently, it does not appear that differences in environmental policies related to nitrogen fertilizers can explain the differences in corn yield trends over the past two decades.

Nonlinear Yield Trends. Estimating yield trends has been the subject of extensive previous research.[23] A crucial research decision in estimating yield trends is the selection of the functional form used to track the relationship between yields and time. It is unclear whether yield trends should be estimated using linear or nonlinear functions. Technological change is often gradual and influenced by learning processes. As a result, nonlinear yield trend models may be more representative of actual yield experiences.

Figure 3. US Corn Yield and Trend, 1961–2016

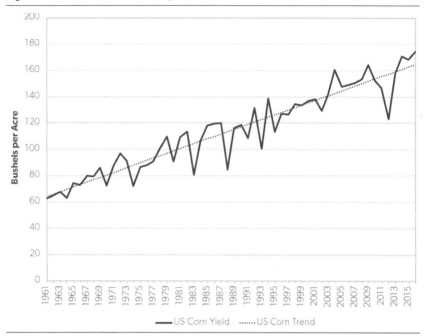

Source: Gary W. Brester et al., "An Examination of the Influence of Genetic Modification Technologies on U.S. and EU Crop Yields," *Journal of Agricultural and Resource Economics,* forthcoming.

Either way, this is an empirical issue that can be resolved using careful statistical analyses.

Nonlinear Corn Yield Trends. The linear approach to yield trend estimation provides evidence that US and EU corn yield trends have diverged since the introduction of GM technologies in the United States. The results presented in Figure 3, however, show that using a less-restrictive, nonlinear functional form results in the same estimate for US corn yields trends (1.83 bushels per acre annually) as the estimates obtained using a linear functional form.[24]

Using predictions from the linear trend line, US corn yields increased 28.5 percent, or 37 bushels per acre, between 1996 and 2016. Conversely, the EU corn yield trend is more accurately represented by a nonlinear trend (Figure 4). Corn yields in the European Union continue to trend upward,

Figure 4. EU Corn Yield and Trend, 1961–2016

Source: Gary W. Brester et al., "An Examination of the Influence of Genetic Modification Technologies on U.S. and EU Crop Yields," *Journal of Agricultural and Resource Economics*, forthcoming.

but at a decreasing rate. Thus, when the trend in EU corn yields is modeled more accurately as a nonlinear relationship, the decline in EU yields relative to US yields is more substantial than the differences indicated using linear trend analyses. The nonlinear trend relationship for EU yields indicates that average EU corn yields increased by 19 bushels per acre between 1996 and 2016, a 20.5 percent increase.

GM technologies are not used in the European Union. Thus, these yield increases result from factors such as improved conventional seed technologies, changes in input or output prices, and improvements in other production practices. Similar factors could also be responsible for yield increases in the United States. To the extent that technologies and production practices are readily transferable between the United States and the European Union, however, the difference of 18 bushels per acre between the two regions since 1996 is likely attributable to the US adoption of GM technologies.

Figure 5. US Minus EU Corn Yield and Trend, 1961–2016

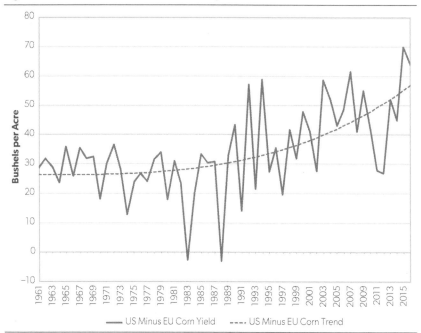

Source: Gary W. Brester et al., "An Examination of the Influence of Genetic Modification Technologies on U.S. and EU Crop Yields," *Journal of Agricultural and Resource Economics*, forthcoming.

A more direct approach to test for divergent annual yields is to consider the *difference* between US and EU corn yields using the data presented in Figure 2. The nonlinear model illustrated in Figure 5 indicates that the difference between US and EU corn yields has been increasing. Much of the increase appears to have occurred over the past two decades—the period over which GM corn has been almost completely adopted in the United States but banned in the European Union. The trend line shows that the predicted difference between US and EU corn yields in 1996 (34.2 bushels per acre) had increased to 56.8 bushels per acre in 2016. The 22.6 bushel per acre increase in the difference between US and EU corn yields since 1996 is similar to the difference obtained by comparing the results of separate trend models of the levels of EU and US corn yields.

Figure 6. US and EU Wheat Yields and Trends, 1961–2016

Source: Gary W. Brester et al., "An Examination of the Influence of Genetic Modification Technologies on U.S. and EU Crop Yields," *Journal of Agricultural and Resource Economics*, forthcoming.

Wheat Yields. Factors other than GM technologies could be responsible for changes in yields between regions or countries. For example, both the United States and the European Union have experienced major changes in agricultural policies over the past several decades. In addition, labor, food safety, or production scale differences may have developed over time.

One way to assess whether the substantial differences in US and EU corn yield trends since 1996 have been caused by factors other than GM technologies is to examine yield trends for a major crop that is produced in both regions but not affected by GM technologies. Wheat is a major commodity produced in both the United States and the European Union, but it is not commercially produced using GM technologies in either region. Thus, wheat provides a potential metric for comparison.

Figure 6 presents data on US and EU wheat yields from 1961 to 2016. Because much of the US wheat crop is raised in semiarid regions, EU

Figure 7. EU Minus US Wheat Yield and Trend, 1961–2016

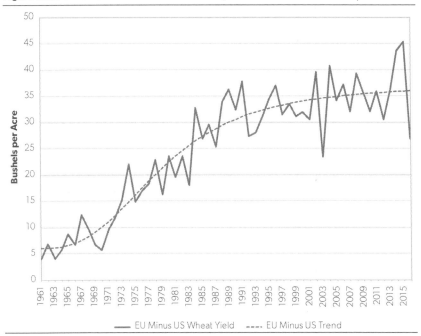

Source: Gary W. Brester et al., "An Examination of the Influence of Genetic Modification Technologies on U.S. and EU Crop Yields," *Journal of Agricultural and Resource Economics*, forthcoming.

wheat yields exceed those in the United States in every year. A linear trend model best explains the US data and indicates an annual yield increase of 0.38 bushels per acre. However, EU wheat yields have followed a sigmoid functional form since 1961. Note that EU wheat yields have continued to increase over the past several years, albeit at a decreasing rate. Nonetheless, the recent trend appears to be somewhat steeper than that of the United States.

Another way to consider these changes is to estimate a trend for the difference between EU and US wheat yields. Figure 7 indicates that the difference between EU and US wheat yields has continued to widen, although at a decreasing rate. These results provide a counterfactual supporting the hypothesis that GM technologies in the United States explain why US corn yields have increased relative to EU corn yields.

Figure 8. US and EU Soybean Yields and Trends, 1964–2016

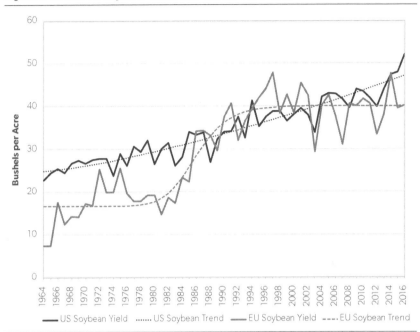

Source: Gary W. Brester et al., "An Examination of the Influence of Genetic Modification Technologies on U.S. and EU Crop Yields," *Journal of Agricultural and Resource Economics*, forthcoming.

Soybean Yields. The GM technologies that help control weed and insect problems in corn have likely increased yields. However, weed control in corn through a combination of broadleaf and grass herbicides and mechanical cultivation was relatively effective before GM technologies were introduced. For example, Elizabeth Nolan and Paulo Santos used experimental plot data to conclude that GM corn yield increases were more highly influenced by GM insect-control traits than herbicide-tolerant traits.[25]

However, weed control in conventional soybean varieties was more difficult before GM technologies were introduced because selective broadleaf herbicides were only partially effective.[26] Therefore, if GM technologies increase crop yields, it would likely be more apparent in crops for which traditional methods of weed control were less effective.

Figure 8 presents soybean yield data for the United States and the European Union between 1964 and 2016. Data on EU soybean yields are not

Figure 9. US Minus EU Soybean Yield and Trend, 1964–2016

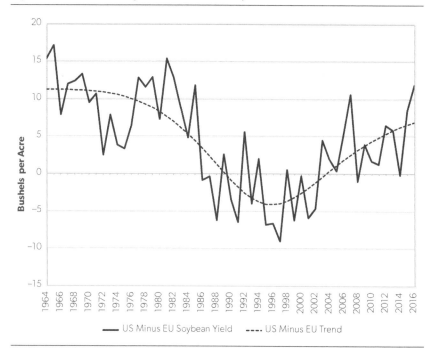

Source: Gary W. Brester et al., "An Examination of the Influence of Genetic Modification Technologies on U.S. and EU Crop Yields," *Journal of Agricultural and Resource Economics*, forthcoming.

available before 1964. In addition, only 10,000 acres of soybeans were planted in the European Union in 1964, as it was a new crop for the region. It was not until 1980 that EU farmers planted close to one million acres, and in 2016 they planted only two million acres. By comparison, the US planted 32 million acres of soybeans in 1964 and almost 83 million acres in 2016.[27]

Figure 8 indicates that the estimated nonlinear US soybean yield trend has only a small degree of curvature and is similar to a linear trend. However, EU soybean yields have followed a sigmoid functional form. Specifically, the EU yield trend has been almost flat since the mid-1990s. In contrast, US soybean yields have been increasing since 1996, when GM soybean technologies were introduced.

Figure 9 presents the annual differences between EU and US soybean yields between 1964 and 2016. Between 1964 and the mid-1980s, US soybean yields were larger than EU yields. However, between 1986 and 2002, EU yields were generally larger than US yields. Since 2002, US soybean yields have generally exceeded EU yields. The trend line based on differences between US and EU soybean yields clearly indicates the difference has increased since 1996.

Summary

Although yield trends are often estimated using linear functional forms, such trends may actually be nonlinear. For the United States, however, a linear trend for corn yields fits the data better than a nonlinear trend and indicates that US corn yields have increased 37 bushels per acre (28.5 percent) since the introduction of GM technologies in 1996, although the increase may not be entirely attributable to GM technologies. The EU corn yield trend is more accurately modeled as a nonlinear relationship that indicates that the annual rate of growth in EU corn yields has flattened over the past two decades. Between 1996 and 2016, EU corn yields increased by 19 bushels per acre (20.5 percent), as compared to the 37 bushel (28.5 percent) growth in US average corn yields over the same period.

If the *difference* in yields since 1996 between the United States and the European Union is attributable only to GM technologies, then US corn yields have increased by 23 bushels per acre more than EU yields since the adoption of GM varieties. This represents a net 18 percent increase in US corn yields, an impact similar to those reported by Lusk, Tack, and Hendricks, who used county-level data,[28] and Nolan and Santos, who used experimental plot data,[29] but smaller than those estimated by Zheng Xu et al., who used Corn Belt county-level data.[30]

GM technologies' impact on soybean yields may be even more substantial than their impacts on corn yields because traditional weed-control technologies are less effective for non-GM soybeans. The estimated trend models show that the United States had a substantial yield advantage over the European Union until the mid-1980s. For the next 20 years, EU soybean yields exceeded those of the United States. However, since the introduction of GM soybean technologies, EU soybean yields have remained flat, while US yields have increased and now exceed those of the European Union.

Factors other than GM technologies could be responsible for flattening EU corn and soybean yield trends. However, such factors should have similar effects on other crops, including those for which GM technologies are not commercially available in the United States. For instance, trend analyses indicate that EU wheat yields continue to increase relative to those of the United States. Hence, if factors other than GM technologies have been responsible for widening US and EU corn and soybean yield trends, they have not had a similar effect on US and EU wheat yield trends.

Agricultural yield trend increases are not fait accompli.[31] The remarkable sustained crop yield gains experienced in developed countries over the past six decades have occurred because of new technologies. Although some yield gains may be accomplished by more effectively using previously developed technologies, increasing yield trends can only continue an upward trend if new technologies are developed.

Any country or region certainly has the right to ban new technologies. The result of such constraints, however, is that productivity growth rates in these regions will not continue along their historical trends. The ultimate effect of banning agricultural yield-enhancing technologies is that food crop production will be lower than would otherwise be the case. Without genetic crop variety improvements, more water, land, and other inputs will be needed to increase global food production.

The trade-offs associated with banning GM technologies involve lower worldwide food output, higher production costs, higher food prices, increased input usage, and, especially for the world's poorest citizens, more food insecurity, hunger, malnutrition, and the attendant consequences for the health and productivity of those populations. As is often the case, inadequate and ill-informed analyses can lead to agricultural policy outcomes that harm the world's most food-insecure human populations.

Notes

1. World Health Organization, "Frequently Asked Questions on Genetically Modified Foods," May 2014, http://www.who.int/foodsafety/areas_work/food-technology/faq-genetically-modified-food/en/.

2. US Department of Agriculture, Economic Research Service, "Recent Trends in GE Adoption," July 12, 2017, https://www.ers.usda.gov/data-products/adoption-of-

genetically-engineered-crops-in-the-us/recent-trends-in-ge-adoption/; and Hugh J. Beckie et al., "GM Canola: The Canadian Experience," *Farm Policy Journal* 8, no. 11 (Autumn 2011), http://www.canolawatch.org/wp-content/uploads/2011/10/20110309_FPJ_Aut11_Beckie.et_.al_.pdf.

3. Danny Hakim, "Doubts About the Promised Bounty of Genetically Modified Crops," *New York Times*, October 29, 2016, https://www.nytimes.com/2016/10/30/business/gmo-promise-falls-short.html.

4. Jacob Bunge, "Behind the Monsanto Deal, Doubts About the GMO Revolution," *Wall Street Journal*, September 14, 2016, https://www.wsj.com/articles/behind-the-monsanto-deal-doubts-about-the-gmo-revolution-1473880429; Jonathan Foley, "GMOs, Silver Bullets and the Trap of Reductionist Thinking," Ensia, February 25, 2014, https://ensia.com/voices/gmos-silver-bullets-and-the-trap-ofreductionist-thinking/; and Doug Gurian-Sherman, *Failure to Yield: Evaluating the Performance of Genetically Engineered Crops*, Union of Concerned Scientists, April 2009, http://www.ucsusa.org/sites/default/files/legacy/assets/documents/food_and_agriculture/failureto-yield.pdf.

5. Jean-Paul Chavas, Guanming Shi, and Joseph Lauer, "The Effects of GM Technology on Maize Yield," *Crop Science* 54, no. 4 (July–August 2014): 1331–35, http://corn.agronomy.wisc.edu/Pubs/JL_JournalArticles/cs-54-4-1331.pdf.

6. Elizabeth Nolan and Paulo Santos, "The Contribution of Genetic Modification to Changes in Corn Yield in the United States," *American Journal of Agricultural Economics* 94, no. 5 (October 2012): 1171–88, https://academic.oup.com/ajae/article-abstract/94/5/1171/93467.

7. For example, see Langdon Winner, "Do Artifacts Have Politics?," in *Readings in the Philosophy of Technology*, ed. David M. Kaplan (Lanham, MD: Rowman & Littlefield, 2009), 251–63.

8. Zvi Griliches, "Research Costs and Social Returns: Hybrid Corn and Related Innovations," *Journal of Political Economy* 66, no. 5 (1958): 419–31.

9. Yujiro Hayami and Vernon Wesley Ruttan further noted that the important factor in sustaining productivity is allowing such technologies to be transferred between regions so that a region can economize on its most limiting input factor. Yujiro Hayami and Vernon Wesley Ruttan, "Factor Prices and Technical Change in Agricultural Development, the United States and Japan, 1880–1960," *Journal of Political Economy* 78, no. 5 (1970): 1115–41. A. L. Olmstead and Paul W. Rhode investigated US agricultural technological change and noted that changing crop patterns and investments in biological technologies explain much of the change in relative input usage between 1880 and 1980. A. L. Olmstead and Paul W. Rhode, "Induced Innovation in American Agriculture: A Reconsideration," *Journal of Political Economy* 101, no. 1 (1993): 100–18, https://experts.umich.edu/en/publications/induced-innovation-in-americanagriculture-a-reconsideration.

10. E. D. Perry, G. Moschini, and D. A. Hennessy, "Testing for Complementarity: Glyphosate Tolerant Soybeans and Conservation Tillage," *American Journal of Agricultural Economics* 98, no. 3 (2016): 765–84.

11. Andrew R. Kniss, "Long-Term Trends in the Intensity and Relative Toxicity of Herbicide Use," *Nature Communications* 8 (2017), https://www.nature.com/articles/ncomms14865.

12. A more comprehensive approach to considering a new technology's effects is to

examine multifactor productivity growth rates, which encompass both yield outcomes and the amount of inputs used to obtain those outcomes. For example, see Julian M. Alston, Matthew A. Anderson, and Philip G. Pardey, "The Rise and Fall of U.S. Farm Productivity Growth, 1910–2007," University of Minnesota, Department of Applied Economics, January 2015, https://ageconsearch.umn.edu/record/200927/files/Alston%20 et%20al%202015%20UMN%20--%20The%20Rise%20and%20Fall%20of%20US%20 Farm%20Productivity%20Growth%201910_2007.pdf.

13. Food and Agricultural Organization of the United Nations, FAOSTAT, http://www. fao.org/faostat/en/#data.

14. Hectograms per hectare are converted to bushels per acre by first multiplying by the hectogram-to-pound conversion rate (0.220462). Given that corn averages 56 pounds per bushel, bushels per hectare are then obtained by dividing by 56. One hectare equals 2.47105 acres. Therefore, bushels per acre are obtained by dividing the previous result by 2.47105. Because these values are constants, the conversion of hectograms per hectare to bushels per acre is simply a scaling process that does not affect regression analyses and is used only to make the discussion more transparent.

15. Hakim, "Doubts About the Promised Bounty of Genetically Modified Crops."

16. National Academies of Sciences, Engineering, and Medicine, *Genetically Engineered Crops: Experiences and Prospects* (Washington, DC: National Academies Press, 2016), https://www.nap.edu/catalog/23395/genetically-engineered-crops-experiences-and-prospects.

17. Jose B. Falck-Zepeda, "Experiences and Prospects of Genetically Engineered Crops," *Choices* (2016), http://www.choicesmagazine.org/choices-magazine/theme-articles/a-future-informed-by-agricultural-sciences/experiences-and-prospects-of-genetically-engineered-crops.

18. Jorge Fernandez-Cornejo, Seth J. Wechsler, and Michael Livingston, "Adoption of Genetically Engineered Crops by U.S. Farmers Has Increased Steadily for over 15 Years," US Department of Agriculture, Economic Research Service, March 4, 2014, https://www. ers.usda.gov/amber-waves/2014/march/adoption-of-genetically-engineered-crops-by-us-farmers-has-increased-steadily-forover-15-years/.

19. US Department of Agriculture, Economic Research Service, "Feed Grains: Yearbook Tables," https://www.ers.usda.gov/dataproducts/feed-grains-database/feed-grains-yearbook-tables/.

20. Jayson Lusk, Jesse Tack, and Nathan Hendricks, "Adoption of Genetically Engineered Corn on Yield and the Moderating Effects of Weather, Soil Characteristics, and Geographic Location" (working paper, Department of Agricultural Economics, Oklahoma State University, December 29, 2016).

21. US Department of Agriculture, Foreign Agricultural Service, Production Supply and Distribution, https://apps.fas.usda.gov/psdonline/app/index.html#/app/advQuery.

22. Hans van Grinsven et al., "Losses of Ammonia and Nitrate from Agriculture and Their Effect on Nitrogen Recovery in the European Union and the United States Between 1900 and 2050," *Journal of Environmental Quality* 44 (2015): 356–67, https://www. researchgate.net/publication/271471074_Losses_of_Ammonia_and_Nitrate_from_ Agriculture_and_Their_Effect_on_Nitrogen_Recovery_in_the_European_Union_and_ the_United_States_between_1900_and_2050.

THE IMPACT OF GENETIC MODIFICATION TECHNOLOGIES 165

23. See, for example, Marco Bianchi, Martin Boyle, and Déirdre Hollingsworth, "A Comparison of Methods for Trend Estimation," *Applied Economic Letters* 6 (1999): 103–9, https://people.cs.pitt.edu/~chang/265/proj10/sisref/3.pdf; J. R. Kruse, "Trend Yield Analysis and Yield Growth Assumptions," Food and Agricultural Policy Research Institute, June 1999; and Alston, Anderson, and Pardey, "The Rise and Fall of U.S. Farm Productivity Growth, 1910–2007."

24. For estimation details, see Gary W. Brester et al., "An Examination of the Influence of Genetic Modification Technologies on U.S. and EU Crop Yields," *Journal of Agricultural and Resource Economics*, forthcoming.

25. Nolan and Santos, "The Contribution of Genetic Modification."

26. Edward D. Perry, GianCarlo Moschini, and David A. Hennessy, "Testing for Complementarity: Glyphosate Tolerant Soybeans and Conservation Tillage," *American Journal of Agricultural Economics* 98, no. 3 (2016): 765–84, https://www.card.iastate.edu/faculty/profiles/giancarlo_moschini/Am-J-Agr-Econ-2016-Perry-765-84.pdf.

27. Food and Agricultural Organization of the United Nations, "FAOSTAT," http://www.fao.org/faostat/en/#data.

28. Lusk, Tack, and Hendricks, "Adoption of Genetically Engineered Corn."

29. Nolan and Santos, "The Contribution of Genetic Modification."

30. The US Corn Belt is a highly productive corn-growing region. Zheng Xu et al., "The Realized Yield Effect of Genetically Engineered Crops: U.S. Maize and Soybean," *Crop Science* 53, no. 3 (2013): 735–45, https://www.card.iastate.edu/faculty/profiles/giancarlo_moschini/Xu-et-al-Crop-Science-2013.pdf.

31. Philip G. Pardey et al., "Long-Run and Global R&D Funding Trajectories: The U.S. Farm Bill in a Changing Context," *American Journal of Agricultural Economics* 97, no. 5 (2015): 1312–23, http://www.instepp.umn.edu/products/long-run-and-global-rd-fundingtrajectories-us-farm-bill-changing-context.

Section III

Conservation and the Environment

6

The Farm Bill, Conservation, and the Environment

ERIK LICHTENBERG

On January 6, 1936, the US Supreme Court ruled the Agricultural Adjustment Act of 1933—which authorized the federal government to prop up farm prices by paying farmers to reduce planted acreage and kill off livestock—unconstitutional. Four days later, Secretary of Agriculture Henry Wallace unveiled a proposal for a replacement that empowered the federal government to pay farmers to replace soil-depleting crops with grass and legumes as a means of conserving soil. Funding for the program would come from the federal government, while the program itself would be administered at the local level by soil conservation district committees elected by and from the farm community. On February 27, 1936, Congress adopted Wallace's replacement program by enacting the Soil Conservation and Domestic Allotment Act.[1]

The Soil Conservation and Domestic Allotment Act's explicit goal was to increase farm income by cutting production to achieve a ratio of prices received to prices paid to that which prevailed during August 1909–July 1914.[2] From the beginning, then, federal agricultural conservation policy in the United States has been intertwined with farm income support. The waxing and waning of conservation in subsequent farm bills bears out that close connection: The cropland diversion provisions of the 1936 act were retained in the 1938 Agricultural Adjustment Act. They were suspended from 1940 until the mid-1950s as World War II, war devastation in Western Europe, and the Korean War heightened demand for US agricultural commodities. They were reintroduced in the form of the Soil Bank Program in the Agricultural Act of 1956, when US agriculture again faced reduced export demand due to recovery in Europe and the end of wartime while increases in US farm productivity increased supply.

Income support has never been the sole motivating force for conservation programs. The 1936 act built on the Soil Conservation and Domestic Allotment Act of 1935, which established an administrative structure for helping farmers control and prevent soil erosion, to "preserve natural resources, control floods, prevent impairment of reservoirs, and maintain the navigability of rivers and harbors, protect public health, public lands and relieve unemployment."[3]

Enacted in the shadow of the Dust Bowl, the 1935 legislation created the Soil Conservation Service (since renamed the Natural Resource Conservation Service) in the US Department of Agriculture (USDA) and authorized it to provide technical assistance to farmers for planning and installing erosion control and other conservation measures. The 1936 legislation augmented that technical assistance role with financial support in the form of cost sharing provided via the Agricultural Conservation Program (ACP), the principal forerunner of today's Environmental Quality Incentives Program (EQIP). As with land retirement, funding for the ACP that Congress appropriated was allocated to states, distributed by states to counties, and administered by county-level associations of agricultural producers.

Beginning around 1960, US grain exports and farm income entered an extended period of growth. Existing Soil Bank Program land retirement contracts were maintained, but new enrollments were discontinued. The ACP remained in effect, and a variety of similar cost-sharing programs, mainly focused on specific regional concerns, were added to the USDA portfolio; none received significant funding. During the 1970s, a boom in export demand made shortages rather than surpluses the concern of the day. Then, in the early- and mid-1980s, US grain exports collapsed due to contracting foreign demand, an overvalued dollar, and high interest rates. The collapse of grain exports triggered a financial crisis throughout the farm sector.[4]

In the 1980s, as in the 1930s, hard times in agriculture brought conservation back into prominence, with an emphasis once again on paid land retirement. The secretary of agriculture already had the authority to require farmers to limit specific land-planted crops as a condition of receiving farm subsidies. The Food Security Act of 1985 resuscitated the Conservation Reserve Program (CRP), a component of the 1950s-era Soil Bank Program, and authorized the USDA to enroll a total of 40 million acres of highly erodible cropland in long-term rental contracts. Farmers entering into those contracts were required to convert enrolled cropland into an approved conservation use such as vegetative cover. Up to half the costs of establishing those approved conservation uses were shared by the department.

A notable new feature of the CRP was a broadening of goals to encompass environmental concerns, with improvements in water quality and protection of fish and wildlife habitat being added to the more traditional goals of protecting cropland productivity, reducing sedimentation, curbing surplus production, and supporting farm income. Despite these new concerns with water quality, though, CRP enrollment was directed largely toward the wheat-growing areas of the High Plains and Palouse regions—wind-erosion-prone areas that had been the center for erosion-control attention during the Dust Bowl years.

Environmental concerns were also addressed by other provisions of the 1985 act, notably the sodbuster and swampbuster provisions that rendered farmers who converted virgin grassland or wetlands to crop production ineligible for any farm program benefits, including price supports, crop insurance, disaster payments, and some federally guaranteed loans. New cost-sharing programs (e.g., the Water Quality Incentives Program) aimed specifically at protecting water quality were added to the USDA portfolio later in the 1980s. The Federal Agriculture Improvement and Reform Act of 1996 combined the ACP, the Water Quality Incentives Program, and several smaller regional programs into a larger, consolidated conservation cost-share program, the Environmental Quality Incentives Program (EQIP).

As with the CRP, the erosion-control programs of the 1930s remained the rootstock of these cost-share programs, with environmental concerns grafted on. EQIP, for instance, provides technical and financial assistance (up to 75 percent of approved costs) to farmers for projects that protect or improve soils (and thus agricultural productivity), conserve water, and improve other natural resources, as well as help farmers meet environmental-quality regulations. The administrative structure of the 1936 legislation—federal appropriations of funds allocated to states and then counties by formula and administered locally—also remained largely intact.

Figure 1. Direct Farm Program Payments to Farmers, 2000–16

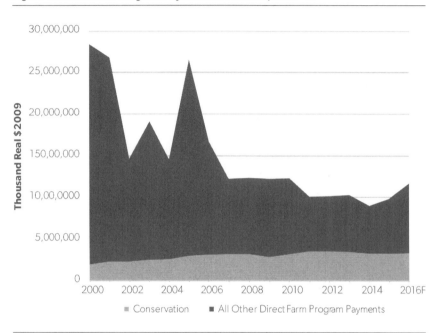

Source: US Department of Agriculture, Economic Research Service.

Recent Trends

Spending on conservation has remained a robust component of direct payments to agricultural producers in recent years, even as the overall level of farm support has fallen. Between 2000 and 2015, for instance, federal direct payments to farmers in all farm programs fell at an average annual rate of about 7 percent. Conservation payments, in contrast, rose at an average annual rate of more than 3 percent during that period (Figure 1). As a result, conservation program spending has risen markedly as a share of overall farm support, increasing from 7 percent of direct payments to farmers in 2000 to 33 percent in 2015.[5]

From 1985 until 2008, agricultural conservation policy stressed cropland retirement over subsidies for conservation on working farmland. The past two farm bills have reversed that emphasis. From its inception, CRP acreage was capped at 39.2 million acres. While that cap was never attained, CRP enrollment did grow from about two million acres in 1986 to almost 37 million acres in 2007. The CRP has been shrinking ever since. The 2008 Food, Conservation, and Energy Act reduced the overall cap on CRP enrollment from 39.2 million acres to 32 million acres. The 2014 Agriculture Act cut that cap further to 24 million acres by fiscal year (FY) 2018.

Enrollments in smaller land retirement programs have slowed as well, although overall caps on enrollment in those programs have not been cut. The 1990 Food, Agriculture, Conservation, and Trade Act created the Wetlands Reserve Program (WRP) with a goal of reconverting an eventual total of 1.075 million acres of cropland that had been wetlands before cultivation. The 2002 Farm Security and Rural Investment Act raised the cap on WRP acreage to 2.025 million acres and added a Grassland Reserve Program (GRP) aimed at converting an ultimate total of two million acres of cropland back to its original grassland status.

Both programs featured long-term contracts with annual rental payments and established cost sharing in a manner similar to the CRP. The 2014 Agriculture Act merged these two programs with the much smaller Farm and Ranchland Protection Program into the Agricultural Conservation Easement Program (ACEP). New enrollments in the WRP and GRP fell from a combined total of 191,000 acres in 2009 to 144,000 acres in 2014, while total enrollment in the two programs rose from 1.96 million acres in 2008 to 3.043 million acres in 2014.

Funding for EQIP, in contrast, grew from $77,000 in 1997 to $50 million in 2002, $686 million in 2008, and $724 million in 2014 (i.e., roughly tenfold over 20 years). The 2002 Farm Security and Rural Investment Act added a new conservation incentive program for working farmland, the Conservation Security Program. Appropriations for the program, which provided incentive and cost-share payments for both existing and new conservation practices on working farmland in selected watersheds, were set initially at $202 million in FY2005, rising to $382 million in FY2008.[6] The 2008 Farm Bill replaced the Conservation Security Program with a new Conservation Stewardship Program (CSP); CSP spending rose from $294 million in 2011 to $763 million in 2014.

The result of these changes has been a marked difference in conservation spending priorities. In the late 1990s, the CRP accounted for almost all spending under the conservation title of the farm bill. By 2014, it accounted

Figure 2. Allocation of Authorized Farm Bill Conservation Spending, 1996–2018

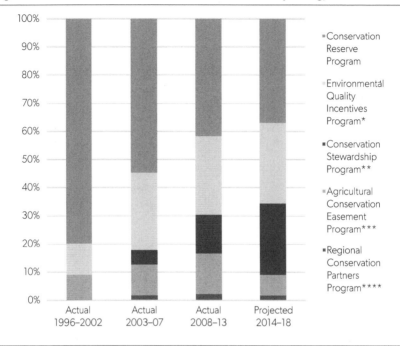

Note: *Includes EQIP and the Wildlife Habitat Incentives Program for 1996–2013. **Includes the Conservation Security Program for 2002–07. ***Includes the Wetland Reserve Program, Farmland Protection Program, and GRP (easement portion) for 1996–2013. ****Includes the Agricultural Water Enhancement Program, Chesapeake Bay Watershed Program, Cooperative Conservation Partnership Initiative, and Great Lakes Basin Program for 1996–2013.
Source: Economic Research Service analysis of Office of Budget and Policy Analysis on actual expenditures for 1996–2013; and spending levels provided in the 2014 Farm Act and Congressional Budget Office estimates for 2014–18.

for less than half, while EQIP and CSP combined accounted for more than two-fifths (Figure 2).

Economic Efficiency Rationales for Agricultural Conservation Programs

The stated rationales for conservation programs in the farm bill are (1) to prevent farmland degradation to preserve productivity and (2) to mitigate environmental externalities, notably damage to water quality, wildlife habitat, and air quality. It is worth examining the extent to which each of these is truly subject to market failure. It is equally worth examining the extent to which any market failures are national in scope and thus best addressed by federal programs rather than programs at the state or local level.

Soil Erosion. The case for public provision of technical assistance is straightforward: Information about how best to protect land from degradation is a public good. The case for public provision of financial assistance for conservation measures aimed at protecting farmland productivity is not at all obvious, at least under current circumstances. Economic theory indicates that well-functioning land markets provide landowners strong incentives to invest in soil protection and enhancement measures as a means of preserving (or increasing) the value of land.[7]

Land price statistics bear this out; high-quality farmland commands a substantially higher price than low-quality farmland. Tenants, of course, have less incentive than owners to invest in measures that protect land productivity beyond expected lease termination dates.[8] But landlords can counteract any underinvestment in conservation by tenants by leasing on shares rather than cash or by imposing lease terms that require using conservation practices that leave a durable imprint on the landscape and are thus verifiable.[9]

Achieving efficient levels of private investment in measures that reduce erosion or otherwise prevent land degradation requires that capital markets and land markets function well: Land prices may signal to landowners that conservation is a good investment, but landowners are likely to draw on credit to make that investment. Rural credit markets were not functioning well when the Dust Bowl struck in the 1930s.[10] They are much stronger today due to the creation of the federally backed Farm Credit System, relaxation of constraints on interstate banking, and greater access to broader capital markets. One indication of that strengthening is that the rural credit system weathered the farm financial crisis of the 1980s much better than it did the financial travails of the 1920s and 1930s.[11]

Even so, private-sector lenders might be unwilling to finance conservation investments adequately due to insufficiently longtime horizons, excessive risk aversion, or the availability of lending options with higher rates of return. But the appropriate government response in such cases would be to provide loan guarantees or otherwise reduce private-sector lending costs for conservation rather than providing subsidies to farmers. Overall, then, the case for subsidizing measures that prevent land degradation to protect farmland productivity is poor in the context of financial markets that exist in the US today.

Environmental Externalities. There is a much stronger rationale for government programs that mitigate environmental damage from agriculture. The farm sector is a major contributor to many important environmental problems. In terms of water-quality impairment problems in the US, for instance, agriculture accounts for an estimated 70 percent of the nitrogen and phosphorus creating the dead zone in the Gulf of Mexico and 40–50 percent of nitrogen phosphorus pollution in the Chesapeake Bay.[12] Farming and ranching involve conversion of naturally occurring ecosystems to artificial ones; destruction of wildlife habitat is collateral damage in that process.

In many parts of the US, ongoing processes of converting land to agricultural uses and maintaining those uses is a major threat to endangered species.[13] In the Dust Bowl years, farming was a major contributor to air pollution nationwide, as dust storms carried particulates into major urban areas throughout the country. Today, ammonia and particulates, notably from concentrated animal feeding operations (CAFOs), are important sources of air-quality problems in some areas, with damage to human health and quality of life.[14]

The extent to which these environmental problems are national in scope varies, suggesting that some deserve attention at the federal level while others are most appropriately addressed at the state or local level. The case for federal policy to address water-quality impairment is quite strong. Water-quality impairments in the Gulf of Mexico, Great Lakes, Chesapeake Bay, and other major estuaries are clearly national in scope, coming as they do from sources distributed across numerous states. The states that contribute to those water-quality impairments have different stakes in maintaining water quality. Those differences in incentives make it difficult to coordinate cleanup efforts, accentuating the importance of federal intervention. Protecting habitat for migratory waterfowl along major flyways is clearly national in scope as well. Endangered species protection is an obligation under the federal Endangered Species Act.

The case for federal—rather than state or local—intervention to pre-serve habitat in cases other than endangered species, migratory fauna, or other environmental amenities of importance to the general population is less clear. Localities may want to preserve habitat for its scenic beauty, for instance—which may well be important for local residents or for a local tourist industry but may not spill over state lines.[15] Air pollution damage from CAFOs and other farming and ranching activities may similarly be confined to relatively small local areas, in which case state or local actions (as California, Idaho, and Minnesota have all undertaken) may be more appro-priate than federal ones.

Agri-Environmental Policy Design—Conceptual Considerations

While agriculture is responsible for a large share of many environmental problems—most notably water pollution—agricultural production has up until today remained largely exempt from environmental regulation.[16] That is not a matter of law: The Clean Water Act, for example, specifies that all emitters face limits on Total Maximum Daily Loads of nutrients and other pollutants discharged into waterways. Instead, it is a matter of practicality.

Agricultural emissions are nonpoint sources. Unlike point sources, there is no clear "end of pipe" where effluent can be monitored. Farms gener-ally do not discharge directly into water bodies. Instead, nonpoint sources are spread out over the landscape. Nutrients from fertilizer and livestock waste infiltrate into the soil, dissolve in water, and travel through the water table until they discharge into surface waters. The diffuse nature of nonpoint sources makes it impossible to monitor them with any accuracy. Dissolved nutrients also degrade as they move across the landscape, so emissions from different locations can correspond to markedly different deliveries to receiv-ing water bodies. And degradation rates vary with temperature, precipita-tion, and other randomly occurring conditions.

Further, farms in many regions are quite heterogeneous in terms of soils, crop choices, farming practices, and other conditions that affect both pro-duction conditions and runoff. These features combine to make it difficult to identify how much each farm contributes with any accuracy and thus to write regulations that are both reasonable and effective.

The difficulty of crafting regulations to address nonpoint source pollution has meant that agricultural conservation programs have remained the de facto principal instruments for addressing environmental problems in agriculture. We address threats to water quality, wildlife habitat preservation, and air quality from farming by paying farmers to convert environmentally sensitive land to conservation uses via the CRP and ACEP and share the costs of adopting conservation measures on working farmland via EQIP and CSP. These conservation programs differ from most environmental regulations in two important ways: (1) They subsidize farming practices that are believed to reduce environmental damage from farming in some way rather than placing limits on (or taxing) the practices farmers can use, and (2) participation in conservation programs and hence uptake of farming practices that reduce environmental damage is voluntary rather than mandatory. Both features have implications for how well we might expect conservation programs to perform in delivering environmental protection.

Taxes Versus Subsidies. That agricultural conservation programs are incentive based gives them an advantage over direct regulation. But that they are subsidy based rather than penalty based suggests that they will not be as efficient as possible in addressing environmental-quality problems.

Economic theory indicates that regulating farms directly will generally be less efficient than using incentives such as subsidies or taxes because farms tend to be heterogeneous, numerous, and highly dispersed geographically. Direct regulation typically runs into problems in squaring efficiency and equity when emitters are heterogeneous. In such cases it is efficient to treat different emitters differently. But writing regulations that address those differences effectively and efficiently is difficult to do.

Moreover, while it may be efficient to write regulations that specify differential treatment, differential treatment appears unfair because in effect some emitters would be treated more leniently than others. In principle, incentive-based regulations using subsidies or taxes do not face these problems, as they leave emitters free to adjust their production practices optimally to suit their own conditions in the face of the same tax or subsidy rate (i.e., under equal treatment).

Economic theory indicates further that a fundamental asymmetry between taxes and subsidies makes subsidies generally less effective than taxes. In principle, both have the same effects on the intensive margin. Maximizing profit or minimizing cost implies equating the marginal cost of abating the last unit of pollutant emitted with the tax or subsidy rate equivalently. That the tax is an explicit cost while the subsidy is an implicit one (consisting of lost potential revenue) should make no difference to the decision.

Taxes and subsidies have different effects on the extensive margin, though. A tax reduces profitability and should thus lead to some shrinkage of the industry over the long run while a subsidy increases profitability and should thus lead to industry expansion over the long run.[17] In the agricultural context, the long run can be as short as the next growing season, and industry expansion can take the form of increases in newly cultivated acreage. Such slippage can offset at least in part any increases in environmental protection that the subsidy achieves.[18]

A final consideration in optimal policy design is that nonpoint source pollution is an example of what economists call "team production." It is the joint product of many agents (farmers) whose actions (farming practices) all influence the outcome (e.g., water quality). The effects of those individual actions are hard, if not impossible, to disentangle. And emissions result from activities that are widely dispersed in space and time, making them extremely costly, again if not impossible, to observe. In such cases, economic theory indicates that policies should be based on overall performance (e.g., ambient water quality) rather than individual effort (farmers' choices of farming practices).

Additionally, policies should be applied collectively to all agents that contribute to the outcome (e.g., all farmers in a watershed). For example, an efficient policy could pay all farmers in a watershed a bonus based on achievement of ambient water-quality standards, in the spirit of Bengt Holmstrom.[19] Alternatively, an efficient policy could impose a tax or penalty on all farmers in a watershed if ambient water-quality standards were not achieved, as Kathleen Segerson suggests.[20] To achieve a first best, any penalty should be set at marginal damage from ambient water quality at the level of the standard while a bonus should be set correspondingly at marginal damage avoided, evaluated at the same level of ambient water quality.

The collective nature of first-best taxes or subsidies creates some obvious political difficulties. First-best taxes may well be prohibitively costly for farmers. First-best subsidies may be prohibitively expensive for the government. It is thus likely that any incentive-based scheme that is practical to implement will not be first best. It is important in such cases to avoid letting the perfect be the enemy of the good.

Mandatory Versus Voluntary Uptake. That agricultural conservation programs are voluntary rather than mandatory also suggests that they cannot deliver improvements in environmental quality efficiently. The biggest environmental problems created by agriculture are nonpoint sources in nature, which imply that mandatory policies are needed to achieve efficient outcomes. Further, participation in voluntary programs is subject to self-selection, raising questions about additionality (i.e., how much of the conservation effort that subsidies pay for is above and beyond what participating farmers would have done without those payments).

The question of additionality speaks to whether we essentially get what we pay for. It is not obvious that we would: One would expect that these programs would be most attractive to farmers who would profit from conservation even without being paid by the government. It is quite possible, for instance, that cropland enrolled in the CRP or ACEP would have been diverted to non-crop use even if that land were not enrolled in either program because non-crop uses would have been more profitable uses than any crop-based alternative. Similarly, farmers who receive cost sharing for adopting conservation practices from EQIP or CSP possibly would have used those same (or similar) conservation measures even without cost sharing because those practices increase long-run profitability.

CRP, ACEP, EQIP, and CSP all include screening protocols to make sure that enrollment achieves some environmental benefit. Parcels offered for enrollment in the CRP, for instance, must be classified as highly erodible and have been cropped three of the previous five years. Further, the conservation use proposed for the parcel must be evaluated by National Resources Conservation Service (NRCS) technicians and scored using an Environmental Benefits Index (EBI) that characterizes levels of wildlife habitat protection, water-quality benefits, erosion reduction, air-quality benefits, and carbon sequestration, with adjustments for cost. NRCS technicians also screen conservation projects for cost-sharing eligibility under EQIP or CSP; one would expect that screening to weed out projects whose environmental benefits are too scanty to merit subsidies. But those protocols are not designed to assess additionality: In none of these cases does NRCS attempt to assess the extent to which the projects or land uses proposed would be undertaken without enrollment.

There are also conceptual reasons for believing that additionality in these voluntary programs can never be complete. Each farmer knows his or her own situation in ways that the government does not; hence he or she knows what to do without enrolling in a land retirement program or receiving cost sharing for installing conservation practices, while the government does not. That asymmetry of information prevents the government from offering a contract that pays each farmer for only additional environmental benefits. Instead, second-best contracts will generally need to pay for some non-additional environmental benefits, even in cases in which payments are differentiated on the basis of some observable characteristics.[21]

More concretely, the screening protocols that CRP, ACEP, EQIP, and CSP use to evaluate environmental benefits are necessarily incomplete because they cannot take into account factors from farmers' private information. For example, while the government evaluates parcels offered for enrollment in the CRP based on evaluations, environmental benefits, and information about average land rental rates in the relevant neighborhood, it does not know the minimum rental payment each farmer is willing to accept—and it cannot estimate that amount accurately, because it depends on the farmer's skill and more detailed information about the land and microclimate than can be observed.

Similarly, the NRCS can evaluate environmental impacts of proposals for cost sharing under EQIP or CSP but cannot (and does not try to) evaluate the minimum payment each farmer is willing to accept. These considerations suggest that farmers enrolled in these programs will generally receive some information rent—or, put another way, some payment for non-additional environmental benefits.

Evaluating the degree of additionality achieved is difficult because it requires estimating counterfactuals that have not occurred in practice and can thus not be observed directly. Econometric methods can be used to construct such counterfactuals and thus estimate additionality retrospectively. Evidence from econometric studies can thus be useful in screening conservation projects for potential additionality, but such screening will necessarily be imperfect. We consider the currently available econometric evidence below.

Conservation Programs in the Farm Bill Today:
Structure and Performance

The stated rationale for CRP, ACEP, EQIP, CSP, and other conservation programs in the farm bill is that the conservation measures they induce farmers to undertake are close complements to environmental protection, so that the subsidies for conservation via these programs help protect the environment. The conceptual arguments in the preceding section suggests that unavoidable defects in the design of these programs means that it should be possible to achieve the same level of environmental protection at lower cost. As a practical matter, it is important to consider how much inefficiency they involve (i.e., how much environmental benefit they generate both absolutely and relative to cost). This section examines the empirical evidence currently available, both descriptive and econometric, with a focus on the CRP and cost-sharing programs such as EQIP and CSP.

The Conservation Reserve Program. The basics of the CRP are as follows. Farmers enrolling land in the CRP enter into long-term (10- to 15-year) contracts with the USDA under which they agree to convert cropland to vegetative cover or other approved conservation use and maintain it as such over the life of the contract. In return, they receive an annual rental payment and subsidies covering half the cost of establishing the approved conservation use. To be eligible for enrollment in the CRP, parcels of land must be classified as highly erodible.

Participation is voluntary: Farmers offer parcels for enrollment along with a desired rental rate. NRCS technicians evaluate each parcel offered to determine the extent to which it meets each of the CRP's multiple objectives that the EBI measures. The USDA ranks the entire national pool of parcels offered according to the EBI (which includes cost in addition to environmental features) and offers contracts for parcels with the highest EBI scores.

The initial enrollments of the CRP (1986–90) were criticized heavily as getting too little in the way of environmental benefits for the money. Simulations using data on parcels offered for enrollment indicated that those initial CRP enrollment decisions were more consistent with getting as much land as possible into the program than maximizing environmental benefits.[22] Those initial CRP enrollments featured a disproportionately large share of

Figure 3. Conservation Reserve Enrollment by County as of March 31, 2016

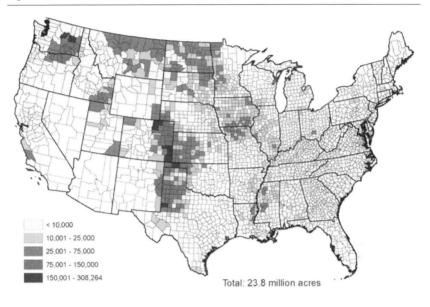

< 10,000
10,001 - 25,000
25,001 - 75,000
75,001 - 150,000
150,001 - 308,264

Total: 23.8 million acres

Source: US Department of Agriculture, Farm Services Agency.

land in the High Plains, which had cheap land but little social damage from erosion. Other simulation studies using data on parcels offered for enrollment showed that the CRP could have obtained much greater social benefits from its budget or its acreage cap had spending been directed to the Corn Belt and Eastern Seaboard states, where water-quality problems are more pressing and affect a much larger share of the US population.[23]

The USDA responded to those criticisms in 1991 by creating the EBI and using it to rank all parcels offered for enrollment on a nationwide basis. The EBI is an additive index consisting of six factors: wildlife habitat, water quality, soil erosion, air quality, enduring benefits, and cost. Wildlife habitat receives between 10 and 100 points: up to 50 points for the presence of wildlife habitat, up to 20 points for any enhancements, and up to 30 points for location in a wildlife priority zone. Water quality receives between 0 and 100 points: up to 30 points for location, up to 45 points for surface-water-quality protection, and up to 25 points for groundwater-quality protection. Soil erosion, measured by the ratio of erosion potential to erosion tolerance, receives

Figure 4. Shares of Total Acreage Enrolled in the CRP, 2016 Versus 1990

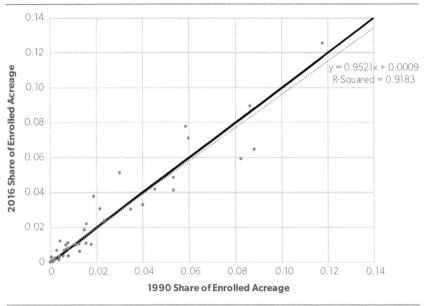

Source: US Department of Agriculture, Farm Services Agency.

between 0 and 100 points; the allocation of points exhibits sharply increasing marginal returns for erodibility indexes between 4 and 17, increasing in proportion to the square of the erodibility index over that range. The number of points awarded for erosion hardly increases at all for index values above 17, however, so that land that is exceptionally vulnerable to erosion does not receive substantially more credit than land that is somewhat less vulnerable.[24]

Air-quality benefits from reduced wind erosion receive between 3 and 45 points, with up to 25 points for wind erosion potential, up to 5 points for being on a list of soils susceptible to wind erosion, up to 5 points for location in an air-quality nonattainment zone, and 3–10 points for carbon sequestration potential. Enduring benefits (the likelihood that certain practices will remain in place beyond the CRP contract period) receive between 0 and 50 points. Cost has two components: the difference between the rental rate offered and the maximum rental rate in the relevant county (0–25 points) and the rental rate itself. In 2014, the rental rate received up to 125 points, with deductions proportional to the ratio of the rental rate offered and the cutoff level of $220 per acre. The 2016 guidelines state that the point value will be determined at the end of the enrollment period based on actual offer data.[25]

Despite this elaborate evaluation process, CRP enrollment remains concentrated in portions of the High Plains, notably eastern Colorado, western Kansas, the Oklahoma and Texas panhandles, the Palouse, and a northern tier running from northwest Minnesota through North Dakota and into central Montana (Figure 3). Enrollment remains low in the eastern half of the country, including the Chesapeake and most of the Mississippi watersheds, as well as on the West Coast. In fact, the geographic distribution of CRP enrollment today looks almost identical to that of 1990, as can be seen from Figure 4, which plots the share of CRP acreage in each state in 2016 against the corresponding share in 1990. The points are clustered closely around a 45 degree line. The trend line has a slope of 0.95, an intercept close to zero, and an R-squared of 0.92. Deviations from the 45 degree line are at most 2 percentage points.

Just as in the early sign-up period, then, CRP enrollment remains concentrated in semiarid, wind-erosion-prone parts of the country with low population density, as can be seen from Figure 4. The main reason? The way the EBI is constructed. Characteristics commonly exhibited by parcels classified as highly erodible in the High Plains (notably wildlife habitat, wind erosion, groundwater quality, and cost) are awarded a great deal of weight. Wildlife habitat and recreational hunting account for about 60 percent of the environmental benefits of enrolled parcels.[26] The portions of the Plains with high CRP enrollment are lightly populated and thus have a lot of wildlife habitat. Points are awarded for the presence (or potential presence) of wildlife habitat in a parcel but not by the quality of that habitat. Thus, benefits from that habitat are not weighted by factors such as risk to wildlife from habitat loss or by human population or human visitation rates (which affect total benefits from the presence of additional wildlife habitat).

Like wildlife habitat protection, erosion, water quality, and air quality are evaluated largely on the basis of parcel characteristics with little weight placed on the potential productivity of cropland or the number of people affected, respectively. The EBI considers only potential soil loss without regard to the productivity of the land. Parcels located in the semiarid High

Plains can thus receive as many or more points for erosion as parcels with similar potential soil loss located in the Corn Belt or Great Lake states, where productivity is much higher due to more favorable soils and climate.

Further, the EBI places a high weight on moderate erosion (erodibility index is four) and relatively little additional weight on more severe erosion (erodibility index of five or more). Surface and groundwater quality are given roughly equal weight. Maximum weight for surface water is given to parcels located in approved water-quality zones, while groundwater-quality impacts are evaluated using an index of potential leasing and whether groundwater is used for drinking water. In neither case is the number of people affected by water quality accorded any weight.

Almost three-fifths of the points for air-quality impacts are determined by parcel-level wind-erosion potential. Since wind-erosion potential is also included in the erosion factor, this procedure essentially amounts to double counting wind-erosion potential. Only a fifth of the points for air quality are awarded to parcels that contribute particulates to air-quality nonattainment zones; as with the remainder of the EBI, the size of the population affected is not taken into account.[27] Finally, setting a cap on rental rates and assigning points for cost proportional to the rental bid as a share of that cap biases the EBI toward parcels with low rental rates—and thus low agricultural productivity.

In sum, the CRP continues to favor enrollment of low-productivity cropland in the sparsely populated High Plains at the expense of cropland close to more densely populated areas where water-quality problems are greatest and wildlife habitat is most at risk. In other words, the original critique of the initial CRP sign-ups continues to hold today: Despite the incorporation of environmental benefits into enrollment decisions via the EBI, it seems likely that we could get substantially more environmental benefits from a CRP of the same acreage or same cost. The principal culprit appears to be the design of the individual components of the EBI, which place too little weight on populations affected or wildlife at risk; for example, simulations using CRP-bid data indicated that small changes in relative weights of the components of the EBI would have little or no effect on the geographic distribution of enrollment.[28]

Aside from questions about the appropriate geographic distribution of enrolled parcels, there are also questions about how well the CRP performs in terms of additionality achieved in sign-up and the degree of slippage occurring post sign-up. Both can be evaluated only by using econometric studies to construct counterfactuals for comparison.

The econometric evidence about additionality is mixed. Estimates based on data from individual landowners exiting the CRP indicate that as much as 42 percent of land enrolled in the CRP would have been put into conservation uses anyway.[29] That estimate suggests additionality on the order of only 58 percent. Estimates based on individual parcels selected for inclusion in the National Resource Inventory conducted by NRCS give a more optimistic picture. Those estimates indicate that only 9 percent of land enrolled in the CRP would have been put into conservation uses otherwise, suggesting additionality of more than 90 percent.[30]

Econometric studies of slippage suggest that it was quite substantial during early CRP sign-ups. Regressions using county-level data for the 1982–92 period derived from Natural Resource Inventory sites in the Corn Belt, Great Lake states, and Northern Plains states indicate a slippage rate of about 20 percent.[31] Regressions using a panel of individual farm data for the entire US from the Census of Agriculture over the same period indicate a slippage rate of roughly the same magnitude.[32] These estimates have not been updated, at least to my knowledge, and likely vary with the outlook for grain markets.

The Environmental Quality Incentives and Conservation Stewardship Programs. CRP enrollment decisions are made on a national basis using an auction mechanism. Cost-share funds awarded under EQIP and CSP are not; instead, funds for both technical assistance and direct payments to farmers are allocated to states on a formula basis. While those formulas incorporate as many as 20 individual factors, most of those factors are measures of farming activity, many of which are highly correlated. Measures of farming activity are accorded most of the weight in the formulas that determine allocation of funds. Environmental-quality factors, in contrast, receive a relatively small share of the weight.

For example, the 2009 EQIP formula used to distribute financial assistance funds to states includes the number of farms and ranches, the number of specialty crop farms, acres of grazing land, acres of irrigated cropland, acres of nonirrigated cropland, livestock numbers (in animal units), cropland

Figure 5. Relationship Between EQIP Spending and Number of Farm Operations by State

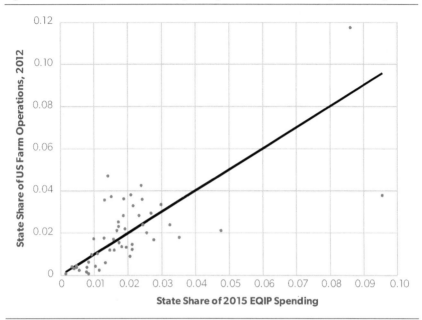

Source: Natural Resource Conservation Service; and US Department of Agriculture, "Census of Agriculture 2012: Summary and State Data," May 2014, https://www.agcensus.usda.gov/Publications/2012/Full_Report/Volume_1,_Chapter_1_US/usv1.pdf.

eroding at greater-than-soil-loss tolerance, and the number of nutrient management plans in place. Together, these measures of agricultural activity accounted for about five-eighths of the total weights in the formula. Environmental factors (air-quality nonattainment area, the number of at-risk species, an index of impaired streams, and acres of wetlands) account for about one-sixth of the weights.[33]

The result is an allocation of EQIP funds that largely tracks the number of farm operations in each state (Figure 5). Each state is guaranteed a minimum share of funds, which not only causes some deviation from apportionment according to the number of farm operations but also tends to diminish the importance of environmental-quality factors. The most recent farm bill also requires 60 percent of EQIP funds to be spent on measures related to livestock, which induces additional deviations from apportionment of funds strictly on the basis of the number of farm operations in general.

Figure 6. Relationship Between Conservation Stewardship Spending and Farmland by State

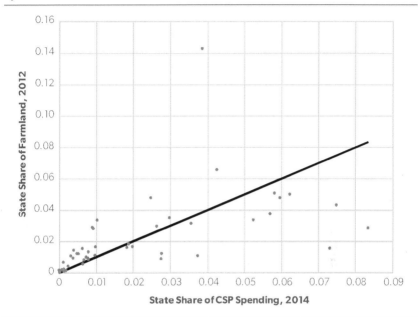

Source: Natural Resource Conservation Service; and US Department of Agriculture, "Census of Agriculture 2012: Summary and State Data," May 2014, https://www.agcensus.usda.gov/Publications/2012/Full_Report/Volume_1,_ Chapter_1_US/usv1.pdf.

The formula for allocating CSP funds to states has similarly been determined by relative amounts of farming activity. In the first CSP sign-up, for instance, NRCS allocated acreage for enrollment across states in proportion to each state's share of the country's agricultural land base.[34] Adjustments for factors including minimum funding for each state cause some deviation from a strict apportionment by farmland shares, but the relationship is still quite close (Figure 6).

Within states, the bulk of cost-share funds are allocated by formula to counties, again based on how much farming activity is present in each. While applications are screened for eligibility and ranked for performance by NRCS technicians, allocation of EQIP and CSP funds to eligible projects in each county is in the hands of county-level committees elected from and by those with local agricultural business interests.[35] Some oversight of those county committees is conducted by state technical committees, but they, too, are selected from those with agricultural business interests. It is only natural that this administrative arrangement would favor projects oriented toward enhancing the productivity of farms and distributing income to farmers who are tied into the existing farm business networks rather than toward protecting water quality or at-risk species.

Data for constructing counterfactuals to assess additionality and slippage in EQIP and CSP are generally lacking because the programs only recently received significant amounts of funding. Maryland, which has used cost sharing for conservation practices aggressively for 30 years to meet its obligations for meeting Chesapeake Bay water-quality goals, is an exception.[36] The Great Miami River watershed, which provides cost sharing for conservation as part of its regional water-quality trading program, is another.

Several econometric studies suggest that additionality is likely higher for cost-sharing programs than for the CRP but still far from perfect. A switching regression study using data from a 1998 survey of Maryland farmers found that receipt of cost-share funds affected the likelihood that a farmer used cover crops and strip cropping or contour farming (treated as an aggregate) but did not affect the share of acreage allocated to either type of practice.[37] A subsequent switching regression study using data from a 2010 survey of Maryland farmers found a high level of additionality in cover crop adoption among farmers who received cost sharing specifically for cover crops, about 95 percent.[38]

A propensity score matching study using data from a 2009 survey of farmers in the Great Miami River watershed found lower levels of additionality for both EQIP and CSP, on the order of 85 percent for filter strips, 70 percent for grid sampling, and 65 percent for grass waterways. Additionality for conservation tillage was much lower, on the order of 20 percent for EQIP and 30 percent for CSP.[39]

While additionality for cost sharing appears to be high, the evidence also suggests that cost sharing can induce a high level of slippage. An econometric analysis using data from the 1998 survey of Maryland farmers found that receipt of cost sharing in programs similar to EQIP and CSP was associated with large reductions in vegetative cover, consistent with conversion to crop use.[40] That finding was corroborated by the results of an econometric study using data from the 2010 survey of Maryland farmers, which found losses in share of land in vegetative cover associated with the receipt of cover crop cost sharing to be roughly half the size of increases in the share of land on which cover crops were used.[41] The intuition is that conservation subsidies can make it profitable for farmers to begin cultivating some highly erodible land previously used only for grazing. The net effect is an offset in any reductions in nutrient runoff, since runoff from land on which crops are grown exceeds runoff from vegetative cover on the same land.

Implications for Policy Reform

From the beginning, conservation provisions in the farm bill have been linked to farm income support. In 1936, faced with legal obstacles, the Roosevelt administration used soil conservation as the vehicle for carrying its supply control and price support program until the administration could craft an alternative that the Supreme Court would accept. For many years thereafter, funding for conservation shrank during times of farm prosperity and expanded when times were hard.

Over the past 10–15 years, though, spending on conservation programs in the farm bill first rose and then remained relatively stable even in the face of budget retrenchments, so that conservation now accounts for roughly a third of direct farm program payments. One hypothesis is that this development, too, is tied to income support considerations, since conservation payments are classified as non-distortionary under World Trade Organization (WTO) rules and thus not subject to WTO limitations on farm support.[42] That hypothesis is consistent with the culture of the USDA as an institution: The department was created to serve the farm community, and finding ways of channeling funds to farmers is a core feature of its institutional DNA.

There are clear economic efficiency grounds for policies that address environmental externalities from agriculture. We know from numerous agronomic studies that there are complementarities between many agricultural conservation measures and reductions in environmental damage, implying that conservation can play a productive role in addressing environmental externalities. And the USDA has taken some significant strides in reorienting conservation programs toward environmental goals.

The CRP notably incorporated environmental-quality considerations as explicit goals. Using the EBI to evaluate CRP bids was an important step toward increasing the role of environmental-quality criteria in making enrollment decisions; after its adoption, enrollment in the Corn Belt and Great Lake states did increase, suggesting a corresponding increase in water-quality benefits. The incorporation of some environmental-quality criteria into formulas for allocating EQIP and CSP funds among states is similarly a positive step forward.

Together, these considerations suggest that prioritizing conservation spending, as the most recent farm bills have done, has been a good thing. Conservation spending deserves to be maintained if not increased in absolute and real terms. That said, conservation spending has not allocated those funds in ways that adequately prioritize environmental quality at the national level. Reform of funding allocation mechanisms is needed to improve the efficiency of conservation spending in the sense of getting the most environmental-quality protection for the money we spend.

Specifically, the USDA should make significant changes to the criteria used to enroll cropland in programs such as the CRP and allocate cost-share funds under EQIP, CSP, and similar programs. Three general kinds of changes are needed: (1) giving more weight to ambient environmental considerations, notably upgrading the importance of water quality and at-risk species while downgrading wildlife habitat generally and all measures of farming activity; (2) incorporating enrollment and funding allocation formulas into factors that measure aggregate benefits such as the size of affected human populations and the presence of at-risk species (i.e., evaluating environmental impacts at the landscape, or watershed, scale rather than at the scale of an individual parcel); and (3) making all funding decisions at the national (rather than state or local) level.[43]

These reforms can be made administratively for the CRP: The CRP is already administered at the national level, and bids are already evaluated using the EBI, so all that would be needed would be changing the EBI. Legislative action, though, would be needed for cost-sharing programs such as EQIP, CSP, and ACEP since farm bills have followed the precedent set in the 1936 legislation by specifying that funding decisions for these programs be made at the state and county levels.[44] Allocating funds according to national environmental priorities rather than by formula funding for states thus requires a change in legislative mandate, giving the USDA the authority to allocate funding centrally using national priority rankings the way that the CRP uses the EBI.

Changes such as these are problematic politically because they involve shifting funds away from many states where farm constituencies have a strong political voice in favor of states where agriculture has less political clout. The culture of the USDA as an institution representing farm interests suggests that reorienting conservation spending toward national environmental priorities is unlikely without some pressure from outside the farm community.

The natural source of that pressure is, of course, the Environmental Protection Agency (EPA), which has a statutory mandate for regulating air and water quality and has an institutional culture oriented toward regulation. As noted earlier, the practical difficulties involved in regulating nonpoint source emissions have, until recently, led the EPA to exempt agriculture from regulation under the Clean Water Act and Clean Air Act. The growing expense and technical difficulty of achieving further reductions in point source emissions, combined with advances in modeling, have made it practical to begin discontinuing that de facto exemption. In the Chesapeake Bay watershed, for instance, it is no longer feasible to meet water-quality goals by reducing point source emissions alone; Total Maximum Daily Load (TMDL) regulations that include agriculture are currently under development. Shrinking the dead zone in the Gulf of Mexico will likely also require TMDL regulations covering agriculture, as will meeting water-quality standards in several other interstate watersheds.

Voluntary efforts like those incentivized by conservation programs in the farm bill have proved unable to achieve reductions in emissions large enough to meet water goals, even in places such as Maryland, which has provided cost-share funds to a much greater extent than other states. Voluntary programs of sufficient scale will be extremely expensive. They are also subject to inherent inefficiencies from self-selection, resulting in imperfect additionality and slippage.

There are also equity considerations: It seems only fair that polluters pay something toward cleaning up the environmental damage they create. These considerations suggest that meeting goals for water quality and other environmental amenities will require mandatory adoption of farm practices that reduce runoff and other forms of environmental degradation. Shifting from voluntary to mandatory environmental compliance would have the additional advantage of shifting incentives away from expanding agricultural production at the extensive margin (i.e., reducing slippage). While paid conservation measures will unlikely be adequate to meet agriculture's obligations under TMDL regulation, conservation programs in the farm bill could help farmers bear the regulatory burden in much the same way that EPA grants help fund municipal sewage treatment.

Notes

1. John C. Culbert and John Hyde, *American Dreamer: A Life of Henry A. Wallace* (New York: W. W. Norton & Company, 2000).

2. Murray R. Benedict, *Farm Policies of the United States, 1790–1950: A Study of Their Origins and Development* (New York: Twentieth Century Fund, 1953).

3. Soil Conservation and Domestic Allotment Act of 1935, Pub. L. No. 74-46, 49 Stat. 163.

4. Charles W. Calomiris, R. Glenn Hubbard, and James H. Stock, "The Farm Debt Crisis and Public Policy," *Brookings Papers on Economic Activity* 2 (1986): 441–79.

5. US Department of Agriculture, Economic Research Service, "Farm Income and Wealth Statistics," March 8, 2017, https://www.ers.usda.gov/data-products/farm-income-and-wealth-statistics.aspx.

6. Tadlock Cowan, "Conservation Security Program: Implementation and Current Issues," Congressional Research Service, April 24, 2008, http://nationalaglawcenter.org/wp-content/uploads/assets/crs/RS21740.pdf.

7. Kenneth E. McConnell, "An Economic Model of Soil Conservation," *American Journal of Agricultural Economics* 65, no. 1 (February 1983): 83–89, https://www.researchgate.net/profile/Kenneth_Mcconnell/publication/245315879_An_Economic_Model_of_Soil_Conservation/links/5592b08408aed7453d4637cb/An-Economic-Model-of-Soil-Conservation.pdf?origin=publication_detail.

8. Meredith J. Soule, Abebayehu Tegene, and Keith D. Wiebe, "Land Tenure and the Adoption of Conservation Practices," *American Journal of Agricultural Economics* 82, no. 4 (November 2000): 993–1005.

9. It is also possible that some individual landowners have incentives to over-conserve soil. Most eroded soil is redistributed from uphill parcels to downhill parcels in a watershed so that external benefits accrue to owners of downhill parcels. Conservation by owners of uphill parcels may thus result in more erosion control than is socially optimal. Douglas Allen and Dean Lueck, "Contract Choice in Modern Agriculture: Cash Rent Versus Cropshare," *Journal of Law and Economics* 35, no. 2 (October 1992): 397–426, http://www.sfu.ca/~allen/allenlueckjle92.pdf; Pierre Dubois, "Moral Hazard, Land Fertility and Sharecropping in a Rural Area of the Philippines," *Journal of Development Economics* 68 (2002): 35–64, http://citeseerx.ist.psu.edu/viewdoc/download?doi=10.1.1.463.5784&rep=rep1&type=pdf; Erik Lichtenberg, "Tenants,

Landlords, and Soil Conservation," *American Journal of Agricultural Economics* 89, no. 2 (May 2007): 294–307; and Stanley W. Trimble and Pierre Crosson, "US Soil Erosion Rates—Myth and Reality," *Science* 289, no. 5477 (July 2000): 248–50, http://www.wou. edu/las/physci/taylor/g473/refs/trimble_crosson_2000.pdf.

10. Raghuram Rajan and Rodney Ramcharan, "The Anatomy of a Credit Crisis: The Boom and Bust in Farm Land Prices in the United States in the 1920s," *American Economic Review* 105 (2015): 1439–77, https://faculty.chicagobooth.edu/raghuram.rajan/research/papers/land_sales_14.pdf.

11. Charles W. Calomiris, R. Glenn Hubbard, and James Stock, "The Farm Debt Crisis and Public Policy," *Brookings Papers on Economic Activity* 2 (1986): 441–79.

12. Richard B. Alexander et al., "Differences in Phosphorus and Nitrogen Delivery to the Gulf of Mexico from the Mississippi River Basin," US Geological Survey, 2009, https://water.usgs.gov/nawqa/sparrow/gulf_findings/; and Chesapeake Bay Total Maximum Daily Load, "Sources of Nitrogen, Phosphorus and Sediment to the Chesapeake Bay," Environmental Protection Agency, December 29, 2010, https://www.epa.gov/sites/production/files/2014-12/documents/cbay_final_tmdl_section_4_final_0.pdf.

13. Brian Czech, Paul R. Krausman, and Patrick K. Devers, "Economic Associations Among Causes of Species Endangerment in the United States," *BioScience* 50 (2000): 593–601.

14. Stacy Sneeringer, "Does Animal Feeding Operation Pollution Hurt Public Health? A National Longitudinal Study of Health Externalities Identified by Geographic Shifts in Livestock Production," *American Journal of Agricultural Economics* 91, no. 1 (February 2009): 124–37.

15. In some cases, people may value the continued existence of environmental amenities they will never visit or otherwise use in some way. In such cases, environmental amenities that may appear to be strictly local in scope may in fact be of interest at the national level.

16. The most notable exception is large CAFOs, which are required to have permits for discharges into waterways under the Clean Water Act.

17. William J. Baumol and Wallace E. Oates, *The Theory of Environmental Policy* (Englewood Cliffs, NJ: Prentice-Hall, 1975).

18. JunJie Wu, "Slippage Effects of the Conservation Reserve Program," *American Journal of Agricultural Economics* 82, no. 4 (2000): 979–92.

19. Bengt Holmstrom, "Moral Hazard in Teams," *Bell Journal of Economics* 13, no. 2 (1982): 324–40, https://faculty.fuqua.duke.edu/~qc2/BA532/1982%20Rand%20Holmstrom%20team.pdf.

20. Kathleen Segerson, "Uncertainty and Incentives for Nonpoint Pollution Control," *Journal of Environmental Economics and Management* 15, no. 1 (1988): 87–98.

21. John K. Horowitz and Richard E. Just, "Economics of Additionality for Environmental Services from Agriculture," *Journal of Environmental Economics and Management* 66, no. 1 (2013): 105–22.

22. A more cynical interpretation is that CRP spending from 1986 to 1990 was directed to areas hardest hit by the farm financial crisis. In that view, the CRP was simply used as a vehicle to funnel support to important farm constituencies. That view is consistent with some other features introduced after the initial sign-up in 1986 but later discontinued,

most notably disallowing any bids asking for rental rates above the county average regardless of environmental benefits. Those bid caps became local public knowledge quite rapidly. As a result, price competition at the county level all but disappeared as virtually all parcels were offered at rental rates at or close to the bid cap. Katherine Reichelderfer and William G. Boggess, "Government Decision Making and Program Performance: The Case of the Conservation Reserve Program," *American Journal of Agricultural Economics* 70, no. 1 (1988): 1–11.

23. Marc O. Ribaudo, "Consideration of Offsite Impacts in Targeting Soil Conservation Programs," *Land Economics* 62, no. 4 (1986): 402–11; and Marc O. Ribaudo, "Targeting the Conservation Reserve Program to Maximize Water Quality Benefits," *Land Economics* 65, no. 4 (1989): 320–32.

24. The erodibility index is calculated using the Universal Soil Loss Equation for areas subject to water erosion and the Wind Erosion Equation for areas subject to wind erosion.

25. US Department of Agriculture, Farm Service Agency, "Conservation Reserve Program 49th General Enrollment Period Environmental Benefits Index (EBI)," December 2015, https://www.fsa.usda.gov/Assets/USDA-FSA-Public/usdafiles/FactSheets/archived-factsheets/crp_49th_GEP_EBI.pdf.

26. LeRoy Hansen, "Conservation Reserve Program: Environmental Benefits Update," *Agricultural and Resource Economics Review* 36, no. 2 (2007): 267–80, http://ageconsearch.umn.edu/record/44702/files/hansen%20-%20current%20-%20pp%20267-280.pdf.

27. The remaining points, amounting to a little over one-fifth of the total, are awarded for carbon sequestration potential. Grassland can get up to half those points, while tree planting can get the full amount.

28. Andrea Cattaneo et al., "Balancing the Multiple Objectives of Conservation Programs," US Department of Agriculture, Economic Research Service, May 2006, https://www.ers.usda.gov/webdocs/publications/45394/29439_err19_002.pdf?v=41471.

29. Michael J. Roberts and Ruben N. Lubowski, "Enduring Impacts of Land Retirement Policies: Evidence from the Conservation Reserve Program," *Land Economics* 83, no. 4 (November 2007): 516–38.

30. Ruben N. Lubowski, Andrew J. Plantinga, and Robert N. Stavins, "What Drives Land-Use Changes in the United States? A National Analysis of Landowner Decisions," *Land Economics* 84, no. 4 (2008): 529–50.

31. JunJie Wu, "Slippage Effects of the Conservation Reserve Program: Reply," *American Journal of Agricultural Economics* 87, no. 1 (February 2005): 251–54; and Michael J. Roberts and Shawn Bucholz, "Slippage in the Conservation Reserve Program or Spurious Correlation?," *American Journal of Agricultural Economics* 87, no. 1 (2005): 244–50.

32. Shinsuke Uchida, "Indirect Land Use Effects of Conservation: Disaggregate Slippage in the US Conservation Reserve Program," University of Maryland, 2014, http://ageconsearch.umn.edu/bitstream/186644/2/14-05.pdf.

33. While the exact formulas used to allocate funds among states vary from year to year, the relative weight of farming activity remains roughly the same. For example, the 2006 formula contained a larger number of factors, most of which are subdivisions of the agricultural activity factors included in the 2009 formula. As was the case in 2009, agricultural activities accounted for almost two-thirds of the total weight in the formula. Emily Gilbert et al., "Improving Federal Allocation of EQIP Funding," Duke

Nicholas School of the Environment, April 24, 2013, https://dukespace.lib.duke.edu/
dspace/bitstream/handle/10161/6812/EQIP%20Final.pdf?sequence=1; and Government
Accountability Office, "Agricultural Conservation: USDA Should Improve Its Process for
Allocating Funds to States for the Environmental Quality Incentives Program," 2006.

34. US Department of Agriculture, Natural Resources Conservation Service, "Final
Cost-Effectiveness Analysis for the Conservation Stewardship Program," May 14, 2010,
file:///C:/Users/int8/Downloads/CSP_BCA-FINAL_5-14-10.pdf.

35. Guilherme S. Bastos and Erik Lichtenberg, "Priorities in Cost Sharing for Soil and
Water Conservation: A Revealed Preference Study," Land Economics 77, no. 4 (2001):
533–47.

36. A significant number of Maryland farmers adopt conservation measures without
receiving any government incentives, an indication that conservation is likely profitable for many. Most Maryland farmers use conservation tillage, for instance, because it
is less costly than conventional tillage and because it helps build organic matter and
thus improves the quality of the sandy soils of the coastal plain areas where farming is largely concentrated; few have received cost sharing for it. Self-financed use of
grass or rock-lined waterways is also widespread. Erik Lichtenberg, Doug Parker, and
Sarah Lane, "Best Management Practice Use and Nutrient Management in Maryland:
A 2010 Snapshot," Center for Agricultural and Natural Resource Policy at the University of Maryland, 2012, http://agresearch.umd.edu/sites/agresearch.umd.edu/files/_docs/
2010PolicyAnalysisReport_BMP.pdf.

37. Erik Lichtenberg and Ricardo Smith-Ramirez, "Slippage in Conservation Cost
Sharing," American Journal of Agricultural Economics 93, no. 1 (2011): 1–17.

38. Patrick Fleming, Erik Lichtenberg, and David A. Newburn, "Evaluating Impacts of
Agricultural Cost Sharing on Water Quality: Additionality, Crowding In, and Slippage,"
University of Maryland, 2017.

39. Mariano Mezzatesta, David A. Newburn, and Richard T. Woodward, "Additionality and the Adoption of Farm Conservation Practices," Land Economics 89, no. 4 (2013):
722–42.

40. Lichtenberg and Smith-Ramirez, "Slippage in Conservation Cost Sharing."

41. Fleming, Lichtenberg, and Newburn, "Evaluating Impacts of Agricultural Cost
Sharing on Water Quality."

42. The fact that crop insurance and conservation both surpassed commodity programs in authorized spending in the 2014 Farm Bill lends additional support to this
hypothesis.

43. While carbon sequestration may be a potentially important component of efforts
to mitigate climate change, the evidence suggests that agricultural conservation programs
will unlikely be effective contributors of sequestered carbon. Sequestering carbon will
involve paid conversion of cropland to vegetative cover. As noted earlier, econometric
studies of the CRP raise questions about additionality while indicating that slippage can
be substantial. Policies to promote production of cellulosic bioenergy feedstocks will
likely be more effective than conservation per se for this purpose.

44. Funding allocations for ACEP are made using a combination of national and state
criteria, with each receiving half of the weight in the total.

7

Waters of the US Rule and Clean Water Act and Cost-Effective Approaches to Water-Quality Improvement

One of the most contentious debates between agricultural and environmental interests is about the Clean Water Rule finalized in 2015—commonly referred to as the Waters of the US (WOTUS) rule. The WOTUS rule was a response to uncertainty that previous Supreme Court cases created that found the Environmental Protection Agency (EPA) and Army Corps of Engineers (Corps) had overreached in their definition of jurisdiction provided by the Clean Water Act (CWA). The EPA and the Corps argue that the WOTUS rule provides greater clarification on the jurisdiction of permitting programs and is based on legal precedent and scientific evidence with respect to hydrologic connections. Agricultural interests—among others—argue that the rule represents the government's vast overreach into private landowners' decisions.

The CWA gives the agencies authority to issue permits to protect the water quality of navigable waters. The Supreme Court has recognized that the jurisdiction must expand to non-navigable waters, but much of the debate hinges on whether to use Justice Antonin Scalia's or Justice Anthony Kennedy's test to define jurisdiction. In an opinion, Scalia argued that jurisdiction extends to only waters with a "continuous surface connection" to navigable waters. Kennedy argued that jurisdiction extends to waters that have a "significant nexus" with navigable waters, in which a significant nexus is defined as any water that "significantly affects the chemical, physical, or biological integrity" of downstream waters under the agencies' jurisdiction.[1] The WOTUS rule applied the Kennedy test, and the EPA issued a scientific report documenting the connection of non-navigable waters to navigable waters. The rule leaves a significant amount of jurisdiction to case-by-case examination, so landowners are uncertain about whether they fall within the jurisdiction without obtaining a jurisdictional determination from the Corps.

The main conclusion of this study is that the WOTUS rule would have little to no impact on improving water quality while creating regulatory uncertainty because in many situations whether a government agency has jurisdiction over a body of water has to be determined on a case-by-case basis. This regulatory uncertainty is especially burdensome due to large fines for violations, even if the violators are inadvertent. Additional permitting requirements under the WOTUS rule also create significant application costs and delays to implement activities on private land to obtain permits. David Sunding and David Zilberman[2] estimated the average cost of applying for a general permit from the Corp at $28,915 and 313 days. The average cost of applying for an individual permit was much higher ($271,596), and the process was much longer (788 days).

While such regulatory uncertainty has negative economic impacts, impacts on agriculture are often overstated. Contrary to some claims, the WOTUS rule would not have required agriculture to obtain permits for regular farming activities. Agriculture—except concentrated animal feeding operations (CAFOs)—is largely exempt for permitting requirements under the CWA, and the WOTUS rule did not affect those exemptions. However, there are legitimate concerns that in some settings agricultural exemptions may be undermined by how the EPA and the Corps interpret vague language in the applicable legislation. A prime example is the John Duarte case, in which the Corps determined that plowing a field did not meet the agricultural exemption since the field had not been tilled for 24 years.

While the WOTUS rule has created significant political tension, the fundamental problem with addressing water quality is the lack of secure property rights for agricultural nonpoint emissions. A clear property right would define whether agricultural nonpoint sources have the right to emit pollutants into water or society has the right to have water with few pollutants. Nonpoint source emissions are largely exempt from permitting under the CWA. However, those emissions can be regulated if a body of water is determined to be impaired and the state establishes a Total Maximum Daily Load (TMDL). Some states explicitly exempt agriculture from pollution regulations, while other states have laws that would allow for regulation of nonpoint source emissions.[3]

Insecure property rights often lead to lawsuits and lobbying. Some environmental interests find it more cost-effective to improve water quality by paying lawyers to force the government to enact regulations on agriculture rather than paying landowners to improve water quality. The courts play an important role in deciding cases that define property rights, so lawsuits certainly have merit. However, the CWA's language is unnecessarily vague and has resulted in decades of lawsuits with still-unclear property rights.

There is an alternative to lawyers and lobbyists—harnessing the power of markets to improve water quality. In this solution, environmental interests and agricultural interests work together to find solutions using incentives created through market transactions for water quality. The government need not place a heavy regulatory burden or overlook water-quality concerns. The government simply needs to clearly define the property rights for agricultural nonpoint emissions.

Agriculture and Water Quality

Agricultural production majorly contributes to water pollutants.[4] The key pollutants of concern are nitrogen, phosphorus, pesticides, and sediment. Even though agricultural production practices have changed over time and the CWA has been in place since 1972, there have been few to no observed improvements in water quality over the past 25 years. It is therefore useful to review some basic facts about agriculture and water quality.

First, pollution from agricultural nonpoint sources is costly to measure, and the water-quality impacts of adopting best management practices (BMPs) to mitigate those impacts are highly uncertain. Agricultural emissions, except for CAFOs, are primarily nonpoint emissions because they come from diffuse sources, making them costly to measure. Once a pollutant reaches surface water bodies where its concentration levels can be measured, it is difficult or impossible to determine the original source and location of the pollution.

Water-quality impacts of adopting BMPs are uncertain because the emissions associated with any given practice depend on weather and soil

Figure 1. Trend in Nutrient Concentrations in Streams, 1993–2003

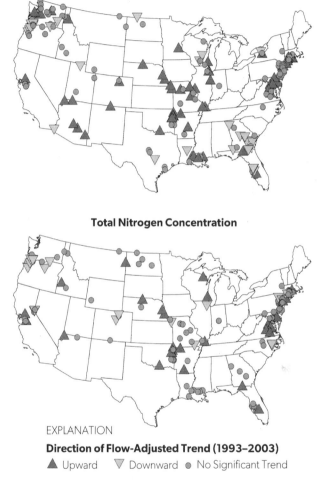

Source: Neil M. Dubrovsky and Pixie A. Hamilton, "Nutrients in the Nation's Streams and Groundwater: National Findings and Implications," US Geological Survey, 2010, https://pubs.usgs.gov/fs/2010/3078/pdf/fs20103078.pdf.

conditions. The impacts are difficult to measure in a real-world setting, and even in a field experiment. For example, nutrient losses from crop fields may enter surface streams directly or enter groundwater that then discharges into surface streams. Researchers have also found it difficult to assess water-quality improvements due to adopting BMPs at the watershed scale.[5]

Second, water-quality impacts from agricultural production occur in both local and distant water bodies. The EPA[6] reported that 100,000 miles of rivers and streams and 2.5 million acres of lakes, reservoirs, and ponds have poor water quality due to excess nutrients. The source of most of these nutrients is from agricultural production in the watershed. However, pollution can also affect distant locations. For example, corn and soybean production in the Corn Belt majorly contributes to hypoxia in the Gulf of Mexico, and agricultural production in six northeast states contributes nutrients to the Chesapeake Bay.

Third, few to no improvements in water quality have been observed over the past quarter century. Figure 1 shows the trend in nutrient concentrations in streams between 1993 and 2003. In many cases, nutrient concentrations have actually *increased* over time, especially in the central United States. The data certainly do not suggest a significant improvement in water quality.

Recent scientific studies also indicate no improvements in water quality. E. G. Stets, V. J. Kelly, and C. G. Crawford[7] found large increases in nitrate concentrations in streams from 1945 to 1980 as fertilizer use increased, but three concentrations have remained relatively stable since 1980. Lori Sprague, Robert Hirsch, and Brent Aulenbach[8] found that nitrate concentrations increased by 10 percent from 1980 to 2008 at the outlet of the Mississippi River into the Gulf of Mexico. Large increases in nitrate concentrations in some agricultural watersheds are of particular concern. Concentrations increased by 76 percent in the Mississippi River at Clinton, Iowa, and by 75 percent in the Missouri River at Hermann, Missouri. In terms of pesticides, Wesley Stone, Robert Gilliom, and Karen Ryberg[9] found that concentrations of several different pesticides increased in streams during 1992–2011.

The Conservation Effects Assessment Project conducted by the Natural Resources Conservation Service found that conservation practices have largely affected water-quality improvements. However, this project used physical process simulation models to estimate water-quality impacts rather than measuring actual changes in watershed water quality. The project also compares only two scenarios—one that included current conservation practices and an extreme case in which no conservation practices were adopted.

Clean Water Act and Agriculture

Three sections of the CWA are particularly relevant for agriculture. Section 402 establishes the National Pollutant Discharge Elimination System permit program. Section 404 establishes a permit program for discharge of dredged or fill material (i.e., sediment). Section 303 gives the states authority to establish TMDLs for a body of water.

The permit programs in Sections 402 and 404 regulate point sources of pollution. A point source is defined by the CWA (Section 502(14)) as "any discernible, confined and discrete conveyance, including but not limited to any pipe, ditch, channel, tunnel, conduit, well, discrete fissure, container, rolling stock, concentrated animal feeding operation, or vessel or other floating craft, from which pollutants are or may be discharged. This term does not include agricultural stormwater discharges and return flows from irrigated agriculture." This definition's last sentence provides an exemption for agriculture.

Whether this exemption applies to agricultural tile drainage was questioned in a recent court case. Des Moines Water Works sued drainage districts in Iowa for discharge of nutrients, arguing that tile drainage is a point source discharge and subject to permitting under the CWA. Des Moines Water Works argued that stormwater discharges cover surface runoff only during a storm event and not flows that were absorbed by the soil and removed using subsurface drainage. They also argued that the exemption applies only to farming and does not apply to Iowa drainage districts.[10] If drainage districts were required to obtain permits and reduce nutrient discharges, then farmers would be implicitly regulated and not exempt from discharges.

In early 2017, the Iowa Supreme Court ruled that Des Moines Water Works was not entitled to collect monetary damages from the drainage districts.[11] Subsequently, in March 2017, the United States District Court for the Northern District of Iowa dismissed the lawsuit on the grounds that drainage districts could not be held liable for any damages.[12] Des Moines Water Works has said that it will not appeal the decision, so the exemption for agricultural tile drainage appears to be settled for now.

Section 404 of the CWA exempts "normal farming activity" from permits for dredged or fill material as long as they are part of an ongoing farming operation. Thus, farmers may continue farming an area that is a wetland without a permit as long as the area has been part of continuous farming activity. Agricultural exemptions do not apply when a wetland designated as a water of the US is converted to crop production.

The case of John Duarte, a farmer in California, is widely cited by agricultural interests as an example in which agricultural exemptions are undermined by the CWA's vague language. Duarte plowed a field in 2012 that contained vernal pools, which are considered wetlands. Duarte instructed the person hired to plow the land to avoid all vernal pools, but some pools were plowed. In 2016, the US District Court for the Eastern District of California sided with the Corps that Duarte violated the CWA because he did not obtain a permit for discharge into waters of the US.[13] The court found that the act of plowing constituted the discharge of dredge and fill material from a point source into waters of the US. The court did not allow the agricultural exemption for plowing because the CWA, not the WOTUS rule, requires the exemption to be part of an "established (i.e., ongoing) farm operation,"[14] and the plowed field had not been in crop production since 1988.

Section 303 of the CWA gives states the authority to establish TMDLs if previous point source reductions have not met water-quality standards and a body of water is listed as impaired. The state establishes a TMDL and defines the total pollutant loads—from both point and nonpoint sources—allowed in a body of water. The state must then allocate TMDLs across point and nonpoint sources. The state could implement incentive-based programs to reduce nonpoint emissions or mandatory programs that require BMPs for agriculture. So although nonpoint source pollution from agriculture is largely exempt from permitting under Sections 402 and 404, it is not necessarily exempt from regulations established to achieve a TMDL under Section 303.

States are given the primary authority related to establishing TMDLs. States determine the list of impaired waters and determine the implementation plan for achieving TMDLs. States also determine if reductions of nonpoint sources of pollution occur through voluntary, incentive-based programs or through regulations.

According to the decision issued in *Gulf Restoration Network v. Jackson*, the CWA also gives the EPA a "backstop role." The EPA has authority under the CWA under Section 303(d), 33 USC §1313(d) to establish its own

TMDL for a body of water if the state fails to implement a TMDL. The EPA must also approve any TMDL proposed by a state and can develop an alternative TMDL if it disapproves. In *Gulf Restoration Network v. Jackson*, several environmental nonprofits sued the EPA for failing to take action to control nutrient pollution into the Gulf of Mexico. These groups argued that the EPA was compelled to act without state action to reduce nutrient pollution given the water-quality concerns in the Gulf. The EPA argued that imposing the necessary regulations would significantly burden the agency and preferred instead to work cooperatively with states. The courts ruled in 2016 that the EPA was not compelled under the CWA to abandon its approach of working with the states.

Cost-benefit analyses of the CWA have not been favorable. One analysis the EPA commissioned found that the costs the CWA imposed to reduce emissions from point sources were greater than estimated benefits.[15] David Keiser and Joseph Shapiro[16] estimate that the CWA has had a statistically significant impact on water quality but find that it is not clear that the benefits from such improvements have exceeded the costs. Keiser and Shapiro[17] also estimate that the CWA's grants to municipal wastewater treatment facilities increased housing prices by only about a quarter of the cost of the grants.

Not all the benefits from cleaner water are likely to be reflected in higher housing prices, but the findings do raise concerns about the program's cost-effectiveness. Looking forward, further reductions in emissions from point sources are likely to come at a high cost with few improvements in water quality since nonpoint emissions and atmospheric deposition are the major contributors to water-quality concerns.[18]

Water-quality permit trading has been proposed to reduce the cost of implementing further regulations on point sources. Current regulations allow point sources to meet their obligations by paying nonpoint sources to reduce their emissions. In some cases, these markets are created due to the establishment of a TMDL for a body of water. However, water-quality trading between point and nonpoint sources has involved little activity.[19]

Trades involving nonpoint sources often require the nonpoint source to implement a new management practice. The EPA allows estimates of nonpoint emission reductions to be used since the change in emissions cannot actually be measured. The EPA also usually requires a larger predicted reduction in emissions from nonpoint sources than those required for the point source due to uncertainty about the actual impact on water quality.[20] However, trading ratios that discount nonpoint pollution may not be optimal since reducing nonpoint pollution can help reduce the variability of emissions.[21]

Definition of WOTUS

The CWA's jurisdiction, known as WOTUS, has been the subject of controversy since the legislation was enacted. Three Supreme Court cases provide important legal precedent. In *U.S. v. Riverside Bayview Homes*, the Supreme Court ruled that the EPA did have jurisdiction over adjacent wetlands that affect navigable waters. This decision provided precedent that the CWA jurisdiction in fact extended to non-navigable waters to control pollution at the source of emissions into navigable waters.

In *Solid Waste Agency of Northern Cook County v. U.S. Army Corps of Engineers*, the Supreme Court said the EPA's jurisdictional rule was too broad. The EPA claimed that a location used as habitat for migratory birds fell within their jurisdiction—known as the "migratory bird rule"—including remote ponds with little connection to navigable waters. The court ruled that this approach could not be reconciled with the legislative authority for regulating navigable waters under the CWA.

In *Rapanos v. U.S.* the Supreme Court again ruled against the EPA's definition of jurisdiction. The court rejected the definition of areas connected to navigable waters through ditches or drains as waters of the US. The *Rapanos* case was decided on a 4–1–4 split with Kennedy writing a separate opinion from the plurality opinion Scalia wrote. Scalia argued that jurisdiction only extends to waters with a "continuous surface connection" with navigable waters and that jurisdiction could not be determined based solely on a hydrological connection.[22] Kennedy's opinion argued that jurisdiction extends to waters with a "significant nexus" to navigable waters.

Following the court rulings, the scope of the CWA jurisdiction appeared to be uncertain, so the EPA proposed a new rule to define WOTUS. The agencies relied heavily on the Kennedy test for defining their jurisdiction because—as they argued—a majority of the court supported the jurisdiction as described in Kennedy's opinion. Furthermore, every federal court that has applied *Rapanos* has found that Kennedy's definition is sufficient to determine jurisdiction.[23] There are questions about whether Kennedy's view has evolved since *Rapanos*. In *Corps v. Hawkes*, Kennedy wrote an opinion that called the CWA's reach "notoriously unclear" and said the CWA "continues to raise troubling questions regarding the Government's power to cast doubt on the full use and enjoyment of private property throughout the Nation."

The 2015 WOTUS rule gives the agencies jurisdiction over navigable waters, interstate waters, and the territorial seas. The WOTUS rule also defines tributaries and adjacent waters within the jurisdiction of the agencies. Tributaries must have physical indicators of flow and contribute to navigable waters. Adjacent waters must be within a defined distance of navigable waters or tributaries or in the 100-year floodplain. The rule also allows waters determined to have a "significant nexus" to any navigable water to fall within the CWA's jurisdiction.

A major controversy with respect to the final rule is that the EPA defined its jurisdiction over waters with a "significant nexus" to any navigable water. It defines a significant nexus as any water that "significantly affects the chemical, physical, or biological integrity" of downstream waters under the agencies' jurisdiction.[24]

The agencies issued a connectivity report to provide scientific evidence that other waters have a significant nexus with navigable waters. The connectivity report reviewed the scientific literature on the connectivity of streams and wetlands on downstream waters. The authors of the report argued that essentially all waters are connected but the degree of connectivity varies. Therefore, the agencies should assess other waters that are under their jurisdiction on a case-by-case basis. Critics of the rule argue that it is unconstitutional because the language of the regulation is too vague and that landowners have little certainty about whether their property is under the CWA's jurisdiction.

The WOTUS rule was finalized on June 29, 2015. In October 2015 the Sixth Circuit Court of Appeals placed a nationwide stay on the rule. On February 28, 2017, President Donald Trump issued an executive order to review the WOTUS rule and requested that the courts put a hold on legal challenges to the rule until the review is completed. Furthermore, the executive order directed the agencies to interpret waters of the US using the Scalia test rather than the Kennedy test until the review is complete. The agencies are now tasked with creating a revised rule that defines the WOTUS consistent with current law. The legality of any revised rule, whether it uses the Scalia or Kennedy test, is almost certain to be challenged in the courts.

Consequences of the 2015 WOTUS Rule

The 2015 WOTUS rule created additional regulatory burden and uncertainty on landowners conducting activities on private property. Since much of the jurisdiction is defined on a case-by-case basis, many landowners would be required to obtain a jurisdictional determination from the Corps. Large penalties for failing to obtain a permit create an incentive for landowners to be excessively cautious in conducting activities and obtaining jurisdictional determinations. For the first offense, negligent landowners could face a fine of up to $25,000 per day of violation for failing to obtain a permit. In his opinion in *Corps v. Hawkes*, Kennedy wrote, "As Justice Alito has noted in an earlier case, the act's reach is 'notoriously unclear' and the consequences to landowners even for inadvertent violations can be crushing."

If private property contains waters of the US according to the jurisdictional determination, then the landowner must obtain a permit for nonexempt activities. For example, a landowner would be required to obtain a permit to construct a building or demolish an old farmstead if the land is under the CWA's jurisdiction. The expanded jurisdiction under the WOTUS rule could require additional permitting requirements for CAFOs, but the EPA stated that there is uncertainty about whether the new rule will require additional CAFO permits.[25]

The cost of obtaining a permit is burdensome. Sunding and Zilberman[26] estimated the cost of preparing a general permit application—for activities that have minimal impacts—was $28,915. The cost of preparing an individual permit application—for activities with greater impacts that receive individual scrutiny—was $271,596. The process of obtaining a permit also requires substantial amounts of time and delays to the proposed activities. Sunding and Zilberman[27] also found an average of 313 days to obtain a general permit and 788 days to obtain an individual permit. These are only the costs of applying for a permit and do not account for any mitigation costs the permit requires.

These new permitting requirements, while costly, are unlikely to result in any significant improvement in water quality. As noted earlier, a primary cause of water-quality impairments is from nonpoint sources, and the WOTUS rule does nothing to reduce pollution from such sources. While the EPA conducted a cost-benefit analysis of the new jurisdictional rule, they have no plausible estimates of the improvement in water quality due to the rule.

The EPA's economic analysis of the rule has several serious flaws. The key assumption in its analysis is that costs and benefits change proportionally to the change in jurisdiction. Its analysis indicates that the benefits of CWA permitting exceed the costs. Thus, a positive economic outcome is baked into the analysis. The EPA methodology would inevitably indicate that any expansion in jurisdiction results in greater benefits than costs. But in practice, it may well be that the incremental benefits of an expanded jurisdiction are smaller than the benefits of a more narrowly defined jurisdiction.

The EPA's economic analysis also assumes implausibly large benefit estimates from wetlands preservation. For example, the analysis assumes that 177 acres—roughly 0.28 square miles—of wetlands in the Midwest will not be destroyed under the expanded jurisdiction. The EPA's estimate of the corresponding aggregate willingness to pay for saving those 177 acres is a whopping $114.4 million, yielding an average willingness to pay $645,445 per acre. As a point of comparison, average land values in Iowa were $7,183 per acre in 2016. The EPA assumption about the value of wetland preservation is crucial to its analysis because roughly 90 percent of the benefits from the expanded jurisdiction occur due to avoided losses of wetland under Section 404 permitting requirements.

Since the WOTUS rule does not change exemptions for agricultural nonpoint emissions, it is not expected to dramatically affect agricultural production—or water quality for that matter. Agricultural interests sometimes claimed that the WOTUS rule would require them to obtain permits for each time they apply pesticides or plow. This is simply not true and exaggerates the impact of the WOTUS rule. To the extent that these farming operations are part of ongoing farming activity, they are exempt from permitting requirements, and no permits or jurisdictional determination are necessary. A permit is required if farmers convert wetlands into farm production that is under EPA jurisdiction. However, given that ongoing farming operations are a major source of water-quality concerns, the WOTUS rule does little to improve water quality.

The concerns expressed by agricultural interests about the WOTUS rule are understandable. The EPA defines exemptions for normal farming activities, and those definitions are subject to change. No list of exemptions can be comprehensive, and current exemptions could be undermined by overly specific interpretations of the CWA language. After all, at one point the EPA interpreted "navigable waters" to mean any pond where a migratory bird landed.

The Duarte case, mentioned previously, is widely cited by agricultural interests as an example of the potential problems WOTUS created. The Corps claimed that Duarte's plowing did not fall under the CWA's agricultural exemption, but another key aspect of the case is that the Corps claimed that the discharge into vernal pools constituted a discharge into waters of the US. The court found that the vernal pools on the land did constitute waters of the US because they have a significant nexus with a tributary of a navigable water.

This definition of waters of the US was based on prior guidance defining waters of the US and not the 2015 WOTUS rule. However, the vernal pools would still constitute waters of the US under the 2015 WOTUS rule since the 2015 WOTUS rule applies the Kennedy test of a significant nexus. The vernal pools would not constitute waters of the US under the Scalia test suggested by President Trump's executive order.

There are also concerns that the WOTUS rule could discourage private conservationists from restoring wetlands on private land.[28] The WOTUS rule expands jurisdiction to many wetlands on private land, so conservationists seeking to restore wetlands would likely need to submit a request for jurisdictional determination to the Corps. If the land is determined to be in their jurisdiction, then a permit is required for any fill material entering waters of the US. Such regulatory costs may well have the unintended consequence of discouraging wetlands restoration.

Other potential impacts are associated with expanded jurisdiction. For example, the rule could increase the number of waters for which TMDLs could be established. However, these waters must be connected to a navigable water, and TMDLs can clearly be established for the navigable water that could affect all upstream sources. Another impact is that additional facilities that produce or store oil could be in the CWA's jurisdiction and be required to implement Spill Prevention, Control, and Countermeasure plans. The EPA claims that requiring these plans could reduce oil spills.[29]

The Real Issue

Clearly defined property rights are a prerequisite for market solutions to water-quality problems. Unfortunately, the CWA does not define property rights for agricultural nonpoint emissions. The property right for nonpoint emissions needs to define whether farmers have the right to discharge into waters of the US or society has the right to water with pollutant levels below certain thresholds. Agricultural nonpoint emissions are largely exempt from permitting requirements under Sections 402 and 404 of the CWA. However, lack of clarity in the language of these exemptions leads to insecurity even in this right. Nonpoint emissions are also not necessarily exempt from regulations under Section 303 when a TMDL is established.

The insecure nature of such property rights has meant that environmental interests have often paid lawyers and lobbyists to regulate agriculture rather than paying polluters to improve water quality by reducing emissions or seeking support for public expenditures to mitigate emissions. Lawsuits can play an important role in defining property rights when legislation is unclear. But the excessive vagueness of the current legal framework creates a situation in which lawyers and lobbyists are too often perceived as the more cost-effective option, and many years are spent in legal battles rather than creating solutions to water-quality problems.

The choice of paying for reduced emissions or paying lawyers and lobbyists is part of a rational decision in which environmental interests seek the least-cost method (to them) to improve water quality. If environmental interests choose to pay for improved water quality, then they incur the cost of estimating water-quality improvements from alternative agricultural practices and providing incentives for farmers to change those practices. If environmental interests choose lawyers and lobbyists, then they incur significant fees and an uncertain outcome of their efforts.

An interview with Des Moines Water Works by MacKenzie Elmer in the *Des Moines Register* on April 11, 2017, illustrates this decision process.[30] The Water Works board of trustees had agreed to spend $1.35 million to pursue the 2015 case against drainage districts. After Water Works lost its lawsuit, the CEO Bill Stowe said "resources would be better spent" on lobbying efforts rather than continued legal action. Des Moines Water Works continues to calculate that changing the property rights represents its least-cost method to improve water quality, but the least-cost method has changed from a lawsuit to lobbying.

Market Solutions to Water Quality

Ronald Coase, a Nobel Prize recipient, famously argued that bargaining could overcome the inefficient welfare losses from pollution (i.e., externalities) when transaction costs are sufficiently small.[31] If farmers are given the right to discharge pollution into water, then cities or environmental interests could pay farmers for changing their management practices to reduce discharges or pay to mitigate the damage through water treatment. Alternatively, if property rights were reversed, then farmers would incur the cost of changing management practices or pay cities to treat the water. While both of these potential solutions require secure property rights, neither require government bureaucrats to determine the optimal outcome.

While government entities—such as cities—may be involved in these transactions, a Coasean solution occurs when (1) neither party in the transaction has regulatory authority over the other and (2) the parties directly related to the damages are involved in the transaction. The lack of regulatory authority implies that the only actions available to the parties are market-related transactions that may include bargaining or cash transfers. Since the parties are directly related to the damages—both those that cause the damages and those affected—the parties have an incentive to find an economically optimal outcome.

Market solutions arising from well-defined property rights have two key advantages over government solutions.[32] First, market solutions are more likely to identify the most cost-effective manner of improving water quality. Consider the example of a city paying upstream landowners to reduce pollution. Entrepreneurial landowners will seek to find the least-cost method to reduce pollution to obtain greater benefits from incentives provided by the city. And the city has an incentive to ensure that their expenditures are resulting in observed improvement in actual water-quality outcomes. Together the city and landowners work to find innovative solutions to the water-quality concern.

Government solutions often either incentivize farmers to adopt certain practices or require them to use certain practices through regulations. The problem with government solutions is that government agencies are poorly suited to determine the most cost-effective practices. Agencies do not know the cost of farmers implementing alternative practices. Nor can agencies quickly adapt to new information about the effectiveness of alternative practices to improve water quality.

Furthermore, government solutions provide no incentive for entrepreneurs to innovate and find new, unique solutions. A caveat is that government solutions can incentivize firms to identify low-cost methods of pollution control if the mandate is placed on emissions or if a technology mandate allows firms to substitute with a better technology. The nature of nonpoint emissions from agriculture prevents the government from placing restrictions on field-specific emissions.

The second advantage of market solutions over government solutions is that markets more optimally evaluate costs and benefits. For example, a city only pays landowners to change practices if the cost of paying landowners is less than the cost to treat the water. Environmental interests concerned about the Gulf of Mexico only pay landowners in the Corn Belt if the benefit from changed practices outweighs the cost of paying the landowners. While everyone desires improved water quality, these improvements come at a cost, and market transactions account for such costs.

Government agencies are often poor at implementing policies based on costs and benefits. One issue is that agencies may lack good information on costs and benefits. The EPA does not possess knowledge about the magnitude of damages from poor water quality. As discussed earlier, economic analysis the EPA conducted estimated that 177 acres of wetlands in the Midwest were worth $114.4 million. Another issue is regulatory capture;

agencies may represent the interest of a powerful special interest group rather than society as a whole. Thus, the agencies implement regulations that please the interest group rather than select a regulation based on costs and benefits. A core problem is that agencies that implement environmental policies are not determining how much they would be willing to pay with their own money to improve water quality or preserve wetlands. The EPA often reduces pollution by mandating practices or setting thresholds for pollutant levels, but neither of these approaches forces an interested party to face the difficult trade-off between costs and benefits of alternative actions.

An important condition for Coasean bargaining to reach an economically optimal solution is that transaction costs must be sufficiently small. At first glance it appears difficult for all persons affected by water quality to bargain with farmers, but, in many cases, organizations are formed to represent the interests of affected individuals. City governments that treat water represent the interests of urban residents who drink water.

The Mississippi River Collaborative and the Gulf Restoration Network represent individuals with an interest in the environmental quality of the Gulf of Mexico. The Environmental Defense Fund collaborates with companies such as Walmart, Smithfield Foods, General Mills, and United Suppliers to provide incentives for agriculture to reduce nutrient pollution. Ducks Unlimited has a long history of representing the interests of hunters in protecting migratory bird habitat.

In addition, several voluntary markets currently exist. The nonprofit organization Forest Trends has documented a significant number of ecosystem markets in place throughout the US, most of which are related to water quality.[33] Some of these markets are driven by the need for compliance with government regulations—not surprisingly given the lack of secure property rights—but there are at least 52 examples of voluntary watershed markets.

Another central question is how to define the property rights. Farmers could have the right to discharge, or society could have the right to water with few pollutants. Economically optimal outcomes can occur regardless of how the property rights are defined.[34] So this decision is primarily a choice for society about the preferred method to distribute costs of improved water quality. If farmers are given the property right, then the beneficiary of improved water quality incurs the cost. If society is given the property right, then farmers incur the cost to mitigate damages or compensate society for damages.

Three important considerations have to be addressed in defining the property rights. First, agricultural nonpoint sources have faced minimal restrictions on discharges—effectively providing them with the right to discharge. The CWA explicitly provided this right in Sections 402 and 404. A reversal of this implicit property right is better defined through expressing the will of the people rather than a government agency reinterpreting different sections of the CWA. Second, how property rights are defined may affect transaction costs. For example, environmental interests may be more likely to provide incentives to farmers in a relevant watershed to improve water quality than farmers are to compensate individuals affected by their discharges.

Third, providing farmers payments to reduce emissions on a per-acre basis could incentivize an increase in agricultural production that undermines the impacts of the emissions reduction. Erik Lichtenberg and Ricardo Smith-Ramírez[35] find that payments to farmers in Maryland to implement conservation practices in crop production led farmers to switch from vegetative cover to cropland. This adverse effect of payments may be avoided through enforcement by the party providing payments.

Clearly, the most significant challenge to achieve market solutions is the political battle associated with defining the property right. Environmental interests would lobby to avoid giving the right clearly to agriculture. Agricultural interests would lobby against any action that would not give them the right to discharge. In addition, the property right needs to be established by states since the CWA gives states authority to implement many aspects of the legislation.

Besides defining property rights, the government could take a number of steps to encourage market solutions. The government could implement policies to reduce transaction costs. In some cases, transaction costs could be reduced by developing new local institutions that represent the collective interests of those affected by poor water quality. The government could also provide enforcement for market transactions. For example, the government could enforce a contract to ensure farmers actually make the changes in management practices to which they have agreed.

In addition, there could be a role for the government to provide financial incentives in certain cases. Free riding presents a major challenge in achieving optimal private transactions for water-quality improvements. Consider the case of water quality affecting recreational users of a lake. A nonprofit organization could form to represent its interest, but free riding would result in suboptimal donations to improve water quality. In this case, the government could use tax dollars to improve water quality.

Agricultural interests promote using conservation payments in the farm bill, but these programs are ineffective at achieving improvements in environmental quality. A key reason for these farm bill programs' failures is that the party providing the incentive (i.e., the federal government) is not directly affected by any damages, so they have little interest in ensuring that the payments achieve the desired outcome.

Rather than directly compensating farmers, the government could provide grants to parties affected by poor water quality. These parties could then use the funds to make transactions with farmers to alter management practices. This approach is more likely to result in water-quality improvements because the party providing the incentive has a strong interest to ensure the payment results in improved water quality.

A Tale of Two Cities

Des Moines and Wichita both face water-quality problems and significant expenditures to treat their water. Des Moines and Wichita both face upstream agricultural production that hurts water quality. But Des Moines and Wichita have pursued different routes to improve the quality of their water.

Des Moines Water Works sued upstream drainage districts in Iowa. Most corn and soybean production in Iowa has subsurface tile drains to remove excess moisture from the soil, which often also contains significant amounts of nitrates. As discussed earlier, Des Moines Water Works argued that tile drainage does not qualify for the CWA exemption for agricultural stormwater discharges. Now that Des Moines Water Works lost its lawsuit, it intends to spend resources lobbying. Alternatively, Des Moines Water Works could provide incentives for farmers to change management practices to reduce nitrate loads or pay the cost of water treatment, depending on which strategy reduces nitrates at the least-cost. But Des Moines decided that the least-cost method to improve water quality was to hire lawyers to test farmers' property rights to discharge nitrates. Unfortunately, the case pitted farming interests against urban interests and delayed improvements in water quality.

In contrast, the city of Wichita has implemented a program that provides incentives for farmers to change management practices to reduce the level of atrazine—a popular herbicide—in surface water. The city has estimated that the cost of providing incentives for farmers is less than the cost of treating the water. The program was featured on the front page of a recent agricultural magazine with the headline "Program Benefits Urban and Rural Interest."[36] An advantage of this approach is that Wichita will monitor water-quality conditions and adjust or end the program based on a comparison of costs and the benefits from observed changes in water quality.

Conclusion

Even though the president recently signed an executive order to begin dismantling the WOTUS rule, the debate on WOTUS is far from over. The executive order asks the EPA to rewrite the WOTUS rule and use the Scalia definition of jurisdiction. Crafting and editing a revised rule will take significant time and effort. Once a revised rule is finalized, lawsuits will immediately follow, and the rule will likely make its way once again to the Supreme Court. All this could take 10 or more years, and the legal battles over the interpretation of language in the CWA will bring no changes in the nation's water quality.

The WOTUS rule did nothing to resolve the core issue of insecure property rights for nonpoint emissions. If anything, the WOTUS rule created even greater uncertainty in terms of the exemption from permitting requirements for nonpoint emissions. A revised rule using the Scalia test would reduce regulatory uncertainty by providing a clearer definition of the EPA's jurisdiction. But a revised rule using the Scalia test will not resolve the issue of insecure property rights for nonpoint emissions.

The current regulatory uncertainty has created an incentive for environmental interests to pursue lawsuits to regulate agricultural discharges, as in the case of Des Moines Water Works. But market solutions to improve water quality are possible, as in the case of Wichita. Clearly defining property rights for agricultural discharges will result in fewer conflicts like in Des Moines and more cooperation like in Wichita.

Too often agricultural interests dismiss water-quality concerns by arguing that farmers are excellent stewards of the environment because they rely on the land and water. And too often environmental interests see regulatory action as the only way to improve water quality. An alternative path is to pursue market solutions in which parties causing the damages and those affected by the damages agree to a transaction that improves water quality. The key to unleashing the power of the market for water quality is to clearly define the property rights for agricultural nonpoint emissions. Then we will see innovative, new solutions that bring together agricultural and environmental interests to achieve a common goal of improving water quality in a cost-effective manner.

Notes

1. Department of the Army, Corps of Engineers, and Environmental Protection Agency, "Clean Water Rule: Definition of 'Waters of the United States,'" *Federal Register* 80, no. 124 (June 29, 2015): 37054–127, https://www.federalregister.gov/documents/2015/06/29/2015-13435/clean-water-rule-definition-of-waters-of-the-united-states.

2. David Sunding and David Zilberman, "The Economics of Environmental Regulation by Licensing: An Assessment of Recent Changes to the Wetland Permitting Process," *Natural Resource Journal* 42, no. 1 (2002): 59–90, https://are.berkeley.edu/~sunding/Economcs%20of%20Environmental%20Regulation.pdf.

3. James Boyd, "The New Face of the Clean Water Act: A Critical Review of the EPA's Proposed TMDL Rules," Resources for the Future, 2000, http://ageconsearch.umn.edu/bitstream/10850/1/dp000012.pdf.

4. Environmental Protection Agency, "National Water Quality Inventory: Report to Congress for the 2004 Reporting Cycle," 2009, https://www.epa.gov/waterdata/national-water-quality-inventory-report-congress.

5. David J. Mulla, Adam S. Birr, and Newell R. Kitchen, "Limitations of Evaluating the Effectiveness of Agricultural Management Practices at Reducing Nutrient Losses to Surface Waters," in *Final Report: Gulf Hypoxia and Local Water Quality Concerns Workshop*, ed. J. L. Baker (St. Joseph, MI: American Society of Agricultural and Biological Engineers, 2008): 189–212.

6. Environmental Protection Agency, "Nutrient Pollution: Where This Occurs," 2017, https://www.epa.gov/nutrientpollution/where-nutrient-pollution-occurs.

7. E. G. Stets, V. J. Kelly, and C. G. Crawford, "Regional and Temporal Differences in Nitrate Trends Discerned from Long-Term Water Quality Monitoring Data," *Journal of the American Water Resources Association* 51, no. 5 (2015), http://onlinelibrary.wiley.com/doi/10.1111/1752-1688.12321/full.

8. Lori A. Sprague, Robert M. Hirsch, and Brent T. Aulenbach, "Nitrate in the Mississippi River and Its Tributaries, 1980 to 2008: Are We Making Progress?," *Environmental Science and Technology* 45 (2011): 7209–16, http://pubs.acs.org/doi/abs/10.1021/es201221s.

9. Wesley W. Stone, Robert J. Gilliom, and Karen R. Ryberg, "Pesticides in U.S. Streams and Rivers: Occurrence and Trends During 1992–2011," *Environmental Science and Technology* 48 (2014): 11025–30, http://pubs.acs.org/doi/abs/10.1021/es5025367.

10. Jonathan Coppess, "Dead Zones & Drinking Water: An Update on the DMWW Lawsuit," *farmdoc daily* 7, no. 24 (2017): 109, http://farmdocdaily.illinois.edu/2017/02/dead-zones-drinking-water-update-dmww-lawsuit.html.

11. Kristen A. Tidgren, "Parties in DMWW Lawsuit Disagree as to Meaning of Iowa Court Opinion," Iowa State University Center for Agricultural Law and Taxation, February 14, 2017, https://www.calt.iastate.edu/blogpost/parties-dmww-lawsuit-disagree-meaning-iowa-court-opinion.

12. Kristen A. Tidgren, "Why a Federal Court Dismissed the DMWW Lawsuit," Iowa State University Center for Agricultural Law and Taxation, March 18, 2017, https://www.calt.iastate.edu/blogpost/why-federal-court-dismissed-dmww-lawsuit.

13. Tiffany Dowell, "Trial Court Ruling in Duarte Nursery v. Army Corps of Engineers Concerning for Landowners," Texas Agriculture Law Blog, July 11, 2016, https://agrilife.org/texasaglaw/2016/07/11/duarte/.

14. LaJuana S. Wilcher and Roland W. Page, "Memorandum: Clean Water Act Section 404 Regulatory Program and Agricultural Activities," US Environmental Protection Agency and US Department of the Army, 1990, https://www.epa.gov/cwa-404/memorandum-clean-water-act-section-404-regulatory-program-and-agricultural-activities.

15. George L. Van Houtven, Smita B. Brunnermeier, and Mark C. Buckley, "A Retrospective Assessment of the Costs of the Clean Water Act: 1972 to 1997," Environmental Protection Agency, 2000, https://yosemite.epa.gov/ee/epa/eerm.nsf/vwAN/EE-0434-01.pdf/$file/EE-0434-01.pdf.

16. David A. Keiser and Joseph S. Shapiro, "Consequences of the Clean Water Act and the Demand for Water Quality," National Bureau of Economic Research, 2017, http://www.nber.org/papers/w23070.

17. Keiser and Shapiro, "Consequences of the Clean Water Act and the Demand for Water Quality."

18. Environmental Protection Agency, "National Water Quality Inventory."

19. Karen Fisher-Vanden and Sheila Olmstead, "Moving Pollution Trading from Air to Water: Potential, Problems, and Prognosis," *Journal of Economic Perspectives* 27, no. 1 (2013): 147–71, https://www.aeaweb.org/articles?id=10.1257/jep.27.1.147.

20. EPA Region III, "Accounting for Uncertainty in Offset and Trading Programs," Environmental Protection Agency, 2014, https://www.epa.gov/sites/production/files/2015-07/documents/final_uncertainty_tm_2-12-14.pdf.

21. Richard D. Horan and James S. Shortle, "Endogenous Risk and Point-Nonpoint Uncertainty Trading Ratios," *American Journal of Agricultural Economics* 99, no. 2 (2017), https://academic.oup.com/ajae/article-abstract/99/2/427/2875285/Endogenous-Risk-and-Point-Nonpoint-Uncertainty?redirectedFrom=fulltext.

22. Roger A. McEowen, *Principles of Agricultural Law* (Ankeny, IA: McEowen PLC, 2017).

23. McEowen, *Principles of Agricultural Law.*

24. Department of the Army, Corps of Engineers, and Environmental Protection Agency, "Clean Water Rule."

25. Environmental Protection Agency, "Economic Analysis of the EPA-Army Clean Water Rule," 2015, https://www.epa.gov/cleanwaterrule/final-clean-water-rule-e conomic-analysis.

26. Sunding and Zilberman, "The Economics of Environmental Regulation by Licensing."

27. Sunding and Zilberman, "The Economics of Environmental Regulation by Licensing."

28. Jonathan Adler, "Redefining the Waters of the United States," *Property and Environment Research Center* 34, no. 2 (2015), https://www.perc.org/articles/redefining-waters-united-states.

29. Environmental Protection Agency, "Economic Analysis of the EPA-Army Clean Water Rule."

30. MacKenzie Elmer, "Des Moines Water Works Won't Appeal Lawsuit," *Des Moines Register*, April 11, 2017, http://www.desmoinesregister.com/story/news/2017/04/11/des-moines-water-works-not-appeal-lawsuit/100321222/.

31. Ronald H. Coase, "The Problem of Social Cost," *Journal of Law and Economics* 3 (1960): 1–44, https://econ.ucsb.edu/~tedb/Courses/UCSBpf/readings/coase.pdf.

32. For an excellent discussion of the advantages of market solutions to environmental problems, see Terry H. Anderson and Donald R. Leal, *Free Market Environmentalism for the Next Generation* (New York: Palgrave Macmillan, 2015).

33. Genevieve Bennett et al., "An Atlas of Ecosystem Markets in the United States," Forest Trends Ecosystems Marketplace, 2016, http://forest-trends.org/releases/p/atlas_of_ecosystem_markets.

34. Coase, "The Problem of Social Cost."

35. Erik Lichtenberg and Ricardo Smith-Ramírez, "Slippage in Conservation Cost Sharing," *American Journal of Agricultural Economics* 93, no. 1 (2011): 113–29, https://academic.oup.com/ajae/article-abstract/93/1/113/86783/Slippage-in-Conservation-Cost-Sharing.

36. Doug Rich, "Program Benefits Urban and Rural Interests," *High Plains Journal*, January 16, 2017, http://www.hpj.com/ag_news/program-benefits-urban-and-rural-interests/article_811a05c7-0f55-5655-b4f2-f88faeb920fb.html.

8

Biofuels, the Renewable Fuel Standard, and Policy Ineffectiveness

AARON SMITH[1]

Biofuels account for more than 10 percent of farm crop revenue in the United States, so they are an integral part of the farm economy. In 2016, 40 percent of domestic corn production was used to produce ethanol, and a quarter of soybean oil was used for biodiesel. These biofuels are blended with petroleum products—ethanol with gasoline and biodiesel with diesel—and sold as transportation fuels.

The main policy governing biofuels is the Renewable Fuel Standard (RFS), which requires that at least a minimum amount of each category of biofuel be blended into the transportation fuel supply each year. The RFS was established by the Energy Policy Act of 2005 and expanded under the Energy Independence and Security Act (EISA) of 2007. The program sets ambitious standards for biofuel consumption, with the overt goals of reducing greenhouse gas (GHG) emissions and reducing dependence on foreign oil.[2] An additional effect of the program is to expand demand for corn, soybeans, and some other crops grown on US farms.

The RFS is at a crossroads. Until 2013, the fuel industry met the RFS mandates without too much difficulty. However, the mandates now require more biofuel than the fuel industry can easily absorb. As a result, compliance costs have increased, which in turn have increased lobbying pressures on the Environmental Protection Agency (EPA), which administers the program. The EPA, and by extension Congress, faces important decisions about the future path of the RFS.

Farm bills have devoted relatively few federal resources to biofuels. The energy title in the 2014 Farm Bill contained a projected $125 million per year for biofuels, less than 1 percent of projected non-nutrition spending.

221

Actual spending since 2014 has been even lower as appropriations committees have reduced funding. Energy title funding focuses on the development
of non-corn-based biofuels, which have potentially larger GHG reduction
benefits than corn ethanol and which constitute all the RFS-mandated
growth in biofuels after 2015.[3] As such, the energy title is best seen as an
abetment to the RFS.

This chapter addresses two questions:

- What lessons from the RFS are useful for the policymaking process?

- What farm bill initiatives could improve US biofuel policy?

I draw three lessons from the RFS that are relevant to government policymaking in this and other areas:

1. Incorporate uncertainty. Policymakers should make, implement, and
   analyze policy with a view to what might happen, rather than a single
   projection of what will happen.

2. Do not give the regulator too much discretion. Political forces and legal
   challenges can undermine policy if the regulating agency has discretion to repeatedly adjust the policy parameters.

3. Do not mandate things that do not exist. Mandates are an inefficient
   and ineffective method for forcing technological progress.

These lessons relate to details of legislation and its implementation, which
sets this chapter apart from a typical paper on climate policy. Most economic
analysis emphasizes a hypothetical first-best policy and evaluates existing
policies relative to that ideal. For example, Stephen Holland et al. estimate
that the RFS is more than three times more costly than cap and trade for
reducing carbon emissions.[4] This is an important point that should be made
repeatedly, but reiterating it is not the objective of this chapter.

The main potential benefits of the RFS stem from reduction of GHG emissions. Such emissions represent a global externality that can be mitigated by
subsidizing low-carbon fuels. Two other public benefits, both of which are

likely to be small, are often touted by RFS advocates. The RFS could also improve energy security, which can be framed as a public good, and it could improve competition in the fuel sector by preventing the petroleum industry from excluding ethanol. Here, the focus is on greenhouse emission reductions when discussing the public benefits of the policy.

I argue that directing resources to biofuels through the farm bill would produce only small, if any, public benefits. If Congress continues to fund the energy title, it is imperative that Congress target federal resources toward areas with significant public good components. These include research and development, promoting competition, and mitigating network externalities.[5]

In the next section, I present a short primer on climate change before describing the history of the RFS and its recent challenges. With that background, I then identify the three lessons before discussing the farm bill energy title.

A Primer on Climate Change

Greenhouse gases in the earth's atmosphere play a pivotal role in keeping the planet warm enough for life to flourish. They act like a blanket, letting heat from the sun through to earth and then preventing that heat from escaping into space. The more greenhouse gas in the atmosphere, the warmer the planet is. The main greenhouse gas is carbon dioxide (CO_2), but others include methane, nitrous oxide, and water vapor (clouds).

Carbon is absorbed from the atmosphere by living plants and passed along to animals that eat those plants. When these organisms die and decay, their carbon is either trapped underground or mixed with oxygen and emitted as CO_2. Fossil fuels such as oil, coal, and natural gas were formed by decaying organisms that were trapped underground millions of years ago. Using these fossil fuels releases the sequestered carbon back into the atmosphere in the form of CO_2.

The average temperature on earth has risen by 0.85° Celsius in the past century, mostly due to humans burning fossil fuels. Other human activities such as deforestation (especially through burning) and raising livestock have also contributed. Scientists estimate that temperatures will rise another 0.3° to 4.8°C in the next century, depending on the extent of mitigation activities.[6]

Two underreported facts stand out in studies of the economic effects of climate warming. First, the estimated total effects are not catastrophic. Second, there is substantial uncertainty around the consensus estimate.

The consensus estimate under "business as usual" conditions is that average temperature will increase a further 3°C by 2100, which will reduce world gross domestic product (GDP) permanently by 4 percent.[7] The world would prefer not to lose 4 percent of GDP to climate change, and some regions and people will face huge effects. However, it is difficult to argue from that estimate that the aggregate economic effects of climate change will be dire. The reduction is equivalent to the loss of less than two years of average growth.

On the flip side, the cost of mitigating such modest effects should not be crippling, which explains why the estimated social cost of carbon (SCC) is not large relative to the price of fossil fuels. The consensus SCC estimate is presently $37 per ton of CO_2,[8] which translates to 38 cents per gallon of gasoline, 2 cents per kilowatt hour (kWh) of natural gas–generated electricity, and 3.5 cents per kWh of coal-fired electricity. The gasoline and natural gas price effects would be about 20 percent of current retail prices, and the coal price effect would be about 35 percent of current retail prices. Standard economic theory implies that if a carbon tax were imposed so that consumers were to pay 20 percent more for gasoline and natural gas and 35 percent more for coal, then they would be paying for the climate effects of using these fuels. The resulting outcome would be economically optimal.

This first fact suggests that climate change is much less of a problem than implied by the rhetoric used by environmental advocates. However, the second fact has the opposite implication. Estimating the economic impact of climate change requires forecasting decades into the future. Economic forecasters have little success predicting one year into the future, let alone what will occur decades from now. New clean-energy technologies will play an important role in climate-change mitigation, as may new carbon sequestration technologies, but the paths and scope of their development are impossible to predict. Climate systems move more slowly than economic variables but are still difficult to forecast accurately over long horizons.

The extent of the uncertainty about climate change indicates that the economic impacts our descendants experienced will likely diverge substantially from the current consensus prediction. In some plausible scenarios, the effects are benign. In other plausible scenarios, climate change has large, catastrophic effects on the world. The possibility of disaster explains the difference in tone between environmental advocates, who emphasize the worst-case scenario, and cool-headed economists, who tend to focus on the consensus prediction. One theme of this chapter is that economic analysts and policymakers need to think more seriously about the uncertainty rather than focusing on only the expected outcome.

The Renewable Fuel Standard

The 2007 RFS program established ambitious standards for biofuel use, with the goal of increasing consumption to 36 billion gallons (Bgal) per year by 2022. The EPA administers the program, and although the EISA statute provides specific biofuel consumption targets, the EPA is allowed discretion in setting each year's mandates.

The RFS distinguishes among categories of biofuel and sets separate mandates for each. The biofuel categories are: (1) cellulosic biofuel, which can be produced from wood, grasses, or the inedible parts of plants; (2) biomass-based diesel, typically produced from oilseeds such as soybeans or canola, tallow, or used cooking oil; (3) other advanced biofuel, mostly ethanol produced from sugarcane but also any renewable fuels other than ethanol derived from corn; and (4) conventional biofuel, which is essentially ethanol derived from corn. The mandates are nested so that the advanced biofuel mandate can be met with any fuels in the first three categories. The total renewable mandate can be met by fuels in any of the four categories.

The RFS specifies minimum renewable fuel use for each calendar year from 2006 through 2022, as shown in Figure 1. It required 9 Bgal in 2008 and increased this level on an annual basis to 15.2 Bgal in 2012 and 36 Bgal in 2022. However, the RFS specified that no more than 15 Bgal of corn ethanol could count toward the mandate after 2015. The balance of the RFS was to be filled by advanced biofuels, such as biodiesel from soybean oil and ethanol from cellulosic biomass (e.g., switchgrass, miscanthus, and corn stover). By 2022, almost half the mandated renewable fuels will be cellulosic.

The four categories of biofuel differ in their estimated impacts on life-cycle GHG emissions relative to gasoline and diesel. Cellulosic biofuels must

Figure 1. RFS Mandates

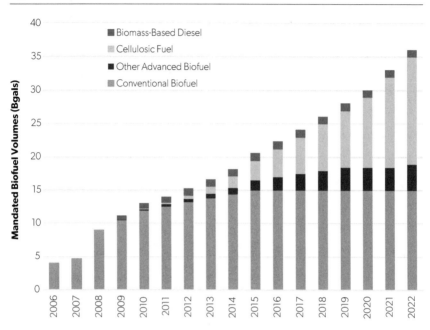

Note: The volumes for 2006 and 2007 come from the first RFS, passed in 2005. The volumes from 2008 onward are from the second RFS, as specified in EISA.
Source: 42 USC § 7545 (o)(2).

generate a 60 percent reduction in emissions to qualify under the program. Biodiesel must generate 50 percent emissions reductions, as must other advanced biofuels. Conventional biofuels must generate at least 20 percent emissions reductions to qualify. The regulation was written this way to encourage a shift toward lower-emission fuels over time.

When President George W. Bush signed the EISA on December 19, 2007, he emphasized two benefits of the RFS. First, it would reduce dependence on foreign oil by expanding domestic fuel production. Second, it would reduce GHG emissions.[9] However, the long history of biofuel lobbying activity suggests a third goal was the catalyst for the standard: increasing the demand for corn and soybeans.

Ethanol made from corn only recently became a significant motor-fuel ingredient in the United States, but it has a long history as a prospective motor fuel. In 1920, the US Geological Survey estimated that peak petroleum production would be reached within a few years. David White wrote, "In fact, it probably is no rash prediction to forecast a world's shortage of petroleum within the next twenty years, with the likelihood that the world's supplies will be insufficient within fifteen years."[10]

At the same time, US agricultural prices had declined as European agricultural production recovered from World War I. Lower prices motivated US agricultural producers to look to ethanol as an alternative use and source of demand for their crops.[11]

The push for ethanol intensified in the 1930s, when the Great Depression brought further hardship to rural America. In the early days of the New Deal, members of the Farm Chemurgic Movement worked closely with the US Department of Agriculture (USDA) on a farm-relief program that would subsidize ethanol production from farm crops.[12] However, by this time large new oil fields had been discovered in Texas, Oklahoma, and California. These discoveries led to high oil production and low prices. Ethanol was not price competitive and faded into the background until the oil shocks of the 1970s.

The first variant of the RFS was created by Congress in 1978. Additional ethanol bills were offered in 1987, 1992, 2000, 2001, 2003, and 2004 and consistently received strong support from the corn lobby.[13] The 1978 Gasohol Motor Fuel Act proposed that production of alcohol motor fuel supply reach at least 1 percent of US gasoline consumption by 1981, 5 percent by 1985, and 10 percent by 1990. This bill never became law, but a weaker version was included in the 1980 Energy Security Act (ESA).

Instead of mandating ethanol production, the 1980 ESA directed the Departments of Energy and Agriculture to prepare and evaluate within the next year a plan "designed to achieve a level of alcohol production within the United States equal to at least 10 percent of the level of gasoline consumption within the United States." However, the ensuing report concluded that this ethanol-use target, "though technologically attainable, is not economically feasible even under optimistic market scenarios."[14] As a result, ethanol constituted less than 1 percent of finished motor gasoline in 1990.

An environmental benefit of ethanol gave the corn-ethanol industry a new argument for favorable legislation. The 1990 amendments to the Clean Air Act required that, in regions prone to poor air quality, oxygenate additives be blended into gasoline to make it burn more cleanly. Ethanol and methyl tertiary butyl ether (MTBE), a natural gas derivative, were the main contenders to fulfill the oxygenate requirement. Ronald Johnson and Gary Libecap document the lobbying battle between advocates for ethanol and those for MTBE.[15] Ethanol received some favorable treatment in the final legislation,[16] but MTBE became the dominant additive because it was less expensive. Subsequently, however, leaks in underground storage tanks lead to MTBE contamination of drinking water, and as a result, at least 25 states banned MTBE.

Without competition from MTBE, ethanol cemented its place as a fuel additive in the 2005 Energy Policy Act. This law included the first RFS, mandating that 4 Bgal of ethanol be used in 2006 and gradually increasing to 7.5 Bgal per year by 2012. This 2012 quantity corresponded to 5 percent of projected domestic gasoline use. Thus, it represented a small expansion of the proportion of oxygenates in gasoline. In 2005, US oxygenate production (ethanol and MTBE combined) totaled 4.6 percent of finished motor gasoline supplied. Legislation to increase the RFS was introduced in Congress even before the 2005 Energy Policy Act had passed, and more bills followed in 2006.[17] These proposals led to the current RFS.

The RFS is administered by the EPA through a system of tradable credits, known as renewable identification numbers (RINs). Each gallon of biofuel that is blended into domestic fuel generates an RIN.[18] Obligated parties under the policy, typically oil refiners, must submit to the EPA a certain number of RINs for each gallon of petroleum fuel they sell. For example, in 2016, they were required to submit 0.101 RINs for each gallon of diesel gasoline they sold. These RINs must include at least 0.0201 advanced biofuel RINs. In turn, the advanced RINs must include at least 0.0159 biodiesel RINs and at least 0.00128 cellulosic RINs.

RINs are typically generated by blenders, firms that blend wholesale fuels for sale to gas stations. Thus, to comply with the RFS, oil refiners need to purchase RINs from a blender. Some oil companies have blending operations, so they do not need to purchase RINs from another firm, but there are enough obligated parties without blending operations to ensure a robust market for RINs. The price of RINs is determined by the extra cost of using biofuel in place of petroleum. The blender uses the proceeds from selling RINs to help pay for biofuel (if it is priced higher than petroleum) or to pay distribution costs (if blended fuel is more costly to deliver to consumers than pure petroleum). In effect, the RIN is a subsidy to biofuel funded by a tax on petroleum.

Technical, Political, and Legal Challenges to the RFS

The RFS has run into two barriers. The first is that production of cellulosic biofuel continues to be close to zero, even though the RFS now mandates significant quantities. The second barrier, known as the blend wall, is that regular gasoline can contain up to 10 percent ethanol without affecting engines or fueling infrastructure. Gasoline with 10 percent ethanol is known as E10. The RFS now requires more biofuel than can be consumed in E10. Breaching the blend wall requires either expanded consumption of biodiesel, which does not face any relevant blend restrictions, or increasing sales of a high-ethanol blend of gasoline known as E85, which contains up to 85 percent ethanol and can be used only in flex-fuel vehicles.[19]

The EPA, which administers the RFS, is authorized to set the required biofuel volumes below the mandate if there is insufficient supply. It has used this authority to deal with both barriers, which has not been controversial for the first barrier because of the lack of cellulosic production. However, the insufficient-supply provision has met with stiff opposition when used to deal with the blend wall. In 2013 and 2014, the EPA argued that there is insufficient supply of E85 because the retail fueling infrastructure does not exist to get the fuel to consumers, whereas the ethanol industry argued that there is sufficient supply because there is enough ethanol to make enough E85 to meet the mandate.

The data reported in Figure 2 indicate that the market first hit the blend wall in 2010 and has hugged the blend wall since then. This was feasible under the RFS as long as the required cellulosic volume was set to zero. In 2013, however, the conventional ethanol mandate exceeded the blend wall, even without the cellulosic component. The EPA would either have to force the industry to burst through the blend wall or waive part of the conventional biofuel mandate. In August 2013, the EPA first hinted that it might reduce the 2014 mandate to relieve the blend wall constraint. Then, in October 2013, a Reuters news article leaked an early version of the EPA's

2014 proposed rule. In November 2013, the EPA released a rule proposing to waive the RFS blend-wall quantities of the ethanol mandate for 2014.

Behind-the-scenes lobbying by the oil industry, which wanted the conventional mandate kept below the blend wall, and by the ethanol industry, which wanted to enforce the statutory volumes, prevented the EPA from releasing the 2014 and 2015 rules in a timely fashion. Not until December 2015 did the EPA finalize the rules for 2014, 2015, and 2016. The EPA finalized the 2017 rule in December 2016, so it appeared to be back on track.

Another challenge appeared in 2016 when several oil refiners petitioned the EPA to move the compliance burden from oil refiners to blenders. Rather than oil refiners demonstrating compliance by turning in RINs to certify that sufficient biofuel has been blended into the fuel supply, the petitioners argued that blenders should be the ones to demonstrate compliance. Recalling that the RIN system acts like a subsidy to biofuel funded by a tax on petroleum, this proposal is akin to moving the point at which the tax is assessed. If the fuel system were perfectly competitive, this change would have no effect. In competitive markets, refiners would be compensated for the RIN tax liability by receiving a higher price for their product. The petitioners argue that they are not receiving such compensation and therefore the RFS would be more efficient if blenders were obligated.[20] Recent research suggests some significant market power in parts of the fuel system, although it is unclear whether this lack of competition implies that moving the point of obligation would improve the RFS.[21] The EPA denied this petition in November 2017.

In 2018, President Trump convened several high-profile meetings on RFS reform. Attendees included Sens. Joni Ernst (R-IA) and Chuck Grassley (R-IA) representing agricultural interests and Sens. Ted Cruz (R-TX) and Pat Toomey (R-PA) representing oil interests, as well as EPA Administrator Scott Pruitt and USDA Secretary Sonny Perdue. Initially, it appeared that the two factions had agreed on a deal. To placate agricultural interest, the EPA would relax environmental restrictions that currently prevent mid-blend ethanol fuels such as E15 from being sold in the summer, and for the oil industry, it would allow exported ethanol to count toward RFS compliance. It was unclear whether the EPA could legally make either change without congressional action, but such concerns became moot when the reported deal collapsed in June 2018.[22]

The RFS statute allows the EPA to exempt small refineries if they suffer "disproportionate economic hardship" from complying with the statute, but it had only issued a small number of such waivers in previous years. In April 2018, news broke that the EPA had issued retroactive waivers to several large and profitable firms exempting them from complying with the RFS. The news of these waivers sparked a strong response from ethanol advocates, may result in lawsuits, and has effectively reduced biofuel volumes.

Exempting small refineries reduces the biofuel mandate only when invoked retroactively. If the EPA intends to continue these exemptions in future years, then it has to transfer the biofuel obligations of the exempted firms to the nonexempt firms. Instead, the EPA has claimed that these exemptions are temporary, opening the door to including their volumes in future mandates but secretly planning to grant another exemption next year. Doing so would be a backdoor way to reduce the RFS mandate, but a plain reading of the statute suggests that it would be illegal and would therefore generate legal challenges. Regardless of their legality, these actions absorb scarce EPA resources that could instead be directed toward addressing the blend wall and setting volumes for future years.

The RFS statute specifies that 26 Bgal of biofuel be used in 2018, including no more than 15 Bgal of corn ethanol. The EPA set 2018 volumes at 19.29 Bgal of biofuel, of which at least 4.29 Bgal must be advanced biofuel (i.e., not corn ethanol). The blend wall was projected at 14.3 Bgal for 2018 but is likely slightly higher because low gas prices cause people to drive more. The 0.7 Bgal gap between the blend wall and the allowable amount of corn ethanol will most likely be met by increased biodiesel use, but the gap is large enough that some expansion in E85 sales may be required. Increasing E85 sales would require increasing availability of the fuel. About 6 percent of registered vehicles in the US have flex-fuel capability, but less than 2 percent of gas stations sell E85.[23] Private market investment in E85 infrastructure has been slow, but in early 2016, the USDA spent $100 million to fund installation of E85 fuel dispensers with the goal of doubling E85 retail capacity.

Looking ahead, the EPA may consider reducing the mandate permanently. The RFS legislation states that, if the EPA waives at least 20 percent of the mandated volume for two consecutive years, then it can modify the required volumes for all following years. The 2016 volume of 18.11 Bgal

Figure 2. The Blend Wall

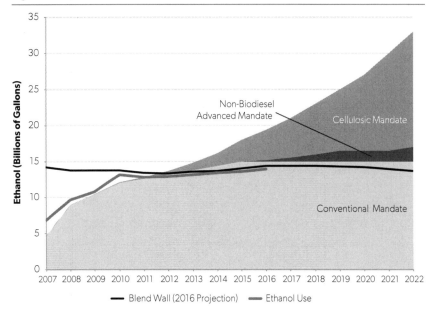

Note: I subtract 1.5 times the biodiesel mandate to get the ethanol mandate. The legislation treats 1 gallon of biodiesel as equivalent to 1.5 gallons of ethanol because biodiesel has a 50 percent higher energy content than ethanol. The biodiesel mandate is set at the levels implied by the EPA final rule through 2016 and 2 Bgal thereafter. The blend wall is 10 percent of gasoline use. After 2016, I use the EIA projection of gasoline use to determine the expected blend wall.
Source: RFS mandates from 42 USC § 7545 (o)(2). Gasoline and ethanol use from US Energy Information Administration, "Petroleum & Other Liquids: Product Supplied," https://www.eia.gov/dnav/pet/pet_cons_psup_dc_nus_mbbl_a.htm; and US Energy Administration, "Oxygenate Production," https://www.eia.gov/dnav/pet/pet_pnp_oxy_dc_nus_mbbl_a. htm. Gasoline projections from US Energy Information Administration, *Annual Energy Outlook 2017,* January 5, 2017, Table 11, https://www.eia.gov/outlooks/aeo/tables_ref.php.

was 19 percent below the statute, and the 2017 volume was 20 percent below.[24] Thus, it appears that the soonest the EPA could reset the volume of total renewable fuel would be for 2019 and later compliance years.

However, waivers for the cellulosic and advanced components of the mandate have been much higher than 20 percent since 2013. Thus, the EPA could permanently reset the cellulosic and advanced components at any time. However, the only way to reduce the cellulosic and advanced mandates while keeping corn ethanol capped at 15 Bgal is to also reduce the total RFS mandate. It is unclear whether the EPA could use such an argument to legally reduce the total mandate before 2019.

Whatever the EPA does, the proportion of ethanol in the gasoline supply seems unlikely to drop much below 10 percent. The fuel system has adjusted its infrastructure to make E10 the standard fuel, and unless there is an extreme spike in relative corn prices, it will remain cost-effective.

Lesson 1: Incorporate Uncertainty

Uncertainty about climate change and its impacts is pervasive. Climate scientists are uncertain about how much warming will occur. Economists estimate the effects of climate change using imperfect models with parameters about which they are uncertain. Prognosticators are uncertain which new modes of transportation, fuel technologies, sources of renewable and fossil fuels, and carbon sequestration technologies will emerge. Forecasters are uncertain about future fuel prices.

Several elements of the RFS legislation and its implementation demonstrate that policymakers have not taken uncertainty seriously.

Blend Wall. The RFS was written in 2006 and 2007 when the economy was expanding and gasoline demand was expected to keep rising. The 2006 EIA projection placed the blend wall at 15.9 Bgal in 2013, rising to 16.5 Bgal in 2016. The corn-ethanol component of the mandate plateaus at 15 Bgal, so if the EIA projection had come true, we never would have hit the blend wall with conventional ethanol. Only the cellulosic component would have required breaching the blend wall.

The actual blend wall was 13.6 Bgal in 2013 and is projected to be 14.3 Bgal in 2018. Rather than being a billion gallons below the blend wall, the mandate was set at more than half a billion gallons above the blend wall. A mandate set above the blend wall raises compliance costs because it forces firms either to invest in the infrastructure to get E85 to market or to use additional biodiesel, which is more expensive than ethanol on a per-gallon basis.

Not only does breaching the blend wall raise compliance costs, but a mandate close to the blend wall also causes volatile compliance costs. Small changes in required volumes can push the industry to the other side of the blend wall and cause large changes in compliance costs. This volatility generates compliance cost uncertainty for firms.[25] This uncertainty means that firms do not receive a strong signal about whether to invest in the infrastructure required to get E85 into the market.

The blend wall and the ensuing uncertainty about compliance costs could have been avoided if the statute had been written as a rate standard rather than as a volume standard. Requiring the market to blend a certain percentage of biofuel rather than a certain volume would have made the blend wall salient and would have clarified when the blend wall would be binding.

Fuel Prices. The EPA no doubt knew the blend wall constraint would be significant but paid little public attention to the issue. In February 2010, the EPA released an extensive regulatory impact analysis (RIA) of the expected benefits and costs of the RFS.[26] The EPA reported large net benefits from the RFS2 in 2022 with estimates ranging from $12.8 billion to $25.97 billion a year. The estimates equal the sum of estimated reductions in fuel costs, improvements in energy security and health, and reductions in GHG emissions attributed to the policy in 2022. Each component is presented as a single number, except for the GHG emissions benefits for which the EPA presents a range depending on the SCC used by the agency.

The reductions in fuel costs attributed to the RFS2 were $11.8 billion, which is almost all the benefits in the low-SCC case and half the benefits in the high-SCC case. The fuel market benefits arose because the EPA estimated that ethanol would be less expensive than oil and therefore that using ethanol would save consumers money. In addition, despite acknowledging the vast uncertainty in projecting feedstock and oil prices in 2022, the EPA limited itself to the central oil price projections from the Department of Energy's *Annual Energy Outlook 2009*,[27] ignoring the high and low projections from that report. When the RIA was written in 2009, world oil markets were coming off a historical volatile period with prices hitting $140 barrel in the summer of 2008 and bottoming out near $40 in January 2009. Despite this volatility, the EPA failed to consider more than one price trajectory.

Figure 3 plots actual ethanol and gasoline prices since 2009 and the prices assumed in the RIA. The EPA used a wholesale gasoline price of $3.42 per gallon (corresponding to a crude oil price of $116 per barrel) and an ethanol price of $1.716 per gallon. In fact, they reported three cases for ethanol, with a comically narrow and precise range of $1.688 to $1.732. Observed ethanol prices ranged from $1.42 to $3.15 over this period, while gasoline prices ranged between $1.02 and $3.31. Moreover, the two prices were positively correlated, with high ethanol prices typically corresponding with high gasoline prices. The RIA would have presented a much clearer picture of compliance costs if it had incorporated price uncertainty into its analysis.

Rather than incorporating price uncertainty, the EPA focused its analysis on detailed modeling of the many potential types of biofuel, their sources, and a thorough accounting of their costs. To do so, the agency relied on a set of large-scale engineering and economic models. Large-scale models require substantial effort to implement, and they generate copious statistics. To cite one of many examples, oil refineries produce two main products (gasoline and distillate) and a slew of minor products. The RIA presents the estimated change in oil refinery production of 47 different products over five regions of the US.[28] Almost all the information is irrelevant to the RFS. Such detailed output creates the impression of rigor and precision when in fact it reflects numerous modeling assumptions made about the relevant economic systems. Moreover, the complexity of the models and the time required to run them preclude reasonable accounting for uncertainty.[29]

A complex model has numerous parameters that interact in often unknown ways. Suppose a modeler were to run the model with three different feasible values of the future price of crude oil. The resulting predictions of the model would depend on other parameters such as the price of ethanol, which necessitates running the model for, say, three different ethanol prices. Now, we have nine possible combinations to run—three ethanol prices for each of three oil prices. The results from these runs would depend on numerous other parameters, such as the prices of each of the refinery's 47 products and many others. Running the model for different values of each parameter may be impractical computationally because some of these models take hours to complete a single run. Even if the computational challenges can be overcome, the modeler is left with hundreds of predictions from the model, each one from a different set of parameter values to which the modeler has no way to assign a probability.[30]

Technology. The gasoline-powered internal combustion engine has reigned supreme for more than a century. Like all dominant technologies, it will eventually be replaced by something better, but no one knows what or when.

Figure 3. Prices of Ethanol and Gasoline

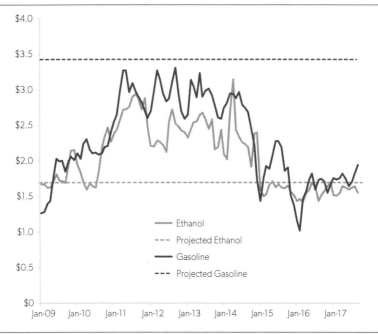

Note: The dashed lines show projected ethanol and gasoline prices in the RIA. The solid lines show actual prices.
Source: Nebraska Energy Office, "Ethanol and Unleaded Gasoline Average Rack Prices," 2017, http://www.neo.ne.gov/statshtml/66.html; and US Environmental Protection Agency, "Renewable Fuel Standard Program (RFS2) Regulatory Impact Analysis," February 2010, https://www.epa.gov/sites/production/files/2015-08/documents/420r10006.pdf.

Plug-in electric cars (including plug-in hybrids) went from essentially zero in 2010 to 3 percent of US car sales in 2015. Solar electricity generation increased more than 20-fold over the same period, and wind generation doubled. This does not mean that electric cars, charged by electricity from the wind and sun, will drive petroleum-powered vehicles out of the market, but it raises the possibility.

Alternatively, new discoveries may keep oil competitive as a fuel source. In recent years, new technology has allowed US oil producers, through a combination of horizontal drilling and hydraulic fracturing, to extract oil from oil shale. US oil production in 2008 was lower than at any time since 1950. With this new technology, 2015 production was 89 percent higher than 2008 and the highest since the previous peak in the early 1970s.[31]

High shale oil production was a major factor in the 50 percent drop in oil prices in late 2014. Lower oil prices made gasoline-powered cars more appealing to consumers. In fact, fewer electric cars were sold in 2015 than in 2014. This does not mean that electric cars are destined to be a niche product, but it does raise that possibility.

Hydraulic fracturing has also generated large increases in US natural gas production. With this jump in supply, natural gas has supplanted coal as the cheapest fuel for electricity generation in many parts of the country. Cheap natural gas has also raised the prospect of expanding its use in transportation, which would reduce carbon emissions relative to gasoline. To date, there has been little expansion in natural gas as a transportation fuel, in part because expansion would require a large investment in refueling infrastructure.[32]

Cellulosic biofuel is another potential new transportation fuel with climate benefits relative to gasoline. In spite of the RFS mandate, this technology has not produced significant amounts of fuel. In 2018, the EPA projects 14 million gallons of liquid cellulosic biofuel will be used in the US, which is about 0.01 percent of gasoline use.[33]

No one knows which technologies will come to dominate in transportation, yet the RFS picks one: biofuel. Reaching the statutory volumes will require breaching the blend wall, which in turn will require substantial investment in new infrastructure at gas stations to dispense high-blend ethanol fuels. In September 2015, the USDA distributed $100 million to fund 4,880 new fuel pumps and 515 storage tanks at 1,486 gas stations around the country.[34] At present, 3,015 of approximately 170,000 US gasoline stations sell E85,[35] so this funding will significantly increase capacity to deliver E85, but many more hundreds of millions will be required to make a substantial dent in the blend wall.

The infrastructure investment will be wasted if cellulosic biofuel does not become an economically viable fuel. This anecdote highlights a drawback of mandates in the presence of uncertainty about technological progress. Mandates encourage the industry to abandon alternative technologies in favor of the mandated technology, which can lead to technological lock-in—in other words, getting stuck with an inferior technology because the infrastructure already exists.

The Obama administration advocated an all-of-the-above approach to energy policy.[36] One interpretation of this principle is that it is open to any potentially useful innovations. Following this principle, analysts would be well served to consider potential new technologies when evaluating new policies. In particular, they should ask whether the policy has a significant opportunity cost because it reduces the option to develop alternative technologies in the future.

Emissions. A further source of uncertainty—one central to climate policy—is the unknown amount of warming caused by carbon emissions and its economic impacts. The equilibrium climate sensitivity is a parameter that describes the long-term increase in the annual global-average surface temperature from doubling atmospheric CO_2 concentration. Scientists estimate that the likely range for this parameter is 1.5°C to 4.5°C.[37] The top of this range is three times the bottom. Economic models of climate change such as the Dynamic Integrated Climate-Economy model[38] specify the economic impact of warming as a quadratic function of the temperature increase, so the top of their range of economic impacts is nine times the bottom of the range. If we then allow for uncertainty about the economic damage function, or any of the other parameters in the model, the range of potential outcomes expands further.

There is no agreement among economists on what this uncertainty means for climate policy. Martin Weitzman argues for aggressive carbon emissions reductions because of what he terms the "dismal theorem."[39] The dismal theorem states that the non-negligible possibility of catastrophe dominates all other considerations in cost-benefit analysis of climate policy. Standard cost-benefit analysis that focuses on the most likely outcome will favor policies that are much too passive.

Robert Pindyck also emphasizes the uncertain effects of climate change but argues that policies with insurance characteristics make more sense for avoiding extreme outcomes, rather than merely increasing the stringency of whatever policy would be applied in a world without uncertainty. He does not recommend specific policies.[40] However, Daron Acemoglou and his coauthors show theoretically how a research subsidy can have large benefits in addition to a carbon tax because it enables avoidance of environmental disaster.[41] Avoiding the potential for environmental disaster through the use of a carbon tax would require a much larger and more costly tax.

Overall, analysts need to think about the distribution of outcomes when formulating and evaluating policy: Focus projections of what could happen, rather than a single estimate of what will happen.

Lesson 2: Do Not Give the Regulator Too Much Discretion

The RFS legislation specifies the number of gallons of renewable fuel to be used each year. To implement the mandate, the RFS charges the EPA with converting the volume standard to a rate standard. Specifically, the legislation directs the EPA to take three steps by November 30 each year:

1. Obtain from the Energy Information Administration "an estimate, with respect to the following calendar year, of the volumes of transportation fuel, biomass-based diesel, and cellulosic biofuel projected to be sold or introduced into commerce in the United States."

2. Divide the RFS-mandated number of biofuel gallons by estimated petroleum fuel use to compute the percentage standard.

3. Require that each obligated party (typically oil refiners) show evidence that enough biofuel entered the market to meet the percentage standard for the petroleum fuel they sold.[42]

There is little discretion in these directions. The legislation gives the EPA a formula and a deadline by which to apply it. However, a subsequent clause introduces discretion: "EPA may waive the statutory volume in whole or in part if implementation would severely harm the economy or environment of a State, region, or the United States, or if there is an inadequate domestic supply."[43]

In 2012, a severe drought hit the Midwest, lowering corn yield by 16 percent from 2011 and generating a spike in prices. Governors from several states, including Arkansas and North Carolina, requested a waiver of the RFS on the grounds that firms in their states would be severely harmed. The affected firms were livestock producers and feed lots that rely on corn as an important source of animal feed. They hoped an RFS waiver would reduce corn demand from ethanol producers and thereby lower the price of corn to livestock producers.

The EPA denied the waiver request on November 27, 2012, and then began developing the 2013 RFS percentage standard. The agency proposed a rule in February, which it finalized in August 2013—after the year was

Figure 4. Price of Conventional Biofuel RINs

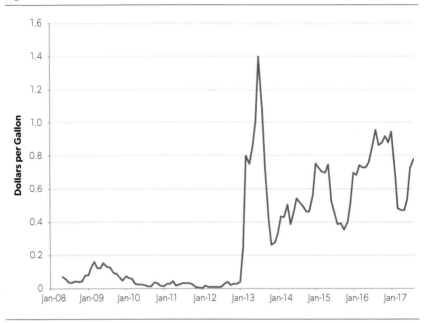

Source: Oil Price Information Service.

two-thirds over. The EPA justified enforcing the rule for the whole year on the grounds that the rule was not a surprise; it was essentially the same rule that had been proposed in February.

Figure 4 shows that RIN prices jumped from less than $0.05 to $1.40 per gallon in early 2013 as the industry realized that an above-blend-wall mandate would be enforced. The price had been below 6 cents per gallon for 2010 through 2012. This was the period when ethanol use was at the blend wall, but the RFS did not require above-blend-wall use of conventional ethanol (Figure 2). Prices were slightly higher in 2009, when oil prices dropped relative to corn prices, causing ethanol to become more expensive than gasoline.

The EPA apparently reversed course in August 2013 when it announced, "EPA anticipates that adjustments to the 2014 volume requirements are likely to be necessary based on the projected circumstances for 2014."[44] This announcement and several other announcements later that year caused RIN prices to crash from a high of $1.40 in July to $0.20 in November.

The biofuel industry reacted forcefully to the possibility of waivers, and the resulting political mayhem prevented the EPA from finalizing the required 2014 and 2015 biofuel volumes in a timely fashion. The industry spent almost two years in limbo, not knowing how much biofuel it should be using. Finally, in June 2015, the EPA proposed volumes for 2014, 2015, and 2016, which it finalized in December 2015. Because 2015 was almost over by this time, it set 2014 volumes at actual 2014 consumption and 2015 volumes at expected consumption.

The proposed 2016 volumes were initially lower than expected, causing RIN prices to drop from $0.75 to about $0.40 in June 2015, but the final volumes turned out higher, causing RIN prices to jump back up to about $0.75 in December.

In their study of the 2013 fluctuations in RIN prices, Gabriel Lade, Cynthia Lin Lawell, and Aaron Smith show how a change in the expected future stringency of the mandate affects current RIN prices and, therefore, current compliance costs.[45] This link arises because RINs can be banked for use in future compliance years, which means that RIN prices adjust to smooth expected compliance costs over time. If compliance is expected to be expensive next year because of the blend wall, then RIN traders will save current RINs, which reduces the number available for current compliance and raises current RIN prices.

The long delays in finalizing percentage standards created uncertainty in the industry. Investments in E85 infrastructure at this time would have made it possible to deliver more E85 to consumers, lowering marginal compliance costs. However, such investment has not yet happened. One problem with the uncertainty created by delays in agency decisions is that it deters investment and thereby undermines the statute.

A larger problem with agency discretion, however, is that it allows industry lobbies to direct policy. This problem is exacerbated if the policy's objectives are murky. Although energy security and climate-change mitigation are the policy's stated objectives, the history discussed earlier indicates that the corn lobby is a dominant driver of this policy. This group is motivated to maximize the amount of corn ethanol used, rather than climate policy. The other important lobby groups are the petroleum industry, which is motivated to minimize its costs of complying with the legislation, and the livestock industry, which is motivated to minimize the amount of corn used for ethanol. It is unlikely that a lobbying battle among these parties will produce effective climate policy because none of them are motivated by climate concerns.

The RFS is not the only legislation that has granted discretionary power to an agency. Both the Affordable Care Act and the Dodd-Frank financial reform act charged agencies with implementing often vaguely written legislation, opening up the opportunity for industry lobbies to drive policy in a nontransparent way.

Regulator flexibility can be beneficial. One way to incorporate uncertainty into policy implementation is to allow the regulating agency discretion to adjust over time. The potential reset of biofuel volumes in the RFS is a good example. If too little biofuel is being produced that the EPA must issue two consecutive 20 percent waivers, then the agency could reset the volumes for all years rather than issue a waiver every year. However, note two features of the reset: First, the statute specifies the formula the EPA should apply to determine whether a reset is required. Second, the purpose of the reset authority is to reduce the burden of annual rulemaking, rather than making the agency issue a new waiver every year.

These features highlight how the RFS could have reduced counterproductive EPA discretion in its implementation. Annual rulemaking has been possible only under perfect conditions. The 2012 drought and the 2013 blend wall caused long delays in setting the percentage standards. One simple fix would be to require percentage standards to be set at less frequent intervals, such as once every three years. Setting percentage standards over a longer horizon would also have the advantage of making the blend wall more transparent so that it operates more like a rate standard.

The clause that allows a waiver if implementation would cause "severe economic harm" has not been useful because it is too vague. It has produced challenges that have only delayed rulemaking. If such a clause were desired as part of the legislation, then it should have taken the form of a price cap on RINs. If costs of compliance exceed the cap, then firms are not forced to comply. Rather than using biofuel at RIN prices above the cap, obligated parties could purchase RINs from the EPA at the cap price. This adjustment would remove EPA discretion and remove the ability for rival industries to lobby the agency for favorable treatment.

Specifying transparent rules and formulas in legislation would place the policy burden on Congress rather than the regulating agency. This is especially important when the agency must mediate among competing industries, none of which has incentives aligned with the EPA, as with the RFS.

Lesson 3: Do Not Mandate Things That Do Not Exist

The RFS requires increasing amounts of cellulosic biofuel, but commercial production of that fuel has not materialized. The statute required cellulosic biofuel beginning in 2010, with volumes rising from 0.1 Bgal in 2010 to 1 Bgal in 2013 and 4.25 Bgal in 2016. Actual cellulosic biofuel use was zero in 2010 and 2013. It reached 0.14 Bgal in 2015 and is slated to reach 0.29 Bgal in 2018.

Originally, the expectation was that the cellulosic mandate would be met with liquid fuels—namely, diesel and ethanol made from cellulosic material such as crop residue, switchgrass, miscanthus, and wood. The EPA's RIA projected that 69 percent of cellulosic biofuel would be cellulosic diesel and the remaining 31 percent would be cellulosic ethanol.[46] However, less than 2 percent of the cellulosic biofuel RINs generated in recent years came from these two sources. The remainder was renewable natural gas (biogas) generated from landfills and other similar facilities.

The high percentage contribution of biogas to the cellulosic mandate was enabled by a rule proposed by the EPA in June 2013 and finalized in July 2014. This rule allowed biogas to count toward the cellulosic mandate by stating that "biogas generated by landfills, municipal wastewater treatment facility digesters, agricultural digesters, and separated MSW [municipal solid waste] digesters are predominantly cellulosic in origin." Before the rule, these fuels, which are used in natural gas–powered vehicles, had qualified as advanced biofuels for RFS compliance.

For 2018, the EPA projected that 4.8 percent of cellulosic biofuel RINs would be generated by liquid fuels. This is 4.8 percent of a cellulosic volume requirement that is 4.1 percent of the statutory volumes; thus, only 0.2 percent of the cellulosic liquid fuels prescribed in the RFS is being used.

The RFS did spur investment in research and development of cellulosic liquid fuels. In 2007, the US Department of Energy Biomass Program provided $385 million to support six large-scale cellulosic ethanol plants. Several hundred million dollars of Department of Energy money followed in later years to support cellulosic research and development. The major oil companies invested more than a billion dollars in biofuels research, much of it in partnership with universities and biofuel companies.[47] Since that time, these companies have mostly divested from cellulosic biofuels, but research continues in universities, institutes, and biofuels firms. Large-scale production of liquid fuels from cellulosic materials remains prohibitively costly.

The RFS has an escape valve that has allowed the EPA to waive the cellulosic mandate due to insufficient supply. Otherwise, the industry would have faced a choice between paying extremely high compliance costs and evading the regulation. Recent examples of such evasion in a similar context include Volkswagen's attempt to evade US air-quality standards by installing software that turns on the vehicle's emissions-control systems only when it is being tested.[48] Another example is automakers sending "golden vehicles" to be tested for compliance with Europe's ever-tightening fuel economy standards. These golden vehicles often have no back seats, nondurable tires, and other features that improve their fuel economy by up to 35 percent over standard road vehicles.[49]

Although it mitigates the potential for fraud and evasion, the escape valve also discourages private industry investment in research and development. If no one invests in the technology, then there will be no supply, and the EPA will waive the mandate. The mandate was not a credible threat.

How the RFS is implemented also limits its effectiveness in spurring the desired amount of investment. In principle, a firm that develops a successful cellulosic biofuel technology could generate a stream of valuable RINs that it could sell to recoup the costs of research and development. In practice, once the new technology has been developed, the firm that created it is unlikely to be able to monopolize it. New firms will enter and produce cellulosic biofuel at a low marginal cost, thereby lowering the price of RINs. Thus, unless firms believe that the patent system would allow them to recoup their investment cost, they will underinvest in the new technology even in the presence of a mandate.

Perhaps researchers will produce a breakthrough that will make cellulosic biofuels feasible. In fact, some recent innovations provide hope. Several firms are producing cellulosic ethanol from the fiber in corn kernels, which would otherwise not be used productively. POET, the country's largest ethanol producer, reported in late 2017 an important breakthrough in pretreatment, which has been the main barrier to commercial-scale cellulosic ethanol production.

Lesson 1 suggests that such research into cellulosic biofuels should continue. However, until it becomes commercially feasible, the cellulosic mandate must be considered a failure. Its only benefit has been to spur investment into cellulosic biofuel technology, but if the government wants to increase funding for research and development, it should fund it directly. If the government wants to encourage private firms to invest in the technology, it should offer matching grants. Policy is better when the policy instrument directly targets the policy objective.

Farm Bill Energy Title

The energy title first appeared in the 2002 Farm Bill, which authorized grants, loans, and loan guarantees to encourage research, development, and adoption of agriculture-based renewable energy. In the 2008 Farm Bill, the energy title shifted toward non-corn-based biofuels. This switch was motivated partly by concerns about economic and environmental consequences from directing such a large proportion of the corn crop into the fuel supply and partly by the impetus to support the RFS goal of expanding production of advanced biofuel. The 2014 Farm Bill extended most programs from the 2008 bill with new funding, although projected spending was less than 1 percent of projected non-nutrition spending in the bill.[50]

In terms of mandatory funding, the three largest programs in the 2014 energy title were the Rural Energy for America Program (REAP, $250 million), the Biorefinery Assistance Program ($200 million), and the Biomass Crop Assistance Program (BCAP, $125 million). These were the only programs with more than $100 million in total mandatory funding in 2014–18.

REAP provides grants and loan guarantees to rural small businesses and agricultural producers for research and development of renewable energy systems. It includes bioenergy, anaerobic digesters, geothermal, hydrogen, solar, wind, and hydropower, but it excludes any mechanism for dispensing energy at retail. The Biorefinery Assistance Program provides loan guarantees for construction or retrofitting of demonstration-scale biorefineries to understand the commercial viability of advanced biofuel production. BCAP offers financial assistance to owners and operators of forest and agricultural land who wish to produce biomass feedstocks.

Beyond the farm bill, the USDA has conducted other initiatives to support biofuels. Most notably, in 2015 the Biofuel Infrastructure Partnership (BIP) supplied $100 million in grants to fund up to half the costs of installing tanks, fuel pumps, and related infrastructure to dispense higher ethanol blends such as E15 and E85 at vehicle fueling locations. The economic argument for such spending is based on a network externality: A retail station will not invest in new infrastructure unless it thinks it will sell a lot of E85 or E15, and consumers are not going to switch to those fuels unless they are widely available.

At the very least, the BIP could have been used to estimate the magnitude of the network externality and the process of new fuel adoption. This would have required detailed data from participating stations on sales and prices before and after the intervention. Even better, the program could have used an experimental design to randomize the allocation of funds in a way that would have enabled researchers to quantify the network externality. Instead, the funds were dispensed with few data requirements and no experimental design.

Can measures such as the farm bill's energy title and the BIP improve the efficiency of the RFS? GHG emissions reductions are the main potential welfare benefit; thus, improving RFS efficiency requires that energy title spending must lower the total cost of achieving those emissions reductions. The RFS will generate substantial emissions reductions only if large volumes of cellulosic biofuels become available.

Significant use of cellulosic fuel first requires that technology and production processes develop sufficiently to make production of the fuel cost-effective. No one knows whether or when that will occur; cellulosic biofuel advocates have overpromised for many years. Significant barriers remain, including the high costs of transporting bulky cellulosic materials to a biorefinery, storing the materials without significant spoilage, and converting cellulosic biomass into fuel.

Most economists recommend subsidizing research into climate-change mitigation technologies, of which cellulosic biofuel is one example. This recommendation stems from the contention that private firms underinvest in research and development because potential spillovers (positive externalities) from new technologies or the inadequacies of patent law would preclude them from extracting the full benefits of their investments. Thus, a case could be made for the federal government to continue subsidizing cellulosic biofuel research and development through programs such as REAP.

However, cellulosic biofuel is just one of many potential climate-change mitigation technologies. It is beyond the scope of this chapter to assess whether the marginal research dollar should be directed toward cellulosic biofuel rather than solar power, wind power, vehicle electrification, or the numerous other possibilities. Moreover, it is *beyond the scope of the farm bill* to make this assessment. Funding for climate-change mitigation research and development would be better handled by an agency that can compare potential benefits across sectors, such as the National Science Foundation or the Department of Energy.

Getting cellulosic biofuel to market also requires the retail infrastructure to deliver these fuels, most likely in E85. It seems unlikely that an absence of retail infrastructure is delaying the development of cellulosic fuels. Such infrastructure could be built quickly if the technology existed to produce the fuel cost-effectively, and private firms would have a strong incentive to make the required investments. Thus, there appears to be little public good benefit to funding retail E85 infrastructure construction now.

In sum, the arguments for significant spending in the farm bill's energy title are unconvincing. If there is to be significant spending, the 2014 Farm Bill at least seems pointed in the right direction—namely, research and development of cellulosic biofuels. To maximize the benefits of such spending, the government should avoid repeating the mistakes of the BIP, which forfeited an opportunity to measure the effectiveness of the program and thereby spend government money more effectively in the future.

Conclusion

The year 2017 was the second-warmest year recorded on earth since at least 1880, ranking right behind 2016. Ranking third and fourth are 2015 and 2014. Eight of the warmest recorded years since 1880 have occurred in the past 10 years. Alarmed by the scientific consensus that carbon emissions from burning fossil fuels are the main cause of this warming, many governments have enacted policies to promote alternative fuels and reduce fossil fuel use.

Researchers have weighed in on the design and effectiveness of these policies. A Google Scholar search for "climate policy" returns about 130,000 hits. These thousands of studies included important points such as (1) the least expensive policy would be to put a price on carbon through a carbon tax or a cap-and-trade program, (2) research and development into clean energy and carbon sequestration technologies is imperative, and (3) carbon emissions represent a global externality, so coordinating policy across countries is vital. Rather than reiterate these well-established points, this chapter is concerned with the lessons we can draw from 10 years of the RFS, which is a centerpiece of US climate policy.

There are three general lessons:

1. Incorporate uncertainty. Policymakers should make, implement, and analyze policy with a view to what might happen, not a single projection of what will happen.

2. Do not give the regulator too much discretion. Political forces and legal challenges can undermine policy if the regulating agency has the discretion to repeatedly adjust the policy stringency.

3. Do not mandate things that do not exist. Mandates are an inefficient and ineffective method of forcing technological progress.

These lessons extend to many policy areas. Specific to the RFS, these lessons produce recommendations that, in hindsight, would have improved the policy. These recommendations are discussed throughout the chapter, but I collect them here to highlight them:

1. The mandate would have been better specified as a rate standard than a volume standard. Compliance costs are driven by the rate of biofuel blending rather than the amount of biofuel. Compliance cost volatility would have been lower, and the industry would have been able to

make investment decisions with a clearer view of future compliance costs (Lessons 1 and 2).

2. Incorporate uncertainty explicitly in future rulemakings. The blend wall and lack of cellulosic constraints would have been more transparent if the regulatory impact analysis had explicitly incorporated uncertainty (Lesson 1).

3. Rather than discretionary waiver authority, the RFS should have tied waivers to compliance costs and set a RIN price cap. If RIN prices rise to the cap, then allow obligated parties to purchase RINs from the EPA at the cap price rather than require additional biofuel (Lesson 2).

4. The EPA should be required to make multiyear rules rather than annual rules (Lesson 2).

5. Research and development of cellulosic biofuel technology should be funded directly, rather than indirectly through the cellulosic mandate (Lesson 3).

Can the farm bill assist in these improvements? I conclude that the only potential contribution from the farm bill's energy title is the fifth recommendation—namely, to subsidize research and development of cellulosic biofuel technology. However, I argue that the farm bill is not the optimal vehicle for funding such research. Rather, it should be handled by an agency that spans all climate-change mitigation technologies and can better assess the payoffs to the marginal research dollar.

Notes

1. This chapter draws heavily from research performed jointly with Gabriel E. Lade and Cynthia Lin Lawell.

2. White House, "President Bush Signs H.R. 6, the Energy Independence and Security Act of 2007," press release, December 19, 2007, https://georgewbush-whitehouse.archives.gov/news/releases/2007/12/20071219-6.html.

3. Douglas W. Elmendorf, letter to Rep. Frank D. Lucas (R-OK), January 28, 2014,

https://www.cbo.gov/sites/default/files/113thcongress-2013-2014/costestimate/hr2642lucasltr00.pdf.

4. Stephen P. Holland et al., "Some Inconvenient Truths About Climate Change Policy: The Distributional Impacts of Transportation Policies," *Review of Economics and Statistics* 97, no. 5 (December 2015): 1052–69, http://www.nber.org/papers/w17386.

5. A network externality exists when the value of a product depends on the number of users. For example, if enough consumers use a new fuel, then sufficient fueling stations will exist to make it appealing for more consumers to adopt that fuel. Network externalities create a chicken-and-egg problem in developing markets for new fuels.

6. Intergovernmental Panel on Climate Change, *Climate Change 2014: Synthesis Report*, 2015, http://ar5-syr.ipcc.ch/.

7. See, for example, William Nordhaus, *DICE 2013R: Introduction and User's Manual*, 2nd ed., Yale University, October 31, 2013, http://aida.wss.yale.edu/~nordhaus/homepage/documents/DICE_Manual_103113r2.pdf.

8. US Interagency Working Group on Social Costs of Carbon, "Technical Support Document: Technical Update of the Social Cost of Carbon for Regulatory Impact Analysis," November 2013, https://obamawhitehouse.archives.gov/sites/default/files/omb/assets/inforeg/technical-update-social-cost-of-carbon-for-regulator-impact-analysis.pdf.

9. White House, "President Bush Signs H.R. 6."

10. David White, "The Petroleum Resources of the World," *Annals of the American Academy of Political and Social Science* 89 (May 1920): 111–34, https://www.jstor.org/stable/1014212.

11. Newspaper articles expressing this expectation include Frederic Hasking, "Big Future for Alcohol," *Los Angeles Times*, November 2, 1919; *Los Angeles Times*, "What's Coming in Fuel Drama?," November 12, 1920; *New York Times*, "Auto Fuel Problem: English Clubs Provide Fund for Research in Alcohol Mixtures," April 27, 1919; *New York Times*, "Alcohol as a Fuel: Chemist Speaker Predicts That It Will Supplant Gasoline," October 19, 1919; Harry A. Mount, "More Alcohol Wanted: But This Demand Is for Cheap Kind as Substitute for Gasoline," *New York Times*, February 13, 1921; and *New York Times*, "Ford Predicts Fuel from Vegetation: He Says Electricity Will Heat Cities in the Future—Tells of Testing a New Flour," September 20, 1925. Michael Carolan studies peer-reviewed and popular press reports from this period and finds that alcohol fuel had strong support among scientists, automobile engineers, and farmers. Michael S. Carolan, "Ethanol Versus Gasoline: The Contestation and Closure of a Socio-Technical System in the USA," *Social Studies of Science* 39, no. 3 (June 2009): 421–48.

12. David E. Wright, "Alcohol Wrecks a Marriage: The Farm Chemurgic Movement and the USDA in the Alcohol Fuels Campaign in the Spring of 1933," *Agricultural History* 67, no. 1 (Winter 1993): 36–66.

13. Bills introduced in Congress include the Gasohol Motor Fuel Act of 1978 (S. 2533), Ethanol Motor Fuel Act of 1987 (H.R. 2052 and S. 1304), Amendment to the Energy Policy Act of 1992 (H.R. 554), Renewable Fuels Acts of 2000 and 2001 (S. 2503 and S. 670.IS), and Energy Policy Acts of 2003 and 2004 (H.R. 4503 and S. 2095).

14. US Department of Agriculture and US Department of Energy, "A Biomass Energy Production and Use Plan for the United States, 1983–90," 1983.

15. Ronald N. Johnson and Gary D. Libecap, "Information Distortion and Competitive

Remedies in Government Transfer Programs: The Case of Ethanol," *Economics of Governance* 2, no. 2 (July 2001): 101–34.

16. Ethanol was allowed a one-pound waiver in the Reid vapor pressure requirement.

17. 20/20 Biofuels Challenge Act of 2005 (S. 1609); and BOLD Energy Act of 2006 (S. 2571.IS and H.R. 5331.IH).

18. A gallon of biodiesel actually generates 1.5 RINs because biodiesel contains 50 percent more energy than ethanol.

19. A third possibility is E15, which is a blend of 15 percent ethanol and 85 percent gasoline. E15 is approved for use in all cars built since 2001, but it has not been adopted by the industry because it requires new tanks and dispensers to be installed at gas stations and fails to meet environmental requirements for summer gasoline (the Reid vapor pressure requirement).

20. The petitioners also make more nuanced arguments that moving the point of obligation to blenders would increase the incentive to blend biofuel and thereby lower RIN prices.

21. Sebastien Pouliot, Aaron Smith, and James H. Stock, "RIN Pass-Through at Gasoline Terminals" (working paper, University of California, Davis, February 22, 2017), https://scholar.harvard.edu/stock/publications/rin-pass-through-gasoline-terminals.

22. Kelsey Tamborrino, "RFS Changes on Hold," *Politico*, June 6, 2018, https://www.politico.com/newsletters/morning-energy/2018/06/06/rfs-changes-on-hold-243068.

23. US Department of Energy, "Alternative Fueling Station Locator," September 28, 2017, http://www.afdc.energy.gov/locator/stations/.

24. In its proposed rule released in June 2015, the EPA proposed waiving 22 percent of the mandate, but the final rule brought the waiver back below 20 percent.

25. Gabriel E. Lade, Cynthia Lin Lawell, and Aaron Smith, "Policy Shocks and Market-Based Regulations: Evidence from the Renewable Fuel Standard," University of California, Davis, November 2016, http://clinlawell.dyson.cornell.edu/RFS_policy_shocks_paper.pdf.

26. US Environmental Protection Agency, "Renewable Fuel Standard Program (RFS2) Regulatory Impact Analysis," February 2010, https://www.epa.gov/sites/production/files/2015-08/documents/420r10006.pdf.

27. US Energy Information Administration, *Annual Energy Outlook 2009*, March 2009, https://www.eia.gov/outlooks/archive/aeo09/index.html.

28. US Energy Information Administration, *Annual Energy Outlook 2009*, 834, Table 4.4-26.

29. For a more detailed discussion of the RIA, see Gabriel E. Lade, Cynthia Lin Lawell, and Aaron Smith, "Designing Climate Policy: Lessons from the Renewable Fuel Standard and the Blend Wall," http://clinlawell.dyson.cornell.edu/Lade_LinLawell_Smith_climate_policy_RFS_blendwall.pdf.

30. Constructing a complex model is like stacking building blocks to make a tower, and uncertainty analysis is like trying to ascertain which blocks can be removed without the tower collapsing, much like in the game Jenga. When building the tower, small errors in the placement of some blocks can compound to make the tower unstable, and the large number of blocks makes it difficult to determine how much each block could be moved without the tower collapsing. It is better to build a simpler tower.

31. In the same paper in which he predicted peak petroleum, David White also wrote, "Plainly, if the United States is to have oil to satisfy its needs in the future, it must secure adequate reserves in foreign countries, buy oil from foreign oil companies, or depend on oil shale production to fill the void." White, "The Petroleum Resources of the World," 129. It took 100 years, but the US has exercised all three of those options.

32 US Department of Energy, "Alternative Fuels Data Center: Natural Gas," August 11, 2017, http://www.afdc.energy.gov/fuels/natural_gas.html.

33. Total cellulosic biofuel use is projected at 288 million gallons, but most of this is renewable natural gas.

34. US Department of Agriculture, Farm Service Agency, "Biofuel Infrastructure Partnership," http://www.fsa.usda.gov/programsand-services/energy-programs/bip/.

35. US Department of Energy, "Alternative Fueling Station Counts by State," https://www.afdc.energy.gov/fuels/stations_counts.html.

36. Jason Furman and Jim Stock, "New Report: The All-of-the-Above Energy Strategy as a Path to Sustainable Economic Growth," White House, May 29, 2014, https://www.whitehouse.gov/blog/2014/05/29/new-report-all-above-energy-strategy-path-sustainableeconomic-growth.

37. Intergovernmental Panel on Climate Change, *Climate Change 2014*.

38. Nordhaus, *DICE 2013R*.

39. Martin L. Weitzman, "Fat-Tailed Uncertainty in the Economics of Catastrophic Climate Change," *Review of Environmental Economics and Policy* 5, no. 2 (Summer 2011): 275–92, https://scholar.harvard.edu/files/weitzman/files/fattaileduncertaintyeconomics.pdf.

40. Robert S. Pindyck, "Fat Tails, Thin Tails, and Climate Change Policy," *Review of Environmental Economics and Policy* 5, no. 2 (2011): 258–74, http://www.nber.org/papers/w16353.

41. Daron Acemoglu et al., "The Environment and Directed Technical Change," *American Economic Review* 102, no. 1 (2012): 131–66, https://economics.mit.edu/files/8076.

42. 42 USC § 7545, https://www.law.cornell.edu/uscode/text/42/7545.

43. 42 USC § 7545.

44. Environmental Protection Agency, "Regulation of Fuels and Fuel Additives: 2013 Renewable Fuel Standards," *Federal Register* 78, no. 158 (August 15, 2013): 49798.

45. Lade, Lin Lawell, and Smith, "Policy Shocks and Market-Based Regulations."

46. US Environmental Protection Agency, "Renewable Fuel Standard Program," 70, Table 1.2-3.

47. Ralph E. H. Sims et al. "An Overview of Second Generation Biofuel Technologies," *Bioresource Technology* 101, no. 6 (March 2010): 1570–80, http://www.sciencedirect.com/science/article/pii/S0960852409015508.

48. Brad Plumer, "Volkswagen's Appalling Clean Diesel Scandal, Explained," *Vox*, September 23, 2015, http://www.vox.com/2015/9/21/9365667/volkswagen-clean-diesel-recall-passenger-cars.

49. Jason Chow, Ruth Bender, and David Gauthier-Villars, "Europe's Auto Makers Keep Test Firms Close," *Wall Street Journal*, September 30, 2015, http://on.wsj.com/1o5h47B.

50. Mark A. McMinimy, "Energy Provisions in the 2014 Farm Bill (P.L. 113-79): Status and Funding," Congressional Research Service, February 22, 2016, http://nationalaglawcenter.org/wp-content/uploads/assets/crs/R43416.pdf.

Section IV

Regulation and Market Performance

9

Futures Markets Regulation

SCOTT H. IRWIN

Commodity futures markets provide both price discovery and risk-management opportunities for agricultural producers and agribusiness managers. It is not an overstatement to say that these markets are the central nervous system for much of the agricultural sector. Modern commodity futures (and options) markets provide key financial and risk-management services to agricultural producers and agribusinesses. For example, these markets are often used to develop forward contract prices for producers, even if agribusinesses do not directly participate in such markets. In addition, commodity futures markets are often used to establish settlement prices and, by extension, indemnity values for many crop insurance contracts. The US Commodity Futures Trading Commission (CFTC) is the primary regulatory agency for these markets.

The regulation of commodity futures and options markets has received considerable scrutiny in recent years, spurred on by the spike in food commodity prices during 2007–08 and several structural changes in the markets. Most notably, corn, soybean, and wheat futures prices all set new nominal price records in 2007–08. It is important to recognize that the history of agricultural futures markets is inexorably bound up with the cycles of agricultural prices. Periods of historically low prices (e.g., 1930s and mid-1980s) and high prices (e.g., late 1940s, mid-1970s, and mid-2000s) have led to public outcries about agricultural futures markets. In what can be considered an anti-speculation cycle (Figure 1), producers have attacked the legitimacy of futures markets when prices are low, and consumers have done so when prices are high.

Whichever situation dominates, the blame for undesirable price levels is not infrequently attributed to manipulation by speculators in futures

Figure 1. The Anti-Speculation Cycle in Commodity Futures Markets

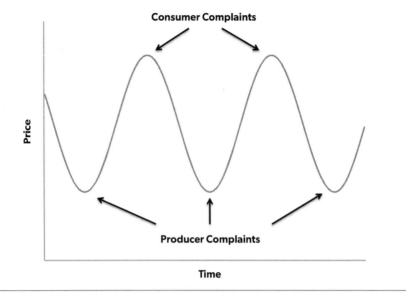

Source: Author.

markets. These complaints have led to attempts to regulate speculative trading in US agricultural futures markets through restrictive position limits, greater margin requirements, and even an outright ban on trading (onions). A discussion of the most salient regulatory issues in recent years follows.

Position Limits

Given the historical cycle between price levels and speculation concerns, it is not surprising that a global uproar about speculation ensued after the spike in food commodity prices during 2007–08. The rapid increase in prices coincided with emerging large-scale participation by a new type of speculator in commodity futures markets: financial index investors. These investors desire long-only exposure to an index of commodity prices for portfolio diversification, inflation hedging, and return enhancement. Concerns emerged in 2007–08 among other market participants, regulators, and civic organizations that the inflow into new commodity index invest-ments was the principal driver of the spike in agricultural and energy prices. This notion is most commonly associated with hedge fund manager Michael Masters and is often referred to as the "Masters Hypothesis."

The Masters Hypothesis essentially argues that unprecedented buying pressure from index investors created massive bubbles in commodity futures prices. In turn, these bubbles were transmitted to spot prices through arbi-trage linkages between futures and spot prices. The end result was that commodity prices—spot and futures prices—exceeded fundamental values by substantial margins, perhaps by as much as 80 percent. Masters used colorful language to draw attention to the issue, labeling index investors the "accidental Hunt brothers," drawing a parallel with the Hunt brothers' famous attempt to corner the silver market in 1979–80.

If the Masters Hypothesis were indeed true, this would raise major ques-tions about the efficiency of price discovery in agricultural futures markets and the usefulness of these markets for managing risk. Some policymakers were quick to adopt Masters-like arguments after the 2007–08 price spikes and pushed for regulations to limit commodity index activity and restrict speculation. Proposals ran the gamut from taxing transactions in commod-ity futures markets in order to cut down on speculation to creating a "vir-tual reserve" whereby a public agency would take futures positions opposite speculators to limit the harmful effects on market prices. It was not uncom-mon during this period to link concerns about speculation to world hunger, food crises, and civil unrest.

In the US, the 2010 Dodd-Frank Wall Street Reform and Consumer Pro-tection Act (Dodd-Frank) was the first major piece of legislation in response to the speculation controversy, and it laid the groundwork for more restric-tive speculative limits on commodity futures positions. The US has had a system of regulating the size of speculative positions in agricultural futures markets since the 1936 Commodity Exchange Act (CEA) passed. These lim-its had never been extended to nonagricultural commodity futures markets when these markets were launched, and, in some cases such as crude oil, they grew enormously. Dodd-Frank directed the CFTC to develop specula-tive position limits for all futures markets for physical commodities.

The CFTC's first attempt at position limit rules for all commodity futures markets under Dodd-Frank was passed after a highly contentious and public debate in October 2011. The rule was quickly challenged by futures indus-try groups and then vacated in September 2012 by US District Court Judge Robert Wilkins on grounds that the CFTC did not establish the necessity of the limits as required by the CEA. "Necessity" in this context refers to the original language in the CEA that grants the CFTC the ability to fix position limits that are necessary to prevent excessive speculation "causing sudden or unreasonable fluctuations or unwarranted changes in the price of [a] com-modity."[1] The CFTC skirted this issue in the proposed rulemaking, claiming that Dodd-Frank requires it to implement the new rules irrespective of the necessary conditions in the original CEA. Judge Wilkins disagreed and indi-cated that the necessity finding was in fact required.[2]

The CFTC both appealed the Court decision and simultaneously formu-lated new position limit rules in 2013. While the CFTC ultimately dropped the Court appeal, it approved the new and revised position limit rules in November 2013. The CFTC subsequently extended or reopened the com-ment period numerous times to provide industry participants ample oppor-tunity to weigh in on the controversial rulemaking.

In 2015, the CFTC formed the Energy and Environmental Markets Advi-sory Committee (EEMAC) to review empirical evidence on speculation and commodity price movements and to make recommendations regarding posi-tions limits. The EEMAC voted overwhelmingly (8–1) to recommend that the CFTC not finalize the proposed position limit rule, relying largely on the fact that the proposed rule fails the necessity finding that the CEA requires due to the lack of empirical evidence. Finally, in December 2016 the CFTC re-proposed its position limits for derivatives but delayed formal consideration of the rulemaking until the Trump administration was in place. As of this writ-ing, no further action has taken place on the December 2016 proposal.

The CFTC does not have an easy task in establishing the necessity described in the CEA and required by the US District Court. An economist's interpretation of excessive speculation as outlined in the CEA represents a relatively high hurdle. First, the speculation must be causing the price fluctuations. Second, the price changes must be sudden, unreasonable, or unwarranted. This definition of excessive speculation seemingly excludes speculation that does not cause price changes and thereby implies a possi-ble temporal ordering. Likewise, the CEA description precludes speculation that warrants price changes—that is, informed speculation.

Fortunately, a large number of studies have been published in the past decade to assist the CFTC in making a necessity determination for expanding position limits to all commodity futures markets.[3] These studies have played an important part in the public debate and the regulatory process. Most of the academic studies fail to find evidence directly tying commodity index funds to agricultural futures price movements, which is obviously inconsistent with the Masters Hypothesis. The basic nature of the findings can be demonstrated graphically.

Before presenting the graphical results, it is helpful to briefly review the available data on index positions. The primary source of data on index positions is the CFTC, which began reporting in 2007 the positions held by commodity index traders (CITs) in 12 agricultural futures markets in the "Supplemental Commitments of Traders" (SCOT) report as a complement to the traditional "Commitments of Traders" (COT) report. The SCOT report is released each Friday in conjunction with the traditional COT report, and it shows the combined futures and options positions of CITs as of Tuesday's market close. A significant limitation of the public CIT data is the lack of data before 2006. The CFTC collected additional data for selected grain futures markets over 2004–05 at the US Senate Permanent Subcommittee on Investigations' request, and these data are used here to supplement the public data.

Figures 2–5 show the weekly net-long positions of CITs and weekly nearby futures prices for Chicago Board of Trade (CBOT) corn, CBOT soybeans, CBOT wheat, and Kansas City Board of Trade (KCBT) wheat from January 6, 2004, through March 14, 2017. Several interesting patterns are apparent. First, the rapid increase in CIT positions occurred from 2004 to 2006. Over this interval, long positions held by index traders quadrupled in corn and CBOT wheat, more than doubled in soybeans, and tripled in KCBT wheat. Clearly, the buildup in CIT positions generally was concentrated in the 2004–06 period, not the 2007–08 period associated with the alleged commodity bubble under the Masters Hypothesis. If CIT buying had a substantial market impact, it would have been most likely during 2004–06 when CIT market holdings increased dramatically. Second, in three of the four markets—corn, CBOT wheat, and KCBT wheat—CIT positions peaked long before the peak of prices during 2007–08. There is more of a parallel buildup in CIT positions and prices during 2007–08 in soybeans.[4]

Figure 2. Weekly CIT Net-Long Position and Nearby Price in the CBOT Corn Futures Market, January 6, 2004–March 14, 2017

Figure 3. Weekly CIT Net-Long Position and Nearby Price in the CBOT Soybean Futures Market, January 6, 2004–March 14, 2017

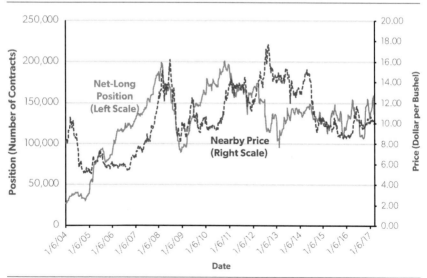

Figure 4. Weekly CIT Net-Long Position and Nearby Price in the CBOT Wheat Futures Market, January 6, 2004–March 14, 2017

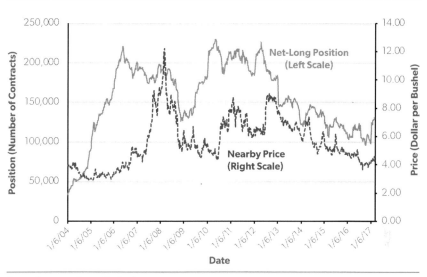

Source: Commodity Futures Trading Commission.

Figure 5. Weekly CIT Net-Long Position and Nearby Price in the KCBT Wheat Futures Market, January 6, 2004–March 14, 2017

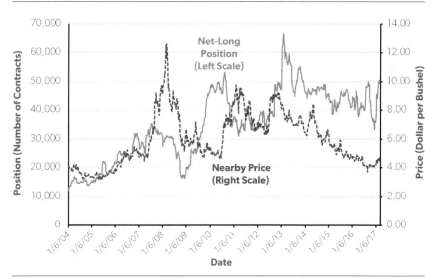

Source: Commodity Futures Trading Commission.

Figure 6. Contemporaneous Relationship Between Weekly Changes in CIT Net-Long Position and Nearby Returns in the CBOT Soybean Futures Market, January 13, 2004–March 14, 2017

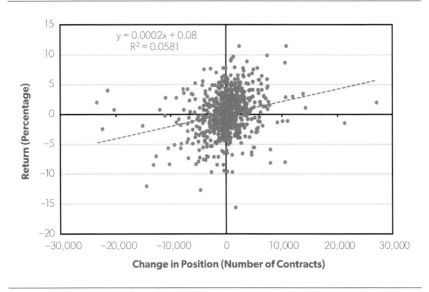

Source: Author's calculations.

Correlation analysis provides a more formal perspective on the relationships in Figures 2–5. As an example, Figure 6 shows that there is a positive contemporaneous association between changes in net positions held by CITs and price changes (returns) in the soybean futures market. The simple correlation coefficient is a moderate 0.24, but the relationship is statistically significant at the 5 percent level. However, this contemporaneous analysis cannot distinguish between the increase in CIT positions and other correlated shifts in fundamentals. In other words, contemporaneous correlation does not imply causation.

A more rigorous test is to correlate the current weekly return with the change in CIT positions lagged by one week. Figure 7 shows that this relatively minor change in timing completely eliminates the contemporaneous relationship estimated in Figure 6. From the perspective of this more rigorous hurdle, there is no evidence that changes in CIT net-long positions lead to higher (or lower) market prices. Similar results are found for the other three agricultural futures markets.

Figure 7. Lagged Relationship Between Weekly Changes in CIT Net-Long Position and Nearby Returns in the CBOT Soybean Futures Market, January 13, 2004– March 14, 2017

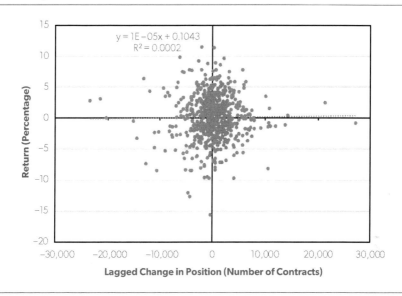

Lagged Change in Position (Number of Contracts)

Source: Author's calculations.

Given the inconsistency of the timing between the period of most rapid buildup in commodity index positions and the spikes in agricultural futures prices, it should not be surprising that most studies fail to find a significant link between index positions and futures price changes. A few studies report evidence of a significant price impact of index positions in agricultural futures markets.[5] However, when interpreting results from these studies, it is important to keep in mind the basic tenants of the Masters Hypothesis. Specifically, the Masters Hypothesis and related concerns about speculative impacts rest on the following assertions: (1) Long-only commodity index funds were directly responsible for driving commodity futures prices higher, (2) the deviations from fundamental value were economically large, and (3) the impact was pervasive across commodity futures markets. That is, empirical evidence should demonstrate a direct link between long-only commodity index positions and commodity futures prices that result in economically large deviations from fundamental value. The few empirical studies that claim to support the Masters Hypothesis tend to fall short on at least two if not all three of these criteria.[6]

In sum, an overwhelming preponderance of evidence indicates commodity index investment was not a primary driver of the agricultural price spikes over the past decade. No smoking gun has been found regarding index investment causing massive bubbles. The evidence simply does not support a necessity finding regarding index trading and "sudden or unreasonable fluctuations or unwarranted changes in the price of [a] commodity." It is hard to argue with the conclusion of Michael Cosgrove—a member of the EEMAC—who after reviewing the empirical evidence noted that "instead of being obvious, it is undetectable. If we claim that elephants were playing in the backyard then we would expect to see their footprints. The alleged excessive speculation, if it is taking place, is leaving no data footprints."[7]

The debate over position limits was long, costly, and, ultimately, unnecessary. In the words of Thomas Glauben, "The alarmism about financial speculation should be classified as a false alarm."[8] It is important to emphasize this does not mean that index investment in commodity futures markets did not have any impact. The rise of large-scale index investment may have had rational, non-bubble impacts in commodity futures markets, such as increasing market integration and reducing risk premiums. These types of market impacts typically come under the heading of "financialization" and may be permanent but relatively small over short time spans. This should not be confused with the large and irrational bubble impacts under the more policy-relevant Masters Hypothesis.

While the acrimonious debate about index investment has ultimately proved unnecessary, it has had the salutary effect of focusing attention on the position limits regime that has been in place for the agricultural futures markets since the 1930s. At the heart of the existing regulations is the definition of a bona fide hedger versus a speculative trader. Making this distinction has always been hard in practice, leading some to question whether it is possible to do so in any meaningful way. For example, Thomas Hieronymus made this argument after another round of legislative changes on the subject in the mid-1970s:

> The definition of hedging in the context of the CFTC Act is extraordinarily difficult, if not impossible. It assumes that

"hedging" and "speculation" are at least different, if not opposite. They are not. All hedges are more or less speculative and all
speculative positions are more or less hedged. There is not a simple solution to the problem of establishing a process for granting
exceptions from speculative position and trading limits.[9]

The controversy surrounding the CFTC's proposal to change existing
rules about aggregating positions for hedgers as part of the recent position limit rulemakings nicely illustrates just how arcane and difficult the
task of defining bona fide hedging positions has become. The problem has
undoubtedly grown over time with the entry of new market participants
such as hedge funds and index funds that blur the distinction between
hedgers and speculators.

The timing seems ripe to reform the current position limit regime for agricultural futures markets. Allen Paul developed a proposal that still provides
a useful starting point. Echoing Hieronymus, the foundation of his proposal
is the impossibility of classifying trading into speculation and hedging:

> Regulation of commodity markets should avoid, where possible,
> classifying trading into the categories of "speculating" and "hedg-
> ing." These terms represent only the polar positions of a large
> continuum. Most business uses of futures trading are combina-
> tions of speculative and hedging elements. Hence, classification
> of commitments into one or the other category often is arbitrary.[10]

Paul emphasizes there is still a need for position limits, but the limits
should be focused on preventing manipulation during the delivery period
of contracts, when the greatest danger for artificiality of prices is present.
He makes no distinction between hedgers and speculators with respect to
manipulation in the delivery period. Historically, hedgers or commercials
have been implicated in more delivery period manipulations than speculators. Paul's proposal is as follows:

> Larger holdings would be permitted early in the life of the con-
> tract and this amount would be reduced to the threshold level at
> the start of the delivery month and then further reduced as the

delivery month progresses. This general constraint would permit much wider business use of futures than now because of the difficulty of qualifying many business uses as bona fide hedges.[11]

In essence, Paul proposes to set wide position limits for *all traders* early in a contract's life and then reduce these in a linear manner as expiration approaches. Such a system would match position limits to a real problem—manipulation in the delivery period—and would eliminate all the problems associated with defining a bona fide hedger.

Non-Convergence

Convergence of cash and futures markets during the delivery period is a bedrock principle of commodity futures markets. In a competitive market, arbitrage will force the futures price at expiration to equal the cash price. A well-designed contract will involve few actual deliveries because the terms of the contract balance the interests of long and short futures position holders. As Hieronymus notes, "A futures contract is a temporary substitute for an eventual cash transaction. In markets that work, delivery is rarely made and taken; futures contracts are entered into for reasons other than exchange of title."[12]

Storable and non-storable agricultural futures markets have a long history of idiosyncratic pricing anomalies that have arisen due to market manipulation in the form of corners and squeezes.[13] In these episodes, a trader or group of traders acquires market power by building up large long positions in futures and the cash market at delivery locations. Once having cornered the market, the trader or group of traders can use their market power to squeeze the shorts in the market and force prices during the delivery period to be much higher.

The classic signature of these episodes is always a short-run artificiality in the level of expiring futures prices compared to cash prices in the delivery area and in the level of the expiring futures prices compared to deferred futures prices. The artificiality seldom lasts more than one contract cycle because of the difficulty of preventing additional supplies from being moved into deliverable position. This is one of the reasons that regulators pay so much attention to the issue of deliverable supply.

CBOT corn, wheat, and soybean futures contracts exhibited dramatic convergence failures over 2005–10. The initial response by exchange staff, market participants, regulators, and academic researchers was to focus on potential structural and manipulation problems with the grain futures contracts. Consequently, the number of warehouse receipts and shipping certificates that a trader could hold was limited, delivery locations were expanded in some cases, and other contract terms were adjusted, all to no avail as the convergence problems continued after changes were made. In particular, the magnitude of the convergence failures was unprecedented, with futures contracts expiring at prices up to 35 percent greater than the prevailing cash grain price. The duration and magnitude of the convergence failures were unlike anything seen in the modern record of grain futures markets and signaled that traditional explanations would not be sufficient to address the problem.

Heated public and academic debate ensued as to the possible causes of the convergence failures. In a twist on the Masters Hypothesis, many blamed new financial index traders in grain futures markets. For example, a report by the US Senate Permanent Subcommittee on Investigations claimed commodity index trading caused the non-convergence in wheat markets.[14] The report maintained that index fund capital overpowered arbitrageurs, who may have been limited by credit constraints and uncertainty over the time it would take to realize arbitrage profits.

Others simply maintained that the grain futures markets were "broken" and questioned whether the contracts would remain a useful hedging tool. Without effective hedging, grain producers, merchandisers, and consumers have less ability to manage risk, a development that could mean potentially serious welfare effects. Likewise, the price discovery function of agricultural futures markets could be seriously threatened. Despite these fears, average daily trading volume in the CBOT corn, soybean, and wheat contracts doubled between September 2005 when non-convergence first appeared and September 2008 when non-convergence was at its worst.

The first major breakthrough occurred when Scott Irwin et al. discovered a direct relationship between the carry and delivery location basis.[15] The term "carry" as used in the grain futures markets refers to the market-determined return of holding stocks of grain. It is measured as the difference in the futures prices between the first deferred contract and the expiring contract.

Figure 8. Basis at Toledo, Ohio, and Percentage of Full Carry on the First Day of Delivery for CBOT Wheat Futures, March 2000–September 2010 Contracts

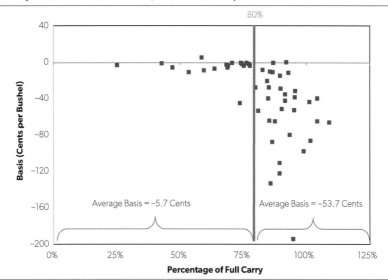

Source: Scott H. Irwin et al., "Spreads and Non-Convergence in Chicago Board of Trade Corn, Soybean, and Wheat Futures: Are Index Funds to Blame?," *Applied Economics Perspectives and Policy* 33, no. 1 (2011): 116–42.

This difference is often stated as a percentage of the "full carry" for storing grain between the delivery period for two contracts. It is computed as the sum of interest opportunity costs for storing grain and the maximum storage rate that can be charged under the contract specifications. The storage rates are necessary to compensate those holding the grain that backs delivery instruments (warehouse receipts or shipping certificates).

Figure 8 shows that non-convergence, or weak delivery location basis, systematically appears in CBOT wheat whenever the carry begins to exceed about 80 percent of full carry.[16] Similar relationships are present in corn and soybeans.

Based on this finding, the CBOT instituted a variable storage rate (VSR) system for the wheat contract in July 2010 that allowed the contract storage rate to adjust up and down based on the percentage of full carry.[17] If the percentage of full carry averaged more than 80 percent during the specified averaging period, the maximum storage rate for the wheat contract increased 3 cents per bushel for the next-to-expire contract; if the percentage of full carry averaged less than 50 percent, the maximum storage rate decreased

3 cents per bushel. The maximum storage rate increased from 6 cents per bushel before VSR to a peak of 20 cents per bushel in a little over a year. Large non-convergence failures subsequently disappeared in CBOT wheat and have not reappeared.

While empirically it was clear that adjusting contract storage rates upward was the key to solving the convergence problems plaguing grain futures contracts during 2005–10, the underlying market dynamics that created the problem in the first place were not yet well understood. The second major breakthrough occurred when Philip Garcia, Irwin, and Aaron Smith developed a dynamic rational expectations model of commodity storage and showed that the convergence failures were generated by a disequilibrium between the price of storage in the physical market for grain and the storage rate paid to holders of the delivery instrument for the grain futures contracts.[18]

Figure 9 illustrates the problem using a classic supply-of-storage framework.[19] The cost of carry on the y-axis represents the equilibrium price paid for storing grain for one period, and the x-axis represents the equilibrium amount of grain inventory that is stored at this price. Panel A shows a case with high inventory and a high price of storing physical grain because the demand for storage is high. The equilibrium price of storing grain in the physical market in this case exceeds full carry in the futures market (determined by the fixed maximum storage rate on the futures contract), and this is the heart of the problem. The futures spread cannot go any higher than full carry; otherwise, risk-free arbitrage would be possible between futures contracts.

But this in turn means that grain hedged in the futures market earns a lower storage return than unhedged grain in the cash physical market. Something has to give to equate the return to storing hedged and unhedged grain, and that something is the delivery location basis, which widens enough to restore equilibrium in the storage market. Panel B shows a case with low inventory carryover and a price of physical storage below full carry on the futures contract. In this case, there is no disequilibrium, and the delivery location basis is zero.

The analysis is more complex for the multi-period case, but the essential insight is that the current delivery location basis widens by the expected value of positive "wedges" between the price of storage in the physical

Figure 9. Convergence and the Price of Storage

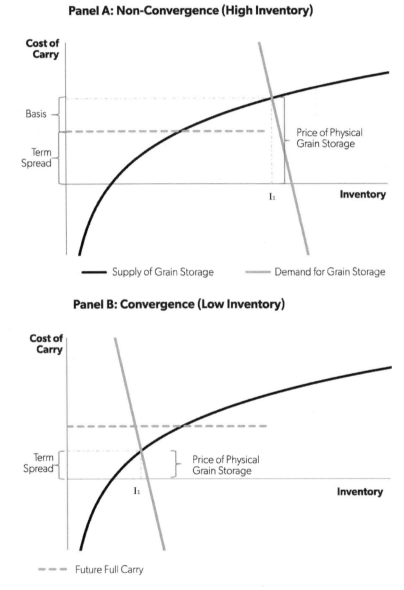

Panel A: Non-Convergence (High Inventory)

Cost of Carry

Basis

Term Spread

Price of Physical Grain Storage

I_1

Inventory

——— Supply of Grain Storage   ═══ Demand for Grain Storage

Panel B: Convergence (Low Inventory)

Cost of Carry

Term Spread

Price of Physical Grain Storage

I_1

Inventory

– – – Future Full Carry

Source: Philip Garcia, Scott H. Irwin, and Aaron Smith, "Futures Market Failure?," *American Journal of Agricultural Economics* 97, no. 1 (2015): 40–64.

market and full carry determined by the fixed contract storage rate. Consider a simple example in which the wedge between the price of physical storage and the maximum storage rate is 5 cents per month, and this wedge is expected to last for 12 months. The current delivery location basis does not widen by 5 cents but instead by 60 cents (5 cents x 12 months = 60 cents) to reflect the cumulative value of the expected disequilibrium. This is an important insight because it shows how relatively modest wedges between the physical price of storage and the contract storage rate can generate a surprisingly wide delivery location basis if the wedges are expected to persist for a long time.

Garcia, Irwin, and Smith conducted econometric tests for CBOT corn, soybeans, and wheat and for KCBT wheat that supported the predictions of their model, with the expected discounted wedge closely mapping the magnitude of non-convergence.[20] They also tested whether commodity index investment contributed to convergence failures as suggested by the US Senate Permanent Subcommittee on Investigations and found no evidence to support this claim. Their work also convincingly demonstrates that the upward VSR adjustments in storage rates for CBOT wheat followed increases in the price of storage in the physical wheat market. Some in the wheat trade have vehemently argued that the causality is reversed, when the evidence clearly indicates this is not the case. Finally, their analysis showed why non-convergence could not be solved by changing delivery points, limiting the holding of delivery certificates, or forcing delivery load-out—as many advocated. Instead, the solution was to simply raise the contract storage rate.

One intriguing puzzle is why grain market futures trading volume could increase in the midst of such severe non-convergence problems. Garcia, Irwin, and Smith's model suggests a solution to the puzzle. In short, traders can do the math and add the difference between market and contract storage rates to the delivery location basis. This requires a certain level of market sophistication regarding the relationship between futures prices, cash prices, and storage rates. Nonetheless, some market participants may have lacked the ability to decode the message from market prices and as a result may have been confused about how to interpret market signals. This could have adversely affected stockholding, price discovery, and risk-management strategies.

Non-convergence problems did not entirely disappear after 2010. In May 2016, another major episode of non-convergence began for the KCBT wheat futures contract. The fixed storage rates for the KCBT contract were raised in the wake of the 2005–10 convergence problems. However, in retrospect the increases were clearly not large enough in light of the size of the 2016 wheat crop and subsequent increases in the demand for storage. The KCBT will implement a VSR system similar to that already in place for CBOT wheat starting in March 2018. The expectation is that this will reduce non-convergence problems in KCBT wheat as it has for CBOT wheat.

At this point there is agreement that recent convergence problems in grain futures contracts were due to contract storage rates that were too low relative to the market clearing price of storage in the physical market. The only real question is what the best approach to adjusting contract storage rates is and whether that approach should be extended to the remaining grain futures markets (CBOT corn and soybeans). One approach is the aforementioned VSR system, which has the advantage of providing market participants with a prespecified rule for adjusting futures storage rates.

However, there can be some added volatility in the price spreads between contracts when the market is close to the threshold for adjusting rates. The other approach is to simply raise and lower fixed contract storage rates as conditions change. This is the system used by the futures exchanges in the US for most of the past 150 years. The advantage of this system is that there is no uncertainty about carry calculations. The disadvantage is uncertainty about whether and when rates will be adjusted by the exchange.

Electronic Trading

Until recently, the basic structure of agricultural futures markets had been remarkably stable over time. Irwin and Dwight Sanders argue that a trader from the latter part of the 19th century magically transported to the trading pits of the waning years of the 20th century might have been surprised by the size of the agricultural futures markets but not by the way trading was conducted or the main types of participants.[21] This would no longer be true with the transition from the telephone and open outcry trading platform to the computer and electronic order matching platform in the past decade—arguably the biggest structural change in the futures markets since they began more than 150 years ago.

Market participants, exchange officials, and regulators have all struggled to adapt to this revolution in the trading environment. In the old open out-cry pit system, capacity was limited by the number of traders and their abil-ity to physically process orders, and trading speed was constrained by the ability to signal trades by hand and voice. In the new electronic markets, trading takes place literally at the speed of light, and there is no theoretical constraint on capacity.

A host of issues have been presented by the transition to electronic trading that go by colorful names such as spoofing, quote stuffing, and predatory trading. However, none have approached the intensity of concern directed toward high frequency traders (HFTs). While widely discussed and debated, there is no agreed-upon definition of an HFT. Albert Menkveld provides a useful perspective:

> A formal definition does not exist but most associate HFT with extremely fast computers running algorithms coded by traders who trade for their own account. Collectively, their participation rate in trades is typically a couple of deciles (SEC 2010). These traders typically do not work at the deep-pocket sell-side banks, but at privately held firms. They therefore need to keep their positions small and short-lived to keep the capital tied up in mar-gin accounts in check. They trade a lot intradaily and avoid car-rying a position overnight. These characterizations suggest that HFTs are best thought of as a new type of intermediary, either benefiting market quality or hurting it.[22]

Concerns about HFTs in agricultural futures markets spilled into the headlines in 2016 when cattle producers pointed the finger at HFTs as the reason for the sharp drop in cattle prices during 2015. The controversy is summarized by Gregory Meyer:

> Cowboys and Flash Boys are headed for a showdown as sav-age price swings whip Chicago's cattle futures market. A US beef industry already squeezed by plunging prices has become

Figure 10. Differenced High-Low Price Volatility for CBOT Corn Futures Around USDA Crop and Inventory Report Announcements, July 2009–14

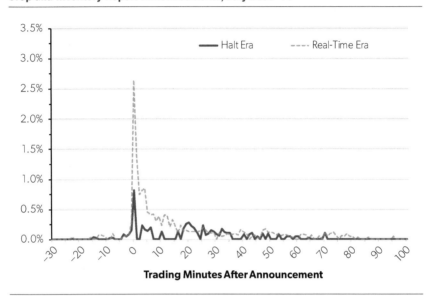

Trading Minutes After Announcement

Note: Significant at the 5 percent level.

Source: Michael K. Adjemian and Scott H. Irwin, "USDA Announcements in Real-Time," *American Journal of Agricultural Economics*, April 26, 2018, https://doi.org/10.1093/ajae/aay018.

aggravated by gyrations on the Chicago Mercantile Exchange. The cattlemen's prime suspect: high-speed trading firms that have marched into futures markets as the old pits fall silent. . . . "We're seeing these limit-up and limit-down [move] with no changes in the fundamentals. There's nothing that would otherwise be driving that kind of action outside of just computers. That's what concerns us," said Colin Woodall, vice-president of government affairs at the cattlemen's association.[23]

It is tempting to dismiss the concerns of cattle producers about HFTs as just another example of the anti-speculation cycle. After all, it is exceedingly difficult to connect a price drop in live cattle futures of $70 per hundredweight over an 18-month period to trading that occurs at the level of a millisecond. But this does not mean HFTs do not raise legitimate policy issues.

The markets are fundamentally different with electronic trading. In particular, speed advantages for the fastest traders allow the potential for a variety of new strategic trading not even imaginable under the old pit trading system.

Electronic trading has also raised policy concerns in other ways. For example, important US Department of Agriculture (USDA) crop and inventory reports have long been released outside the regular trading hours for the CBOT grain futures markets. This allowed market participants a lengthy time-out to read and digest the information provided by these USDA reports before trading resumed. The expansion in trading hours under electronic trading made it much more difficult for the USDA to maintain its decades-old convention of releasing USDA crop and inventory reports outside of trading hours.

Starting in May 2012, the USDA recognized this new reality and began releasing crop and inventory reports in real time during CBOT trading hours. Many market participants expressed concerns about the change to real-time release of USDA reports, in particular, increased price volatility and the economic advantage provided by HFT trading speed. The latter worry is that HFTs could capture the lion's share of the market impact of USDA crop and inventory reports before other more traditional (human) traders have time to react.

Michael Adjemian and Irwin analyzed the impact of the change to real-time release of USDA crop and inventory reports.[24] Figure 10 clearly shows that corn futures prices are more volatile in the minutes immediately following release of USDA reports in the real-time era.[25] Their results confirm that when grain futures markets are permitted to discover prices freely in response to USDA reports, the adjustment process is not instantaneous as markets experience heightened volatility in response to news relative to what was observed during the era of non-real-time release (trading halts). In addition, markets now appear to have more difficulty distinguishing between the newsworthiness of USDA reports, at least in the short run. Figure 10 also shows that these differences persist only for a handful of trading minutes. These mixed results suggest that the debate about real-time release of USDA crop and inventory reports is likely to continue.

Conclusions

Two issues have been paramount in recent years regarding the regulation of futures markets. The first issue is the role that speculation by financial index investors played in the commodity price spikes of the past decade. This was the fuel for the long and acrimonious debate in the US over more restrictive speculation position limits in commodity futures markets. The issue has been more or less settled with the preponderance of evidence indicating that commodity index trading was at most a minor player in recent price spikes. This has left the push for more restrictive limits on speculative trading in commodity futures markets dead in the water.

The second issue is the massive convergence failures in grain futures markets during 2005–10. This is an issue that truly has a happy ending from a regulatory standpoint. It turns out that the problem is relatively simple: Storage rates that are part of contract designs were simply set too low for market conditions. Once contract rules were altered to raise storage rates, the worst of the problems largely disappeared. Recent and more moderate non-convergence problems suggest that the issue needs continued monitoring and that further increases in storage rates may be necessary.

One issue that has emerged in recent years is likely to be the focus of futures market regulation for the foreseeable future. The transition from a telephone and open outcry trading platform to a computer and electronic order matching platform is arguably the biggest structural change in futures markets since they began more than 150 years ago. This is raising issues that could not even be imagined in the old pit trading system. Since the issues with electronic trading are relatively new, there is limited academic or government research that can be used to assess these concerns. This will undoubtedly be a major area of research and regulatory attention in coming years.

Notes

1. Excessive Speculation, 7 USC § 6a (2010).
2. The latest chapter in this ongoing controversy came in January 2017, when the US House of Representatives passed the Commodity End User Relief Act, which, in addition to reauthorizing the CFTC through 2021, directs the CFTC to impose and implement

position limits as it finds necessary, provided the CFTC makes a finding before imposing such limits. In commenting on this latter provision, Rep. Mike Conaway (R-TX) stated from the House floor that "prior to Dodd-Frank, the law was clear: If the Commission wanted to impose position limits, it first had to make a determination that such limits would, in fact, diminish, eliminate or prevent the burdens of excess speculation. Post Dodd-Frank, the courts have ruled that additions to the statute have rendered it ambiguous." If this provision is eventually approved by the US Senate and signed into law by President Trump, it would likely be the final nail in the coffin of current efforts to expand position limits. Charlie Passut, "House Passes CFTC Reauthorization Bill with Amendment Making Position Limits Optional," NGI's Daily Gas Price Index, January 13, 2017, http://www.naturalgasintel.com/articles/109055-house-passescftc-reauthorization-bill-with-amendment-making-position-limits-optional.

3. To gain a sense of how rapidly the academic literature on the subject has expanded, consider that no less than six review papers have been published in recent years: Scott H. Irwin and Dwight R. Sanders, "Index Funds, Financialization, and Commodity Futures Markets," *Applied Economic Perspectives and Policy* 33, no. 1 (2011): 1–31; Bassam Fattouh, Lutz Kilian, and Lavan Mahadeva, "The Role of Speculation in Oil Markets: What Have We Learned So Far?," *Energy Journal* 34 (2013): 7–33; Scott H. Irwin, "Commodity Index Investment and Food Prices: Does the 'Masters Hypothesis' Explain Recent Price Spikes?," *Agricultural Economics* 44 (2013): 29–41; Ing-Haw Cheng and Wei Xiong, "The Financialization of Commodity Markets," *Annual Review of Financial Economics* 6 (2014): 419–41; Matthias G. Will et al., "Is Financial Speculation with Agricultural Commodities Harmful or Helpful? A Literature Review of Empirical Research," *Journal of Alternative Investments* 18, no. 3 (2016): 84–102; and Marco Hasse, Yvonne S. Zimmerman, and Heinz Zimmerman, "The Impact of Speculation on Commodity Futures Markets—A Review of the Findings of 100 Empirical Studies," *Journal of Commodity Markets* 3, no. 1 (2016): 1–15.

4. Nicole Aulerich, Scott Irwin, and Philip Garcia examine the growth of index positions using nonpublic daily position data from the CFTC's Large Trader Reporting System for all 12 agricultural futures markets included in the SCOT report. They show that the fastest period of growth in all but a few of the SCOT markets was during 2004–06. Nicole M. Aulerich, Scott H. Irwin, and Philip Garcia, "Bubbles, Food Prices, and Speculation: Evidence from the CFTC's Daily Large Trader Data Files," National Bureau of Economics Research, May 2013.

5. Miguel Robles, Maximo Torero, and Joachim von Braun, "When Speculation Matters," International Food Policy Research Institute, February 2009; Christopher L. Gilbert, "Speculative Influences on Commodity Futures Prices 2006–2008," UN Conference on Trade and Development, 2010; Christopher L. Gilbert and Simone Pfuderer, "The Role of Index Trading in Price Formation in the Grains and Oilseeds Markets," *Journal of Agricultural Economics* 65, no. 2 (2014): 303–22; and Marco Lagi et al., "Accurate Market Price Formation Model with Both Supply-Demand and Trend-Following for Global Food Prices Providing Policy Recommendations," *Proceedings of the National Academy of Sciences* 112, no. 45 (2015): E6119–E6128.

6. For a detailed discussion of this point, see Dwight R. Sanders and Scott H. Irwin, "Bubbles, Froth and Facts: Another Look at the Masters Hypothesis in Commodity

Futures Markets," *Journal of Agricultural Economics* 68, no. 2 (2017): 345–65.

7. Commodity Futures Trading Commission, Energy and Environmental Markets Advisory Committee, *Report on EEMAC's 2015 Review and Consideration of the CFTC's Proposed Rule on Position Limits*, February 25, 2016.

8. Thomas Glauben et al., "Alarm or Rather False Alarm? A Literature Review of Empirical Research Studies into Financial Speculation with Agricultural Commodities," Leibniz Institute of Agricultural Development in Central and Eastern Europe, December 2012.

9. Thomas A. Hieronymus, *Economics of Futures Trading for Commercial and Personal Profit*, 2nd ed. (New York: Commodity Research Bureau, 1977), 328.

10. Allen B. Paul, *Treatment of Hedging in Commodity Market Regulation (No.1538)*, US Department of Agriculture, Economic Research Service, 1976, iii.

11. Paul, *Treatment of Hedging in Commodity Market Regulation (No.1538)*, 18.

12. Hieronymus, *Economics of Futures Trading for Commercial and Personal Profit*, 340.

13. Hieronymus, *Economics of Futures Trading for Commercial and Personal Profit*, chap. 15.

14. Permanent Subcommittee on Investigations, *Excessive Speculation in the Wheat Market*, US Senate, https://www.hsgac.senate.gov/subcommittees/investigations/hearings/excessive-speculation-in-the-wheat-market.

15. Scott H. Irwin et al., "Spreads and Non-Convergence in Chicago Board of Trade Corn, Soybean, and Wheat Futures: Are Index Funds to Blame?," *Applied Economics Perspectives and Policy* 33, no. 1 (2011): 116–42.

16. Figure 8 was reprinted from Irwin et al., "Spreads and Non-Convergence in Chicago Board of Trade Corn, Soybean, and Wheat Futures."

17. The VSR system was based on a prepublication version of Irwin et al., "Spreads and Non-Convergence in Chicago Board of Trade Corn, Soybean, and Wheat Futures."

18. Philip Garcia, Scott H. Irwin, and Aaron Smith, "Futures Market Failure?," *American Journal of Agricultural Economics* 97, no. 1 (2015): 40–64.

19. Figure 9 was reprinted from Garcia, Irwin, and Smith, "Futures Market Failure?"

20. Garcia, Irwin, and Smith, "Futures Market Failure?"

21. Irwin and Sanders, "Index Funds, Financialization, and Commodity Futures Markets."

22. Albert J. Menkveld, "The Economics of High-Frequency Trading: Taking Stock," *Annual Review of Financial Economics* 8 (2016): 2.

23. Gregory Meyer, "Cattlemen Lock Horns with Futures Exchange over Market Volatility," *Financial Times*, January 25, 2016, https://www.ft.com/content/6eed1268-c130-11e5-846f-79b0e3d20eaf.

24. Michael K. Adjemian and Scott H. Irwin, "USDA Announcements in Real-Time," *American Journal of Agricultural Economics*, April 26, 2018, https://doi.org/10.1093/ajae/aay018.

25. Figure 10 was reprinted from Adjemian and Irwin, "USDA Announcements in Real-Time."

10

Agricultural Contracts and Competition Policies

TOMISLAV VUKINA AND XIAOYONG ZHENG

Aside from land-tenure contracts typical of agrarian economies types, two main versions of contracts that we observe in the modern agriculture in the US are some form of marketing and production contracts, sometimes jointly referred to as alternative marketing arrangements (AMAs).[1] Both of those span the space between markets and hierarchies reserved for the so-called hybrid organizations. As established by a large literature on the trade-off among organizational forms, the leading characteristics of these alignment processes is the degree of asset specificity combined with uncertainty. The main insight permeating this literature is that problems of coordination, combined with risk of opportunism and reinforced by uncertainty, are always pushing in the direction of more centralization.[2] The framework proposed by Oliver Williamson,[3] which correlates asset specificity with transaction costs to explain the trade-offs among markets, hybrids, and hierarchies (firms), can be used to explain the emergence of contracting in agriculture.

As seen from Figure 1, the simple model considers three broad modes of organization: spot (cash) markets, hybrids, and vertically integrated firms. The horizontal axis indicates the degree of intensity of coordination, also interpreted as the degree of asset specificity, whereas the vertical axis measures the cost of governance (transactions) associated with implementation of various modes of organization. Uncertainty could be introduced explicitly into the model, but here it is tacitly subsumed under the effect it has in relation to asset specificity. All three cost curves are positively sloped, indicating that governance cost increases as the centralization of coordination or asset specificity increases.

Under standard assumptions, rational economic agents will seek an arrangement that keeps them on the lower envelope of transactions or

Figure 1. Trade-Off Among Alternative Modes of Organization: Before Regulation

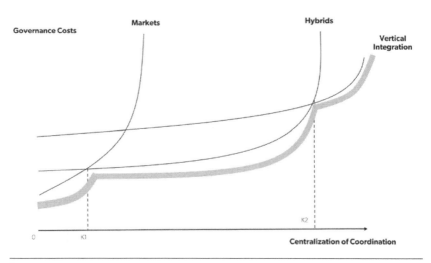

Source: Authors.

governance costs indicated by the thick line. As seen from the figure, hybrids (marketing and production contracts) present the dominant mode of organization of business activities in the K1 and K2 zone in which parties remain legally autonomous and keep control over significant parts of their decision rights while sharing assets that they coordinate via these hybrid arrangements. As will be shown later, this simple stylized model is particularly helpful for illustrating impacts of changes in public policy.

According to James MacDonald and Penni Korb, contract use in agriculture has spread widely since 1969, when the Census of Agriculture first asked about contract use.[4] In 1969, 5 percent of farms used contracts, which covered 11 percent of the total value of agricultural production. These numbers increased to 10 percent of farms covering 28 percent of production in 1991 and to 13 percent of farms and 33 percent of production in 1996. The number of farms with contracts peaked in 1996 and later declined because of the redefinition of farms, which allowed more small entities to be defined as farms. Because only 0.3 percent of farms with sales below $10,000 used contracts in 2013, their expansion in the total farm population reduced the share of all farms with contracts.

In contrast, the share of agricultural production under contracts continued to grow slowly and unevenly until 2011, when 40 percent of the value of production was covered by contracts. Then, in 2013 the share of agricultural production under contracts fell sharply to 35 percent. The main reason for this drop is attributable to changes in relative prices, which led to a substantial increase in the share of crops (especially corn, soybeans, and wheat) in total value of production. With less contracting in crops (again, especially in corn, soybeans, and wheat), the increase in the share of crops in the overall value of production reduced the share of production covered by contracts.

As already hinted above, the use of contracts in agriculture varies significantly across commodities. Contracting is less common in major field crops than in other segments of agriculture. Based on James MacDonald,[5] contracts covered less than a fifth of the total value of corn (17 percent), soybeans (19 percent), and wheat (13 percent) production in 2013, but farms that used contracts placed 49, 60, and 61 percent of their corn, soybeans, and wheat production under contracts, respectively. Contract production leans more heavily toward specialty crops, hogs, and poultry.

For example, contracts accounted for 84 percent of the value of all poultry production in 2013. However, contracts accounted for 100 percent of the value of poultry production on farms that used contracts. The same numbers are 74 percent and 98 percent for hogs and 32 percent and 92 percent for cattle. In peanuts and tobacco, contract use expanded sharply after the elimination of the federal marketing quota programs in the early 2000s. In tobacco, contracts covered virtually all production by 2008, compared to about 25 percent in 2000. In peanuts, contracts covered 60–80 percent of production after 2004 compared to 25–45 percent in the 1996–2002 period.

In addition to variations in contract production across commodities, we also observe significant variations in the types of contracts used. In 2008, all contracts' share in total value of agricultural production was 38.5 percent, of which 21.7 percent belonged to marketing contracts and 16.8 percent to production contracts. The use of marketing contracts favored crops (14.9 percent) against livestock (6.9 percent), whereas the share of production contracts was almost entirely exhausted by livestock production (16.3 percent), with only 0.5 percent belonging to crops.[6]

The main difference between marketing and production contracts is the ownership and control of production factors, which creates the need for different compensation schemes. In marketing contracts, all critical farm-level production factors are owned and controlled by the farmer. Marketing contract represents an agreement (between a farmer and a buyer) that specifies a price or a pricing formula, a delivery outlet, and a quantity to be delivered. Typically, the pricing formula will have some bonus structure that incentivizes the farmer to supply some desired quality attributes. In production contracts, farm-level production factors are shared between a farmer and a contractor, and the contract specifies production (husbandry) practices to which a farmer has to adhere. The compensation schedule is a fee that would typically consist of a piece rate and some type of bonus structure that incentivizes the farmer to produce the commodity efficiently. In general, neither input nor output prices enter the farmer's compensation formula.

Because the objective of this chapter is to provide insights and policy directions on the market competition ramifications of agricultural contracts, we will focus entirely on livestock contracts, where competition issues are more pronounced. The existing literature[7] has shown that producers of the largest field crops move in and out of their contracts easily and that they combine contracts with other marketing channels freely. Moreover, producers typically rely on multiple contracts with different contractors, and various storage options and changes in cropping patterns provide them with further marketing flexibilities.

Except perhaps for specialty crops, buyer concentration and resulting market power does not play an important role. On the other hand, production contracts, predominantly present in livestock production (poultry and hogs), commit contract growers more closely to specific integrators and for longer periods of time. In addition, the fact that significant economies of scale in processing may limit the number of viable integrators in one geographic area and that live animals cannot easily travel long distances raise competition issues to the forefront of policy debates.

The rest of the chapter organizes the material by the type of controversial features surrounding different AMAs. First, we discuss controversies surrounding the AMAs in general and the legislative attempts to ban them. Then, we discuss issues pertaining only to production contracts. The final section concludes with our specific policy recommendations.

AMAs in General

In livestock industries such as cattle, hogs, and broilers, transactions between farmers and packers are completed using either the spot market or AMAs. Spot market transactions refer to transactions that occur immediately, or "on the spot." These transactions usually happen within two weeks of the slaughter date of the animals. And as mentioned above, AMAs refer to all possible alternatives to the spot market and mainly production and marketing contracts. Marketing contracts are formal agreements specifying terms for transfer of livestock using prespecified price or payment formula. Some of these formulas link the final payment to farmers to the price prevailing in the spot market for the same livestock, while others link the final payment to other things such as the price for meat products and feed price. The contracts are usually entered in at any time between placement of livestock on feed and two weeks before the slaughter date.

Production contracts specify the division of production inputs supplied by the two parties, the quality and quantity of a particular output, and the type of the remuneration mechanism for the grower. The livestock are owned by the packer, who also assumes most of the price risk and some of the production risk. Usually packers provide farmers the young animals, feed, and supporting services throughout the production process, while the farmers provide the housing of the animals and the growing services.

The relationship between the spot market and the AMAs is straightforward in terms of quantity transacted. Given the same demand for meat products by the consumers, more transactions through the AMAs mean fewer transactions through the spot market. During the past 30 years, packers have relied more heavily on AMAs to satisfy their slaughter needs. As a result, the share of transactions conducted on the spot market has decreased. For example, in 1999, 36 percent of the market for hogs involved transactions on the cash and spot market,[8] but this share had decreased to 24 percent by 2004–05,[9] to only 5.2 percent by 2010,[10] and finally to 3 percent by 2013.[11]

However, the relationship between the two channels in terms of price is more complicated. Higher transaction prices through the AMAs will attract more farmers to supply the livestock through AMAs. This will decrease both supply and demand to the spot market, resulting in an ambiguous effect on spot market price. Most of the studies of the US-fed cattle market find that AMAs have either a mild negative or an ambiguous effect on the spot market price.[12] On the other hand, the spot market remains important for price discovery.[13]

As mentioned above, many contracts or agreements in AMAs employ the so-called top-of-the-market pricing practice,[14] which links the final price paid to farmers to the spot market price for the same livestock. For example, the US Department of Agriculture's Agricultural Marketing Service (USDA-AMS) groups different kinds of livestock transactions into six marketing channels in its daily mandatory price reporting (MPR). One of the channels is called "market formula purchases," which includes all purchases of livestock by a packer in which the pricing mechanism is a formula price based on a market for the same livestock or the corresponding meat products. About 40 percent of all livestock transactions are conducted in this channel.[15] Because of this link, the spot market price also feeds back to the transaction price in the AMAs.

Benefits of AMAs. In the livestock industries, both farmers and packers face nontrivial risks in their production and marketing activities. For farmers, the main risks involved are production risk, price (both input and output) risk, and marketing timing risk. Production risk mainly comes from the fact that livestock production is a time-consuming and complicated process, and this process can be affected by many factors such as weather and animal diseases over which farmers do not have full control. Price risk comes from uncertainty in both input (feed) and output (livestock) prices. Finally, marketing timing risk can be serious because once the animals reach their optimal weight for slaughter, feed conversion rate starts decreasing, and keeping them on hand is fairly costly to farmers.

Packers face their own risks as well. The meat packing process shows substantial economies of scale in processing and waste management due to the high fixed costs of running the packing plants and the highly automated nature of the production process.[16] Hence, capacity underutilization risk is a major risk for the packers. If packers cannot secure enough hogs with good and uniform quality, their plants cannot run at full capacity, and the associated implicit cost is fairly high. In addition, packers also face price risk, both for inputs (mainly the livestock) and outputs.

AMAs provide farmers and packers a way to attenuate these risks, which is one of the major reasons why AMAs and marketing and production contracts in particular penetrated so fast during the past three decades in the US livestock industries. Marketing contracts are essentially forward sales contracts between farmers and packers. These contracts are usually signed several weeks or months before the animals are ready for slaughter. Hence, the marketing timing and the capacity underutilization risks are eliminated for the farmers and packers, respectively.

Marketing contracts also include clauses on how the transaction price will be determined. For some marketing contracts, the transaction price is linked to the spot market, as mentioned above. For others, formulas such as cost plus, price window, and price floor are used. In cost-plus contracts, prices are determined by the costs of producing the livestock, which include feed, production, and management costs, plus a profit margin. Therefore, the transaction price in cost-plus contacts is independent of the spot market price, and the price risk is eliminated entirely for farmers with this type of contract. Also, no matter whether the production costs are high or low, farmers always obtain a certain profit margin. Packers, however, still face some price risks as livestock production costs still fluctuate over time.

In price-window contracts, there is an upper and a lower bound for the transaction price. If the spot market price is within this price window, the transaction price is the same as the spot market price. Otherwise, the transaction price equals one of the bounds. Price-floor contracts are a special type of price-window contracts in which the upper bound is infinity. Therefore, this type of marketing contract also attenuates price risk for farmers and packers to a certain degree. Overall, transactions conducted through marketing contracts or AMAs in general are associated with fewer price volatilities or risks than transactions completed on the spot market.[17]

Under another important AMA, production contracts, packers own the livestock before slaughter. During the production process, packers provide young animals, feed, vaccination services, transportation services, and so forth, and farmers provide land, labor, and production facilities. When the livestock reach the market weight, they are removed from the farms and transported to the packers' processing and packing plants. Farmers are then compensated for their growing services. Therefore, under production contracts, the price and marketing timing risks are eliminated for the farmers. Their production risk is also reduced.

For the packers, the capacity underutilization and the livestock price risks are eliminated, and since production contracts give them more control over the production process, the livestock produced are more likely to meet their quality requirements. In return, packers take over the input (e.g., feed) price risk and part of the production risk from the farmers. That production contracts' popularity is on the rise in recent years indicates that ensuring the livestock raised is meeting their quality standards is more important for packers.

The reduction in various risks with the use of AMAs increases farmer welfare significantly. Farmers who use AMAs are found to be more risk averse than those who rely on the spot market,[18] and welfare increases for these risk-averse farmers when risks are reduced or eliminated. Although packers or firms are usually assumed to be risk neutral in economic models because firm owners can diversify their portfolio, the reduction in various risks with the AMAs also benefits them because it reduces the risk diversification costs.

AMAs also benefit the packers in the sense that organizing the procurement of livestock through multiple channels mitigates the information asymmetry problems.[19] For example, producing own livestock on packer-owned farms instead of solely relying on outsider producers keeps packers better informed of competitive costs and practices. At the same time, even if own production of livestock is relatively more efficient than relying on outside suppliers (perhaps because of non-contractible, relationship-specific investments), packers would want to at least partly rely on outsiders to keep pressure on in-house management to produce efficiently. In addition, procuring livestock using multiple marketing arrangements enhances packers' bargaining power when negotiating with suppliers. The threat of walking away with no deal and still being able to secure enough livestock through another channel gives a packer an upper hand when negotiating purchases.

The benefits of AMAs do not stop with farmers and packers. They benefit consumers as well. An important advantage of AMAs is that through contracts packers can specify various attributes of the livestock to be exchanged and to specify price premiums and discounts associated with those attributes.

Therefore, packers can incentivize producers to produce better-quality livestock or the kind of livestock that consumers prefer.

Researchers[20] have analyzed quality differences in livestock across AMAs and tested whether various quality attributes used by the industry are significantly different across AMAs. They found that different AMAs are associated with different levels of quality of livestock. Even though the rankings are not unique, they found that marketing contracts (especially other purchase arrangements and other market formula purchases) are consistently associated with higher-quality livestock than negotiated (spot market) purchases. Furthermore, an examination of the relationship between the proportion of AMAs used to procure livestock and the quality of resulting meat products indicates that a higher proportion of AMA use is associated with higher-quality meat products. Therefore, AMAs also benefit consumers as they provide them with better-quality meat products.

Consumers will also see fewer price volatilities in the meat products when more livestock transactions are channeled through the AMAs for two reasons. First, the reduction in capacity underutilization risk for the packers through the use of AMAs means the supplies of meat products will be more stable, and hence their prices will be more stable. Second, fewer fluctuations in the prices packers pay livestock farmers will translate into fewer fluctuations in the prices packers charge the consumers. In the sense that most consumers are believed to be risk averse to a certain degree, reducing the price risks for consumers will increase their welfare.

Concerns About AMAs and Legislative Attempts to Ban Them. Although AMAs bring many of the benefits discussed above, there are also concerns about AMAs. First, a significant share of livestock are formula priced using the reported average spot market price from USDA-AMS's mandatory price reports as a base price in the formulas.[21] However, due to the rising popularity of AMAs, the spot market has become thin.

For example, as mentioned above, the share of hogs transacted through the spot market had decreased to only 3 percent by 2013.[22] This raises many concerns about whether the reported prices still convey useful and accurate market information as they were designed to do when Congress passed the Livestock Mandatory Reporting (LMR) Act of 1999. What are the sources of variations in the reported price? Do changes in reported prices from day to day reflect changing market fundamentals or just nuances of which packers are participating in the spot market each day? Could a particular packer easily manipulate the spot market to its advantage?[23] If reported prices are sensitive to which plants are buying the livestock on any given day, prices may meander from day to day not necessarily because of fundamental changes in supply or demand but because of which plants bought the livestock on the spot market.

For those using USDA-AMS price reports for market information, the reported price change from one day to the next may not be a reliable indicator of evolving market conditions. Also, an increase in the price variation in the spot market price will be translated into an increase in the variation in contract prices through formula pricing agreements. This will increase the price risk for buyers and sellers in the AMAs channel as well. Kayode Ajewole, Ted Schroeder, and Joe Parcell[24] studied the US hog market for these issues and found indeed the publicly reported daily prices are sensitive to which packing plants buy hogs. Furthermore, they found that transaction prices comprising the MPRs are not normally distributed. Hence, reporting the mean and standard deviation of the prices does not give the full picture to market participants.

Second, AMAs depress spot market price for at least two reasons. First, having the majority of their livestock supplies committed through the AMAs, packers have more negotiation power when they come to the spot market. As a result, farmers have to accept a lower price. Second, Tian Xia and Richard Sexton[25] show that when contract prices are linked to the spot price to be determined later, packers have fewer incentives to compete aggressively on the spot market because doing so would increase their purchasing costs for the livestock coming from the AMAs. As a result, farmers receive a lower price. Indeed, Tomislav Vukina et al. found that, as anticipated in the US hog market, an increase in either contract or packer-owned hog sales decreases the spot price for hogs.[26] Specifically, the estimated elasticities of industry-derived demand indicate that a 1 percent increase in contract hog quantities causes the spot market price to decrease by 0.88 percent and that a 1 percent increase in packer-owned hog quantities causes the spot market price to decrease by 0.28 percent.

Third, AMAs tend to benefit farmers with large operations more than their smaller counterparts. As there are significant transaction costs in negotiating and implementing contracts, packers are more likely to form contractual relationships with large producers rather than smaller ones. Therefore, large producers can reap the benefits of AMAs while small farmers take a hit because the cash market remains their main marketing channel for their livestock. This will further widen the income inequality between farmers with large and small operations.

These concerns about AMAs led to a series of legislative attempts to ban their use when the 2002 Farm Bill was under consideration. On December 13, 2001, the United States Senate approved the so-called Johnson Amendment to the Senate Farm Bill, making it unlawful for a packer to own, feed, or control livestock intended for slaughter more than 14 days before slaughter.[27] The amendment includes exemptions for packing houses owned by farmer cooperatives and packers with less than 2 percent of national slaughter. The amendment was approved 51–46 and became part of the Senate Farm Bill.

In early 2002, the amendment language was clarified to prohibit arrangements that give packers "operational, managerial, or supervisory control over the livestock, or over the farming operation that produces the livestock, to such an extent that the producer is no longer materially participating in the management of the operation with respect to the production of the livestock."[28] The new language was approved 53–46 on February 12, 2002. However, this amendment faced strong opposition in the House and was eventually not included in the final version of the 2002 Farm Bill.

There were also similar debates about banning the AMAs when the 2008 Farm Bill was under consideration. In the end, the attempt to ban AMAs failed again. But the 2008 Farm Bill did include several new clauses related to contract farming. It requires packers to maintain written records that provide justification for differential pricing or any deviation from standard price or contract terms offered to different farmers, and it requires packers to file sample contracts with the USDA's Grain Inspection, Packers and Stockyards Administration (GIPSA). It bans certain unfair, deceptive, and unjustly discriminatory practices or devices packers use. It also requires packers to identify their dealers, and it bans packers from purchasing livestock from other packers or dealers associated with other packers. No serious attempts to ban the AMAs were made during the debate, and no new clauses regarding contract farming were included in the 2014 Farm Bill debate. Next, we discuss the controversial issues surrounding the production contracts in particular and the legislative attempts to regulate them.

Production Contracts

The history of attempts to regulate livestock production contracts is rather long.[29] Most of the attempts, either on the state or federal levels, have been deflected by the industry's successful lobbying. The most recent attempt of the federal government to regulate livestock production contracts is the GIPSA 2010 proposal to amend the Packers and Stockyards Act (P&S Act) under the 2008 Farm Bill.

Its intention was to address the increased use of contracting in the marketing and production of livestock and poultry by entities subject to the P&S Act. The stated goal of regulation was to level the playing field between packers, live poultry dealers, and swine contractors and the nation's poultry and livestock producers. Probably the most controversial proposal was to significantly regulate using tournaments in settling poultry contracts. Specifically, the proposed rule said that "if a live poultry dealer is paying growers on a tournament system, all growers raising the same type and kind of poultry must receive the same base pay. No live poultry dealer shall offer a poultry growing arrangement containing provisions that decrease or reduce grower compensation below the base pay amount."[30]

Additional proposals would also require poultry integrators to rank growers in settlement groups only with other growers with similar house types. In December 2011, GIPSA published the Implementation of Regulations Required Under Title XI of the Food, Conservation and Energy Act of 2008,[31] which went into effect on February 7, 2012. Most of the original proposals were dropped or modified. Those that remained were provisions regarding the suspension of delivery of animals, rules about the additional capital investment criteria, provisions regarding the breach of contract, and provisions regarding arbitration. The proposed regulation on the tournament system was among the provisions not included in document. However, GIPSA plans to seek additional public comments related to tournament system with an objective to reconsider possible finalization of this rule in the future. So let's address the issue of tournaments first.

Tournaments. The central feature of the cardinal tournament compensation scheme currently used in almost all broiler contracts is that individual growers are compensated based on their individual performance relative to the group average performance. The existing literature on production tournaments emphasizes their favorable theoretical properties. The main rationale for using tournaments in the context of contracting with risk-averse growers is that they provide income insurance by filtering away common production uncertainty while maintaining a correct incentive structure to mitigate moral hazard.

Theofanis Tsoulouhas and Vukina[32] showed theoretically that, absent bankruptcy concerns, a two-part piece-rate tournament is in fact a linear approximation of the optimal incentive contract. However, risk sharing is not the only rationale for using tournaments. At least two other important advantages of tournaments justify their use in broiler contracts. Both of those work to lower the costs of contracting and are therefore useful in explaining the prevalence of production contracts and the near-complete absence of company-owned chicken farms.[33]

First, payments schemes based on tournaments require no change as technology improves. Since technological change is largely embodied in feed and chicks supplied by the integrator to all growers in a tournament, they represent a common shock that is differenced out, and the contract payments do not have to be renegotiated as technology improves. Second, tournaments commit the integrator to a fixed average payment per pound of live weight (because bonuses and penalties cancel each other out precisely by construction). Hence, the integrator has no incentive to misrepresent the productivity of any individual grower or all growers together.

Despite these favorable properties, many contract producers complain about contract settlements that are based on tournaments. The essence of these complaints is what Armando Levy and Vukina[34] termed the "league composition effect." The problem arises from the possibility that consecutive flocks produced by the same producer with similar production costs may receive substantially different payments because of different composition and, hence, performance of the tournament group.

The welfare comparison between tournaments and simple piece rates depend on the relative magnitudes of common production risk (e.g., weather) and group composition risk. (Sometimes a grower competes against a group of good growers and does poorly; other times a grower competes against a group of not-so-good growers and does well.) Tournaments eliminate common production risk but entail group composition risk. The results showed that when leagues are fixed over time, simple piece-rate contracts improve welfare over tournaments provided that the time horizon is sufficiently long. However, the results also showed that broiler tournament groups are not fixed and that their composition changes significantly from flock to flock, suggesting that the observed broiler industry tournament contracts offer more welfare than piece-rate contracts.

The above-mentioned proposed rule that would prevent poultry companies from offering contracts where bonus/penalty could fluctuate freely above or below the contracted base payment rate was analyzed by Zhen Wang and Vukina.[35] The proposed rule would effectively change the compensation scheme from a standard piece-rate tournament to a truncated tournament in which the below-average performance outcomes would no longer get penalized and only the above-average performance outcomes would be rewarded. That way, the minimum payment per pound of live chickens would be the contractually agreed base payment.

In their model with risk-neutral and heterogeneous abilities agents,[36] they analyzed the principal's problem of optimal choice of contract parameters under both regular and truncated tournament scenarios. The results showed that the principal could significantly mitigate potential welfare losses due to tournament truncation by adjusting the contract parameters. The distributional effects in equilibrium are such that lower- and higher-ability growers are more likely to benefit from regulation, while average-ability growers are expected to lose.

Overall, the proposed truncation policy would not significantly increase growers' incomes, as surely must have been wished for by the policymakers who proposed this regulation, and some producers could end up being worse off than before the regulation. Also, the empirical analysis in Wang and Vukina[37] was based on the assumption that the pool of growers that the principal contracts with stays the same. However, because the results show that the loss due to regulation incurred by the integrator is the largest with the lowest-abilities growers, it is likely that the integrator may seek to terminate the contracts with the lowest-ability types and try to attract higher-ability growers. This could create substantial losses for low-ability types who could permanently lose their contracts and investments in relationship-specific assets while being saddled with mortgage payments from heavily leveraged but now vacant chicken houses.

Finally, the proposal that would require integrators to rank growers in settlement groups only with other growers with similar house types should be eliminated from further consideration. The issue of making tournament groups more homogenous or more heterogeneous has been studied by Vukina and Xiaoyong Zheng.[38] Exactly opposite from the proposed regulation, they showed that for a given average heterogeneity parameter, larger variance (more diverse groups) induces higher optimal growers' effort. Thus, the integrator always wins by mixing growers of different abilities rather than sorting them into more homogeneous groups.

The effect on growers is theoretically indeterminate because higher optimal effort leads to both higher payment and higher cost of effort. However, their counterfactual simulations show that under reasonable assumptions both the integrator and the growers gain when the tournament groups are diversified. Their research also shows that such a practice would be difficult to implement. This is because when the pool of growers under contract with a particular integrator's profit center is fixed, heterogenizing some tournament groups would necessarily require homogenizing other tournament groups, and the effects from different tournaments would cancel each other out.

Additional Capital Investments Requirements, Market Power, and Holdup. The additional capital investment criteria became part of the GIPSA 2008 Farm Bill final rule, which went into effect in 2012. Additional capital investment was defined as a combined amount of $12,500 or more per structure over the life of the contract beyond the initial investment for the grow-out facilities. The term does not include cost of maintenance or repair. The criteria the secretary may consider when determining whether a requirement that a contract grower makes additional capital investments constitutes an unfair practice in violation of the P&S Act include (1) whether a contractor failed to give a grower discretion to decide against investing; (2) whether investment is the result of coercion, retaliation, or threats of coercion or retaliation; (3) whether a contractor intends to reduce or terminate operations at the relevant location within 12 months of requiring additional investment (not counting natural disasters or unforeseen bankruptcy);

(4) whether some growers were required to make investments, whereas other similarly situated growers were not; (5) the age and number of recent upgrades; (6) whether investment costs can be reasonably recouped; and (7) whether a reasonable amount of time to implement these investments was provided.

As explained by Vukina and Porametr Leegomonchai,[39] after housing facilities have been constructed, processors may exploit their advantageous bargaining position by frequently requesting upgrades and technological improvements as conditions for contract renewal. Shira Lewin-Solomons[40] showed that growers may be held up since physical specificity could effectively reduce the growers' compensation without causing additional moral hazard problems. When a contract involves physical asset specificity, the fear of contract termination would induce the agent to exert high effort without the need for efficient compensation. The crux of the problem is that the potential for opportunism can significantly influence contract stipulations even if no actual opportunism occurs. The mere fact that the integrator could act opportunistically helps keep the growers in check.

The above argument is rooted in the standard efficiency wage result.[41] Namely, when incentive problems (caused by the grower's limited liability and the moral hazard problems associated with the fact that effort is unobservable) are sufficiently severe, growers earn positive employment rents. If these rents are high enough, the integrators may hire fewer growers, which would result in the involuntary unemployment for some growers who are perfectly willing to sign a contract but cannot obtain one. The presence of involuntary unemployment creates an additional incentive for the grower to exert high effort because shirking increases the probability of getting fired. Because the grower utility from shirking (exerting low effort) is now lower than before, the incentive-compatibility constraint can be satisfied with the lower wage relative to the situation in which the market clears.

Next, let's add the asset specificity. In this case, the compensation has to be high enough that growers have a sufficient incentive not to shirk and that they earn sufficient quasi-rents to justify the entire investment. Enforcing high effort now becomes cheaper because growers fear that, if terminated, they may lose part of the investment that is relationship specific. The minimum incentive-compatible wage is therefore lower than without the asset specificity, and the need for involuntary unemployment is reduced since termination is costly even with full employment. The threat of having to switch to another integrator may replace the threat of unemployment.

Vukina and Leegomonchai[42] tested the above proposition with the poultry contract grower survey data by looking at the relationship between grower payoffs and the number of substantial upgrade requests per house over the past five years. The results seem to support the above hypothesis that the increase in asset specificity (additional capital investment requirements) enables a fall in grower compensation rates, but only in monopsonistic environments. They found no evidence of such behavior under competitive or oligopsonistic market structures.

The relationship between asset specificity on the grower side of the contract and the exercise of market power of poultry integrators on the market for grower services was also analyzed by MacDonald and Nigel Key.[43] Using the data from the 2006 broiler version of the Agricultural Resource Management Survey, they found that greater integrator concentration results in a small but economically meaningful reduction in grower compensation. Growers who operated in the area with a single broiler company received average fees of approximately 6 percent less than the growers in regions with four or more companies.

Contract Length and Termination. Two other rules adopted by the GIPSA 2012 Final Rule (provisions regarding the suspension of delivery of animals and the breach of contract) are both related to the issue of contract length, suspension, and termination. Virtually all current livestock production contracts exhibit a discrepancy between the duration of the contract and the useful life of a contract's specific assets. A lot of them are actually short term (one flock or one batch at the time); that is, the contract is implicitly renewed when the new batch of animals is brought to the farm, unless explicitly canceled by either party.

Another problem is that even if contracts are explicitly longer term, they never specify the number of batches or flocks of animals that the integrator will deliver to the contract grower per year. According to the new rule, the secretary may consider various criteria when determining whether reasonable notice has been given by an integrator to a grower for suspension of delivery of animals such as the provision of a written notice at least 90 days before the date it intends to suspend delivery of animals and whether the notice adequately stated the reason for the suspension of delivery, the length of the suspension, and the anticipated date when the delivery will resume. In relation to the breach of the contract, the new rule requires the integrator to give the contract grower a written notice of the breach of contracts and a reasonable period of time to remedy a problem that could lead to contract termination.

The problem of contract duration and contract switch from short term to long term was recently studied by Pierre Dubois and Vukina.[44] At the theoretical core of their research is a dynamic decision model in which agents (growers) make three decisions: (1) whether to invest in observable physical capital (e.g., cool cells in chicken houses), (2) how much to invest in their own unobservable human capital, and (3) how hard to work (how much effort to exert). The first decision is discrete; the other two are continuous.

The model links these decisions to the probability of contract renewal and offers predictions about the effects of the contract switch from short term to long term on the agent's behavior. Specifically, the model predicts that a switch to long-term contracts should increase both the effort and the unobservable investment in human capital. The key assumption driving this result is the complementarity between effort and human capital. On the other hand, the effect on observable physical capital will be positive only if the starting level of human capital is high enough to justify the investment. In turn, the new steady-state levels of effort and human capital depend on whether the physical capital increased in response to the change in the probability of contract renewal.

Overall, the research results show potential benefits of long-term contracting relative to short-term contracts but, of course, does not provide any normative prescriptions related to regulatory policy proposals. From what has been said, it seems obvious that mandating the livestock production contracts to be explicitly long term (say, 10–15 years) without requiring that the contract specifies the minimum number of batches or flocks per year that the grower will receive is meaningless. On the other hand, requiring that the contracts specify the exact number of batches per year (e.g., five flocks per year in the case of broiler contracts) would be too intrusive because it would interfere with the integrators' supply response capabilities and could actually lead to more abrupt contract terminations and expensive litigations.

Figure 2. Trade-Off Among Alternative Modes of Organization: After Regulation

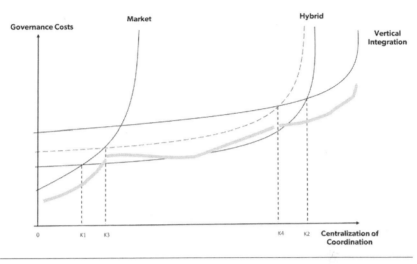

Source: Authors.

Conclusions and Policy Recommendations

When discussing regulatory and policy proposals, it is useful to revisit Figure 1. All policies restricting the use of contracts among parties will tend to shift the AMAs (hybrids) cost curve in the northeast direction on the figure, thereby modifying the distribution of modes of organization. Such a shift is depicted by the dashed curve in Figure 2. As the result of this new regulation, the dashed curve now intersects the other two modes' governance cost curves (which stayed in place) at the abscissa points K3 and K4. Consequently, the region where the AMAs are the most efficient modes of organizing economic activity has shrunk, whereas the area where the other two modes became the most efficient has expanded. This is especially true for vertical integration and to a lesser degree for spot markets.

This insight is especially useful in light of what is as of yet only anecdotal evidence of a strong push by Smithfield Foods (the largest hog company in the world) in North Carolina toward more company-owned farms and away from contracts. If this trend (which could be the result of regulation, constant torts litigation, and many other technological considerations) continues, it could have dire consequences for contract farmers who could lose their existing contracts with no possibility to replace them. Therefore, public policies must be analyzed taking into consideration the effect of regulation on the new distribution of modes of organization that any new policy can create. Considering the above-presented arguments, we feel comfortable formulating the following set of policy recommendations regarding the AMAs in general.

Do Not Ban AMAs. Several attempts were made in the past to ban the use of AMAs by packers. Fortunately, these attempts were not successful. As discussed above, AMAs bring numerous benefits to consumers, packers, and some farmers while hurting other farmers. Overall, the gains by those who benefit far outweigh the losses by those who lose. Indeed, Michael Wohlgenant[45] analyzed the welfare effects of banning the use of AMAs in the US hog industry using simulations and found it would decrease social welfare. The two main sources of welfare loss are the loss in cost efficiency in packer production and a decrease in consumer welfare due to the increase in meat prices. Similar proposals to ban the AMAs in the future should continue to be defeated.

Protect the Spot Market. On the other hand, new regulations should be developed to protect the spot market. If the current trend continues, the spot market will disappear completely in the near future. Packers should be required to purchase a certain minimum percentage of their livestock from the spot market. With more transactions through the spot market, the price discovered in the spot market will be less likely influenced by a particular buyer and more accurately reflect the changes in market fundamentals. Also, the spot market is still the main marketing channel for small farmers. If the spot market disappears, farmers with small livestock operations will be forced to exit the industry altogether.

Furthermore, new regulations should be developed to closely monitor the competition conditions in the spot market and prevent further consolidation of this market. If the spot market becomes concentrated as the current trend continues, then packers could easily manipulate the spot market price to their advantage, and this will harm not only those farmers who rely on the spot market but also the contract farmers, as contract prices are often linked to the spot market price in purchasing agreements. The 2008 Farm

Bill made some progress in this aspect by requiring packers to identify their dealers and banning packers from purchasing livestock from other packers or dealers associated with other packers, and more could be done.

Improve Mandatory Price Reports. One of the main goals of the LMR Act of 1999 was to provide useful and accurate market information to participants in the livestock industries. However, currently, USDA-AMS only reports the quantity and average price of transactions that go through each marketing channel. As discussed above, because of the thinness of certain channels and the high concentration of the livestock industries, the reported average prices may not reflect changes in market fundamentals and not give market participants the whole picture.

New regulations should be developed to amend the LMR Act of 1999 to require AMS to publish more statistics based on the data packers report to them. For example, in addition to the mean, the standard deviation, skewness, and kurtosis of the prices for each marketing channel could be reported. Also, a concentration measure such as the Herfindahl-Hirschman Index of the transactions for each marketing channel could be reported. These statistics are not based on individual transactions, and hence revealing them does not constitute a breach of the data privacy and confidentiality requirements mandated by Titles 13 and 26 of the US Code. With this additional information, market participants can better understand the price information reported in the MPRs, and the livestock markets are expected to operate more efficiently.

In addition, we advance the following set of policy recommendations regarding the production contracts. First, leave tournaments as the dominant mode of settling broiler contracts alone. They have been in use for more than a half century with great success, and their use has spread to Brazil, Europe, and other countries where chickens are produced on a large scale.

Second, because of the increased livestock industries' concentration and the fact that live animals are ill-suited to travel large distances, the concerns about the integrators' market power in the regional markets for contract grower services are well-founded, and some regulatory intervention can be justified on efficiency grounds. Therefore, we support the existing GIPSA rule on the additional capital investment requirements as a sensible (albeit indirect) approach to dealing with this problem. The relationship between the market structure (competition) and the problem of holdup needs to be more carefully studied before proposing more drastic policy interventions.

For example, as indicated by Vukina and Zheng,[46] the post-2012 data and research results seem to indicate that the competition in the markets for grower services in the poultry industry is improving in the core-producing regions of the country as production is gradually shifting from the periphery to the core, and the competition is intensifying in the sense that the number of plants per contract grower is increasing. Of course, some micro-regional competition issues still remain, as well as the potentially more precarious position of the remaining contract growers in the peripheral production regions faced with the prospects of plant closures and permanent loss of contracts. This new asymmetric regional distribution of contract production makes any new regulatory proposal difficult to design and even more difficult to implement and enforce.

Finally, when it comes to contract duration, it has to be recognized that short-term contracts and no guarantees on the number of batches or flocks per year introduce significant degrees of uncertainty and volatility into the contract growers' income streams, yet explicit regulation of these contractual features does not appear to be desirable. Therefore, we believe the existing provisions regarding the suspension of delivery of animals and provisions regarding the breach of contract as promulgated with the new GIPSA 2012 rule are adequate.

Notes

1. AMAs are also referred to as captive supplies in the literature.

2. Claude Menard, "The Economics of Hybrid Organizations," *Journal of Institutional and Theoretical Economics* 160, no. 3 (2004): 1–32.

3. Oliver E. Williamson, "Comparative Economic Organization: The Analysis of Discrete Structural Alternatives," *Administrative Science Quarterly* (1991): 269–96.

4. James M. MacDonald and Penni Korb, *Agricultural Contracting Update: Contracts in 2008*, US Department of Agriculture, Economic Research Service, February 2011.

5. James M. MacDonald, "Trends in Agricultural Contracts," *Choices* 30, no. 3 (2015).

6. MacDonald and Korb, *Agricultural Contracting Update*.

7. MacDonald, "Trends in Agricultural Contracts."

8. Glenn Grimes and Ronald L. Plain, "U.S. Hog Marketing Contract Study," University of Missouri, Department of Agricultural Economics, January 2009, http://hdl.handle.

net/10355/8942.

9. RTI International, "GIPSA Livestock and Meat Marketing Study, Volume 4. Hog and Pork Industries," January 2007.

10. Jong-Jin Kim and Xiaoyong Zheng, "Effects of Alternative Marketing Arrangements on the Spot Market Price Distribution in the U.S. Hog Market," *Journal of Agricultural and Resource Economics* 40, no. 2 (2015): 242–65.

11. Kayode Ajewole, Ted C. Schroeder, and Joe Parcell, "Price Reporting in a Thin Market," *Journal of Agricultural and Applied Economics* 48, no. 4 (2016): 345–65.

12. For example, Emmett Elam, "Cash Forward Contracting Versus Hedging of Fed Cattle, and the Impact of Cash Contracting on Cash Prices," *Journal of Agricultural and Resource Economics* 17 (1992): 205–17; Marvin L. Hayenga and Dan O'Brien, "Packer Competition, Forward Contracting Price Impacts, and the Relevant Market for Fed Cattle," in *Pricing and Coordination in Consolidated Livestock Markets: Captive Supplies, Market Power, IRS Hedging Policy*, ed. Wayne D. Purcell (Research Institute on Livestock Pricing, April 1992), 45–65; Ted C. Schroeder et al., "The Impact of Forward Contracting on Fed Cattle Transaction Prices," *Review of Agricultural Economics* 15, no. 15 (1993): 325–37; Clement E. Ward, Stephen R. Koontz, and Ted C. Schroeder, "Impacts from Captive Supplies on Fed Cattle Transaction Prices," *Journal of Agricultural and Resource Economics* 23 (1998): 494–514; and John R. Schroeter and Azzeddine Azzam, "Captive Supplies and the Spot Market Price of Fed Cattle: The Plant-Level Relationship," *Agribusiness* 19, no. 4 (2003): 489–504.

13. Yoonsuk Lee, Clement E. Ward, and B. Wade Brorsen, "Procurement Price Relationships for Fed Cattle and Hogs: Importance of the Cash Market in Price Discovery," *Agribusiness* 28, no. 2 (2012): 135–47.

14. Tian Xia and Richard J. Sexton, "The Competitive Implications of Top-of-the-Market and Related Contract-Pricing Clauses," *American Journal of Agricultural Economics* 86, no. 1 (2004): 124–38.

15. Kim and Zheng, "Effects of Alternative Marketing Arrangements on the Spot Market Price Distribution in the U.S. Hog Market."

16. RTI International, "GIPSA Livestock and Meat Marketing Study, Volume 4. Hog and Pork Industries."

17. RTI International, "GIPSA Livestock and Meat Marketing Study, Volume 4. Hog and Pork Industries."

18. Xiaoyong Zheng, Tomislav Vukina, and Changmock Shin, "The Role of Farmers' Risk Aversion for Contract Choice in the US Hog Industry," *Journal of Agricultural and Food Industrial Organization* 6, no. 1 (2008): 1–20.

19. Tomislav Vukina, Changmock Shin, and Xiaoyong Zheng, "Complementarity Among Alternative Procurement Arrangements in the Pork Packing Industry," *Journal of Agricultural & Food Industrial Organization* 7, no. 1 (2009).

20. RTI International, "GIPSA Livestock and Meat Marketing Study, Volume 4. Hog and Pork Industries."

21. John D. Lawrence, "Hog Marketing Practices and Competition Questions," *Choices* 25, no. 2 (2010): 1–11; Ron Plain, "U.S. Market Hog Sales, 2002–2014," University of Missouri, Department of Agricultural and Applied Economics, May 2015, http://agebb.missouri.edu/mkt/vertstud14.htm.

22. Ajewole, Schroeder, and Parcell, "Price Reporting in a Thin Market."

23. Nigel Key, "Production Contracts and the Spot Market Price of Hogs" (presentation, Agricultural and Applied Economics Association, Denver, CO, July 25–27, 2010).

24. Ajewole, Schroeder, and Parcell, "Price Reporting in a Thin Market."

25. Xia and Sexton, "The Competitive Implications of Top-of-the-Market and Related Contract-Pricing Clauses."

26. RTI International, "GIPSA Livestock and Meat Marketing Study, Volume 4. Hog and Pork Industries."

27. For more information, see Chuck Grassley, "Grassley Readies Amendments for Farm Bill Debate," press release, December 10, 2011, http://www.grassley.senate.gov/news/news-releases/grassley-readies-amendments-farm-bill-debate.

28. R. A. McEowen, P. C. Carstensen and N. E. Harl, "The 2002 Senate Farm Bill: The Ban on Packer Ownership of Livestock," *Drake Journal of Agricultural Law* 7 (2002): 267.

29. See, for example, Tomislav Vukina, "Vertical Integration and Contracting in the U.S. Poultry Sector," *Journal of Food Distribution Research* 32, no. 2 (July 2001): 29–38.

30. Grain Inspection, Packers and Stockyards Administration, "Implementation of Regulations Required Under Title XI of the Food, Conservation and Energy Act of 2008; Conduct in Violation of the Act," *Federal Register* 75, no. 119 (June 22, 2010): 35352.

31. Grain Inspection, Packers and Stockyards Administration, "Implementation of Regulations Required Under Title XI of the Food, Conservation and Energy Act of 2008; Suspension of Delivery of Birds, Additional Capital Investment Criteria, Breach of Contract, and Arbitration," *Federal Register* 76, no. 237 (December 9, 2011): 76874–90.

32. Theofanis Tsoulouhas and Tomislav Vukina, "Integrator Contracts with Many Agents and Bankruptcy," *American Journal of Agricultural Economics* 81, no. 1 (1999): 61–74.

33. Charles R. Knoeber, "A Real Game of Chicken: Contract, Tournaments, and the Production of Broilers," *Journal of Law, Economics, & Organization* 5, no. 2 (1989): 271–92.

34. Armando Levy and Tomislav Vukina, "The League Composition Effect in Tournaments with Heterogeneous Players: An Empirical Analysis of Broiler Contracts," *Journal of Labor Economics* 22, no. 2 (2004): 353–77.

35. Zhen Wang and Tomislav Vukina, "Welfare Effects of Payment Truncation in Piece Rate Tournaments," *Journal of Economics* 120, no. 3 (2017): 219–49.

36. In this context the standard definition of abilities as innate characteristics or acquired skills based on education, experience, and so forth is extended to include any time-invariant growers' idiosyncrasies such as geographic location, the vintage and quality of production facilities, or similar factors.

37. Wang and Vukina, "Welfare Effects of Payment Truncation in Piece Rate Tournaments."

38. Tomislav Vukina and Xiaoyong Zheng, "Homogenous and Heterogenous Contestants in Piece Rate Tournaments: Theory and Empirical Analysis," *Journal of Business and Economic Statistics* 29, no. 4 (2011): 506–17.

39. Tomislav Vukina and Porametr Leegomonchai, "Oligopsony Power, Asset Specificity and Hold-Up: Evidence from the Broiler Industry," *American Journal of Agricultural*

Economics 88, no. 3 (2006): 589–605.

40. Shira B. Lewin-Solomons, "Asset Specificity and Hold-Up in Franchising and Grower Contracts: A Theoretical Rationale for Government Regulation?," University of Cambridge and Iowa State, September 2000.

41. Carl Shapiro and Joseph E. Stiglitz, "Equilibrium Unemployment as a Worker Discipline Device," American Economic Review 74, no. 3 (1984): 433–44.

42. Vukina and Leegomonchai, "Oligopsony Power, Asset Specificity and Hold-Up."

43. James M. MacDonald and Nigel Key, "Market Power in Poultry Production Contracting? Evidence from a Farm Survey," Journal of Agricultural and Applied Economics 44, no. 4 (2012): 477–90.

44. Pierre Dubois and Tomislav Vukina, "Incentives to Invest in Short-Term vs. Long-Term Contracts: Theory and Evidence," B.E. Journal of Economic Analysis & Policy 16, no. 3 (2016): 1239–72.

45. Michael K. Wohlgenant, "Modeling the Effects of Restricting Packer-Owned Livestock in the U.S. Swine Industry," American Journal of Agricultural Economics 92, no. 3 (2010): 654–66.

46. Tomislav Vukina and Xiaoyong Zheng, "The Broiler Industry: Competition and Policy Challenges," Choices 30, no. 2 (2015): 1–6.

Conclusion

The 19 studies included in this two-volume assessment of agricultural policy in the United States examine a wide spectrum of federal government initiatives that affect, and for the most part substantially benefit, the agricultural sector and related upstream input supply and downstream processing industries. The picture these studies paint consists of a compellingly chaotic, apparently randomly structured collage of individual programs that, nevertheless, almost always serve to benefit carefully selected constituencies at the expense of taxpayers and consumers. In doing so, most of those programs create incentives that result in wasted resources and provide subsidies that overwhelmingly flow to large agribusiness-style farm operations owned by relatively wealthy and very wealthy households (Chapter 1, Volume I; Chapter 2, Volume I).

Despite persistent claims to the contrary by farm interest groups and farm state legislators, farm subsidy initiatives do nothing to alleviate poverty in either rural or urban areas (Chapter 1, Volume II). One exception is the suite of nutrition programs the US Department of Agriculture manages that do help millions of US households in poverty (Chapter 2, Volume II). However, some farm state legislators have regularly sought to shift funds from the Supplementary Nutrition Assistance Program, the largest program that currently helps just under 40 million people, to farm subsidy programs that mainly benefit much wealthier constituents (Chapter 1, Volume I).

Some major subsidy programs (e.g., crop insurance) harm the environment and involve substantial administrative costs (Chapter 3, Volume I). Others address environmental and resource degradation problems in inefficient and inane ways (Chapter 6, Volume II; Chapter 7, Volume II; Chapter 8, Volume II). Many agricultural commodity subsidy and tariff programs also create serious challenges for the United States regarding international trade in agriculture and other commodities and services (Chapter 5, Volume I).

In addition, effective support from agricultural lobbies for public investments in agricultural research and development (R&D) has withered over the past 30 years. Frequently, those lobbies have chosen to trade away from federal spending on agricultural R&D and shift funds to short-term direct subsidy programs. The result has had substantial adverse impacts on productivity growth in the agricultural sector (Chapter 4, Volume II). One R&D policy mistake US legislators have not yet made, but policymakers in other countries have, involves overregulation and even proscription of the development and use of genetically modified organism (GMO) technologies. As Gary Brester and Joseph Atwood discuss (Chapter 5, Volume II), in the United States those technologies appear to have been an important source of productivity growth for corn and soybeans—crops that are mainly used for biofuels and animal feed rather than for human consumption (a purpose for which, in any case, non-GMO varieties of those crops are available).

The various components of US agricultural policy frequently work at cross-purposes, with offsetting impacts that result from delivering benefits to different groups with conflicting objectives. For example, paid land retirement programs encourage soil conservation, while the federal crop insurance program incentivizes farm businesses to plant crops on fragile lands. Nutrition programs, which from a policy perspective are antipoverty programs that help millions of people, somewhat anachronistically continue to be included in farm bill legislation even though they have not measurably affected prices farm businesses receive for their products for at least the past 30 years. In contrast, sugar and dairy product tariffs are explicitly designed to increase domestic food prices and have substantial adverse effects on employment opportunities in the food-processing sector (Chapter 6, Volume I; Chapter 7, Volume I). Further, somewhat ironically, some government funds flow to industry-based organizations for agricultural export promotion (e.g., US Wheat Associates); at the same time, other programs are explicitly designed to impede international trade (Chapter 5, Volume I).

The studies in these volumes reflect several common themes and realities regarding agricultural policy in the United States. First, most policies are largely designed to benefit, and are effectively determined by, relatively small interest groups. Many of these organizations consist of farm businesses (e.g., the National Corn Growers Association, the American Sugar Alliance, the National Cotton Council, the American Soybean Association, the National Milk Producers Federation, the American Farm Bureau Federation, and the National Farmers Union). Others consist of industries that service the agricultural sector, such as crop insurance companies, input supply organizations, and downstream processing companies. These include organizations such as the National Association of Professional Insurance Agents, National Crop Insurance Services, the Fertilizer Institute, the American Bankers Association, and the Food Products Association, as well as large multinational companies with their own lobbyists. When it comes to the inefficiencies and waste associated with US international food aid programs, as Stephanie Mercier, Erin Lentz, and Christopher Barrett discuss (Chapter 3, Volume II), groups such as the National Mariners Association and USA Maritime have pushed to retain mandates that provide rents mainly for shipping companies. Those mandates use up about 30 percent of the federal funds available for such aid and are estimated annually to prevent US international food aid programs from meeting the needs of an additional four million or more people in dire poverty who are experiencing hunger and malnutrition.

Second, other players in the agricultural policy process include environmental and other more broadly focused interest groups such as the World Wildlife Fund and the Sierra Club, as well as other special interest groups such as the Renewable Fuels Association. However, as Erik Lichtenberg points out (Chapter 6, Volume II), often the polices those groups end up supporting involve payoffs to the agricultural sector (e.g., through paid land retirement initiatives such as the Conservation Reserve Program and through subsidies for working-lands programs to encourage the adoption of conservation practices by farm businesses).

These outcomes reflect political compromises between interest groups with otherwise conflicting interests that impose costs on the rest of society. In contrast, pollution in other US economy sectors is typically addressed through government regulations and other approaches (e.g., marketable permits) that require compliance and impose emissions-control costs on polluters rather than taxpayers. The Renewable Fuel Standard, notionally intended to reduce greenhouse gas emissions (Chapter 8, Volume II), also result in similar outcomes. Higher prices for corn and soybeans impose substantial costs on all US consumers in the form of higher food and fuel prices, with substantial adverse environmental effects associated with increased chemical use by farm businesses that produce biofuels crops, especially in the Midwest.

Third, little attention, if any, is given to consumers or the poor in forming and implementing farm subsidy programs or the efficient and effective use of federal resources allocated for humanitarian aid (Chapter 3, Volume II), despite assertions to the contrary from vested farm and other interest groups. Consumers and families in poverty are more likely to be taxed either directly or through higher prices for agricultural commodities.

Fourth, US agricultural policies rarely take account of the international trade relations implications associated with their operations, even though the US is a net exporter of agricultural commodities. Examples include subsidy programs for cotton, dairy products, and major row crops such as corn, cotton, rice, soybeans, and wheat, as well as sugar program initiatives that place arbitrary ad hoc restrictions on imports from trading partners such as Mexico.

Finally, in the vast majority of cases, agricultural subsidies and other policies are deliberately structured to funnel federal funds to a small number of large farm businesses that would be financially successful without any help from the US taxpayer or consumer. Most of these policies have nothing to do with ensuring food security in the United States, the survival of the US agricultural sector, or poverty, and farm interests appear to be increasingly disinterested in policies that do, such as public R&D investments. American farm programs are far more likely to be driven by rent-seeking, through what independent observers have increasingly described as crony capitalism. Thus, it is simply no accident that, as the scholars who have contributed to these volumes document, agricultural policy in the United States remains in disarray.

About the Authors

Joseph A. Atwood is a professor in the Montana State University Department of Agricultural Economics and Economics. He received a Ph.D. in agricultural economics and a bachelor's and master's in science from the University of Nebraska–Lincoln. He has been a faculty member at Montana State University since 1987.

Christopher B. Barrett is the Stephen B. and Janice G. Ashley Professor of Applied Economics and Management at Cornell University.

Gary W. Brester is professor emeritus in the Department of Agricultural Economics and Economics and a distinguished research scholar in the Montana State University Institute of Regulation and Applied Economic Analysis. He received a Ph.D. in economics from North Carolina State University and a bachelor's and master's in science from Montana State University, where he has been a faculty member since 1997.

Joseph W. Glauber is a senior research fellow at the International Food Policy Research Institute and a visiting scholar at the American Enterprise Institute.

Barry K. Goodwin is William Neal Reynolds Distinguished Professor of Agricultural Economics at North Carolina State University and a visiting scholar at the American Enterprise Institute.

Nathan P. Hendricks is an associate professor in the department of agricultural economics at Kansas State University.

Scott H. Irwin is the Laurence J. Norton Chair of Agricultural Marketing and director of *farmdoc* at the University of Illinois at Urbana–Champaign.

He teaches courses on commodity price analysis and futures market research. His research on commodity markets is widely cited by other academic researchers, and his expertise is frequently sought out by market participants, policymakers, and the media.

Erin C. Lentz is an assistant professor at the Lyndon B. Johnson School of Public Affairs at the University of Texas at Austin.

Erik Lichtenberg is a professor in the Department of Agricultural and Resource Economics at the University of Maryland, College Park. He is a fellow of the Agricultural and Applied Economics Association and a former coeditor of the *American Journal of Agricultural Economics*. He has written extensively on environmental issues in agriculture.

Stephanie Mercier is an independent agricultural policy consultant and former chief economist for the Democratic staff of the Senate Agriculture Committee.

Philip G. Pardey is a professor in the department of applied economics at the University of Minnesota; director of global research strategy for the university's College of Food, Agricultural and Natural Resource Sciences; and director of the university's International Science and Technology Practice and Policy (InSTePP) Center.

Diane Whitmore Schanzenbach is the Margaret Walker Alexander Professor and director for the Institute of Policy Research at Northwestern University.

Aaron Smith is a professor of agricultural and resource economics at the University of California, Davis.

Vincent H. Smith is professor of economics in the Department of Agricultural Economics and Economics at Montana State University (MSU), codirector of MSU's Agricultural Marketing Policy Center, and a visiting scholar and director of Agricultural Policy Studies at the American Enterprise Institute.

Daniel A. Sumner is the director of the University of California Agricultural Issues Center and the Frank H. Buck Jr. Professor in the Department of Agricultural and Resource Economics at the University of California, Davis.

Tomislav Vukina is a professor of agricultural and resource economics at North Carolina State University. His research and extension programs are focused on economic organization of agriculture, economics of incentives and information, and personnel economics. He is nationally and internationally known for his work in economics of agricultural contracts and economics of the poultry industry.

Parke E. Wilde is an associate professor in the Gerald J. and Dorothy R. Friedman School of Nutrition Science and Policy at Tufts University.

Xiaoyong Zheng is a professor of agricultural and resource economics at North Carolina State University. He studies markets with asymmetric information. His published and working projects include empirical studies of auctions (public works, timber, and conservation reservation), contracts (marketing and production contracts in agriculture), and insurance (health and crop). He is also an applied econometrician, applying microeconometrics methods to study policy-relevant issues in food demand, health, and international trade.

Acknowledgments

This work would not have been possible without the support and contributions of dozens of gifted individuals. The editors truly appreciate the 17 nationally recognized scholars who as authors have made major contributions to this detailed study of US agricultural policy, and we are especially beholden to them for their focus on making their work accessible to the nonspecialist. Daniel Sumner, in particular, deserves particular recognition for his study of dairy policy and the important insights he shared with the editors drawn from his exceptional understanding of the economics of agricultural policy.

We also owe a major vote of thanks to the many wonderful individuals at the American Enterprise Institute who have helped make this project successful. The AEI in-house editing team has been astonishingly effective in improving the quality of the manuscript, and, as a consequence, we are deeply indebted to Rachel Jelinek, Sarah Crain, and Claude Aubert for their painstaking work, their creative contributions, and, above all, their patience with the foibles of the editors. We also want to thank Michael Pratt, John Cusey, and Emily Rapp for their vision and support in enabling this project to move forward and Ryan Nabil and Isabelle Staff for the extensive logistical support they provided in organizing the workshops and events through which this two-volume study was developed.

Finally, the editors would like to acknowledge their intellectual and personal debts to two giants in the field of agricultural economics, both closely associated with AEI throughout their distinguished careers. The first is D. Gale Johnson, professor of economics at the University of Chicago and past president of the American Economic Association, to whose memory this volume is dedicated. The second is Bruce Gardner, professor of agricultural economics and former undersecretary for economics at the US Department of Agriculture, who succeeded Johnson in leading the AEI agricultural policy program until he passed away in 2009. The intellectual and personal contributions of these two wonderful scholars have influenced every study included in this work, for which we are truly grateful.

Index

of government, 267
of income, 41–43
of interest groups, 7
of legislation, 287–90
of livestock, 36
of poverty, 111–12
of programs, 170–71
of property, 214–16
of R&D, 137–39
of reform, 114–15
of RFS, 32–33, 221–25, 229–33,
    247–49, 307
of SNAP, 43–46, 128
of soil, 194n9
of speculation, 256–57
of subsidies, 305
of trade, 33
in US, 2, 55, 98–99, 143n16,
    217–18
of USDA, 31
of wages, 54–55
of water quality, 198–200,
    211–12, 217–18
of WTO, 4–5, 191
Position limits. *See* Futures markets;
    Regulation
Poverty
    for consumers, 40–41
    culture of, 75–79, 81–83
    data for, 41–43, 57–58, 69, 95–96
    employment and, 90–91
    farm bills and, 3–4, 97, 116
    farming and, 7–8, 47–51, 195n22
    food aid for, 68–73
    history of, 23
    labor and, 51–55

nutrition and, 20–23
policy for, 17–20, 46–58,
    59–61, 106–7
politics of, 111–12
*State of Food Insecurity in the
    World* (2015), 108
subsidies and, 58–59, 308
taxes for, 72–73
in US, 8, 41–43, 87
Prepositioning, 110
Price discrimination, 28–29
Price Loss Coverage (PLC), 4–5
    See also Programs
Pricing
    of commodities, 115
    economics of, 266–67
    investing and, 255–56
    risk in, 286
    storage and, 269–70
    volatility in, 272
Private investing, 175–76
Private R&D, 135
Production
    AMAs for, 283–84
    contracts for, 290–96
    in farming, 9
    incentives for, 35–36
    of livestock, 282, 284–87
    of oil, 237
    policy for, 11–12, 64n38
    regulation of, 28–29
Productivity, 163n9
Programs
    checkoff programs, 31, 141
    for commodities, 20–22
    for cost sharing, 36–37